MathFlare

Name: _______________________

Class: ___________

Teacher: _______________________

<u>Introduction</u>

As parents and educators, we recognize the pivotal role mathematics plays in shaping a child's academic journey and future success. Yet, the path to mathematical proficiency can often seem daunting, fraught with challenges and complexities. That's where the transformative power of MathFlare Workbooks shine through, illuminating the way forward with clarity, precision, and purpose.

Introducing MathFlare Workbooks – a beacon of guidance, a testament to excellence, and a catalyst for achievement. Crafted with meticulous care and expertise, MathFlare Workbooks stand as paragons of educational excellence, designed to nurture young minds, ignite a passion for learning, and develop a deep-rooted understanding of mathematical concepts.

Picture this: your child eagerly delves into the pages of Mathflare Workbook, greeted by a step-by-step guide illuminated with vivid examples that demystify complex mathematical concepts. With each turn of the page, they embark on a journey of discovery, encountering thoughtfully curated practice questions that reinforce learning and hone problem-solving skills. And when they unveil the answers to those very questions, a sense of accomplishment blossoms within them – a tangible reward for their hard work and dedication.

But MathFlare Workbooks are more than just tools for learning; they are pathways to comprehension, fostering a deep-seated understanding of mathematical concepts through a sequential, logical flow. From fundamental principles to advanced problem-solving strategies, every chapter builds upon the last, ensuring a robust foundation upon which future knowledge can be constructed.

As parents, we yearn for nothing more than to see our children thrive, to witness the spark of inspiration ignited within them as they conquer academic challenges with confidence and poise. MathFlare Workbooks serve as partners in this noble endeavor, offering not just practice questions, but the keys to unlocking a world of opportunity.

And for teachers, MathFlare Workbooks stand as invaluable allies in the quest to cultivate mathematical proficiency in the classroom. With answers readily available, instructors can focus on guiding and nurturing their students, confident in the knowledge that MathFlare Workbooks provide a solid framework upon which to build.

In the pages of MathFlare Workbooks, we find not just the promise of academic excellence, but the seeds of a brighter tomorrow. So let us embrace the power of mathematics, let us champion the journey of learning, and let us pave the way for a generation of young minds poised to shape the world. With MathFlare Workbooks as our guide, the possibilities are infinite, and the future, bright.

Table of Contents

MathFlare
Grade 1-2
MATH WORKBOOK
Step by Step Guide and Essential Practice with Answers
Counting and Numbers
Addition and Subtraction
Place Value and Expanded Notations
Understanding Time
MathFlare Publishing

MathFlare
Grade 2
MATH WORKBOOK
Step by Step Guide and Essential Practice with Answers
Addition Subtraction
Multiplication
Place Value and Expanded Notations
Geometry
MathFlare Publishing

MathFlare
Grade 2-3
MATH WORKBOOK
Step by Step Guide and Essential Practice with Answers
Addition Subtraction
Multiplication and Division
Place Value and Expanded Notations
Geometry
MathFlare Publishing

MathFlare
Grade 3
MATH WORKBOOK
Step by Step Guide and Essential Practice with Answers
Multiplication and Division
Decimals
Place Value and Expanded Notations
Fractions and Geometry
MathFlare Publishing

MathFlare
Grade 3-4
MATH WORKBOOK
Step by Step Guide and Essential Practice with Answers
Addition Subtraction
Multiplication Division
Place Value and Expanded Notations
Fractions and Geometry
MathFlare Publishing

MathFlare
Grade 4
MATH WORKBOOK
Step by Step Guide and Essential Practice with Answers
Addition Subtraction
Multiplication Division
Place Value and Expanded Notations
Fractions and Geometry
MathFlare Publishing

MathFlare
Grade 4-5
MATH WORKBOOK
Step by Step Guide and Essential Practice with Answers
Multiplication Division
Place Value and Expanded Notations
Fractions and Geometry
Unit Conversion
MathFlare Publishing

MathFlare
Grade 5
MATH WORKBOOK
Step by Step Guide and Essential Practice with Answers
Multiplication Division
Place Value and Expanded Notations
Fractions and Geometry
Unit Conversion
MathFlare Publishing

MathFlare
Grade 5-6
MATH WORKBOOK
Step by Step Guide and Essential Practice with Answers
Multiplication Division
Place Value and Expanded Notations
Fractions and Geometry
Units and Statistics
MathFlare Publishing

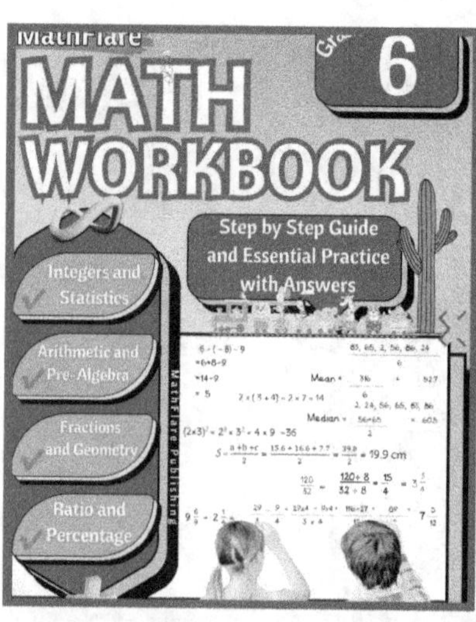
MathFlare
MATH WORKBOOK
Grade 6
Step by Step Guide and Essential Practice with Answers
Integers and Statistics
Arithmetic and Pre-Algebra
Fractions and Geometry
Ratio and Percentage
MathFlare Publishing

MathFlare
MATH WORKBOOK
Grade 6-7
Step by Step Guide and Essential Practice with Answers
Arithmetic and Pre-Algebra
Ratio, Percent Proportion
Geometry
Statistics
MathFlare Publishing

MathFlare
MATH WORKBOOK
Grade 7
Step by Step Guide and Essential Practice with Answers
Pre-Algebra
Ratio, Percent Proportion
Geometry
Statistics
MathFlare Publishing

MathFlare
MATH WORKBOOK
Grade 7-8
Step by Step Guide and Essential Practice with Answers
Pre-Algebra
Ratio, Percent Proportion
Geometry and Cartesian Plane
Statistics
MathFlare Publishing

MathFlare
MATH WORKBOOK
Grade 8
Step by Step Guide and Essential Practice with Answers
Pre-Algebra
Percentage
Linear Equations
Geometry
MathFlare Publishing

MathFlare
MATH WORKBOOK
Grade 8-9
Step by Step Guide and Essential Practice with Answers
Pre-Algebra
Ratio, Proportion and Percentage
Linear Equations
Geometry and Cartesian Plane
MathFlare Publishing

MathFlare
MATH WORKBOOK
Grade 9
Step by Step Guide and Essential Practice with Answers
Equations and Expressions
Linear Equations and Systems
Quadratic Equations
Geometry
MathFlare Publishing

MathFlare
MATH WORKBOOK
Grade 9-10
Step by Step Guide and Essential Practice with Answers
Equations and Expressions
Linear Equations and Systems
Quadratic Equations
Polynomials Geometry
MathFlare Publishing

MathFlare
MATH WORKBOOK
Grade 10
Step by Step Guide and Essential Practice with Answers
Equations and Expressions
Linear Equations and Systems
Quadratic Equations
Polynomials Scientific Notations
MathFlare Publishing

Chapter. 01

Equations and Expressions

Simplifying expressions

It involves combining like terms and performing operations to make the expression easier to understand and work with.

Let's simplify the expression:

$$2x - 2x + 8 + 4$$

- **Combine like terms:** First, we look for terms with the same variable and exponent. In this expression, $2x$ and $-2x$ are like terms, so they can be combined:

$$2x - 2x = 0$$

- **Substitute the simplified terms:** After combining the like terms, the expression becomes:

$$0 + 8 + 4$$

- **Combine the remaining terms:** Now, we add the constants together:

$$8 + 4 = 12$$

Let's solve another problem:

$$-7m - 3 - 3 - 6m$$

combine like terms

$-7m-6m-3-3$

$13m - 6$

Solving Equations

Evaluating expressions involves substituting given values for variables in an expression and then performing the indicated operations to find the result.

For example: Let's evaluate $4x - 10$, when $x = 3$:

Step 1: Substitute the given value for the variable:

Replace every occurrence of x in the expression $4x - 10$ with the given value, which is 3:

$$= 4(3) - 10$$

Step 2: Perform the operations:

Perform the indicated operations according to the order of operations (PEMDAS - Parentheses, Exponents, Multiplication and Division, Addition and Subtraction):

$$= 4 \times 3 - 10$$

Step 3: Simplify:

Calculate the result:

$$12 - 10 = 2$$

Solving Equations (One Side)

Solving one-step equations involves performing a single operation to isolate the variable and find its value.

Let's solve an equation step by step: $16 + x = 31$

1. **Identify the Goal:**

   The goal is to isolate the variable x on one side of the equation.

2. **Simplify the Equation**: Combine like terms on both sides of the equation, if necessary.

   The equation is already simplified.

3. **Undo Addition or Subtraction**: If there's addition or subtraction involving the variable, undo it by performing the opposite operation on both sides of the equation.

   Since x is being added to 16, we'll undo this operation by subtracting 16 from both sides of the equation:

   $$16 + x - 16 = 31 - 16$$

4. **Isolate the Variable**: Ensure that the variable is alone on one side of the equation.

   $$x = 15$$

5. **Check Your Solution**: Substitute the value of x back into the original equation to verify that it satisfies the equation.

   $$16 + 15 = 31$$

   $$31 = 31$$

   The equation is balanced.

Equations (Two Sides)

A two-sided equation is an equation where both sides have expressions with variables and constants. The goal when solving a two-sided equation is to find the value of the variable that makes both sides equal.

For example: Let's solve an equation:

$$9 + 8x + 8 = 64 + x + 2$$

- **Combine Like Terms:** Simplify each side of the equation by combining like terms (terms with the same variable or constants).

$$9 + 8x + 8 = 64 + x + 2$$

$$17 + 8x = 66 + x$$

- **Isolate the Variable:** Use inverse operations to isolate the variable on one side of the equation.

subtract x from both sides:

$$17 + 8x - x = 66 + x - x$$

$$17 + 7x = 66$$

subtracting 17 from both sides:

$$17 - 17 + 7x = 66 - 17$$

$$7x = 49$$

divide both sides by 7:

$$\frac{7x}{7} = \frac{49}{7} = x = 7$$

- **Check Solution:** Once you find the solution, substitute it back into the original equation to ensure it makes the equation true.

Substitute $x = 7$ back into the original equation:

$$9 + 8(7) + 8 = 64 + 7 + 2$$

$$9 + 56 + 8 = 64 + 7 + 2$$

$$73 = 73$$

Verbal Algebra Expressions

Verbal algebra involves translating word problems or verbal statements into algebraic expressions or equations.

For example: The product of the two numbers is 91. One number is six less than the other. What are the numbers?

We're given a verbal description of a problem, and we need to represent it using algebraic symbols and equations.

Let's break down the given problem into algebraic expressions:

- Given that the product of the two numbers is 91, we can write the equation: $xy = 91$
- Also, given that one number is six less than the other, we can write another equation: $x = y - 6$

Now, we can use algebraic techniques to solve the system of equations to find the values of x and y, which represent the two numbers.

$$x(x - 6) = 91$$

1. Solve the equation:

    - Expand the equation:

    $$x^2 - 6x = 91$$

    - Rearrange the equation into standard quadratic form:

    $$x^2 - 6x - 91 = 0$$

    - Factor the quadratic equation:

    $$(x - 13)(x + 7) = 0$$

2. Find the solutions for x:

    - From the factored form, we have two possible values for x:

    $$x = 13 \text{ or } x = -7$$

3. **Check the validity of the solutions:**

- Since one number is six less than the other, we discard the negative solution.

- Therefore, the solution is $x = 13$.

4. **Find the other number:**

- Substitute $x = 13$ into the expression for the other number:

Other number $= x - 6 = 13 - 6 = 7$

So, the two numbers are 13 and 7.

Simplify Expressions

1. $-16m - 5 + 11 - 12m$

2. $-18x + 20 - 3x$

3. $-6y + y$

4. $9 + 15k - 5k$

5. $12y - 20y$

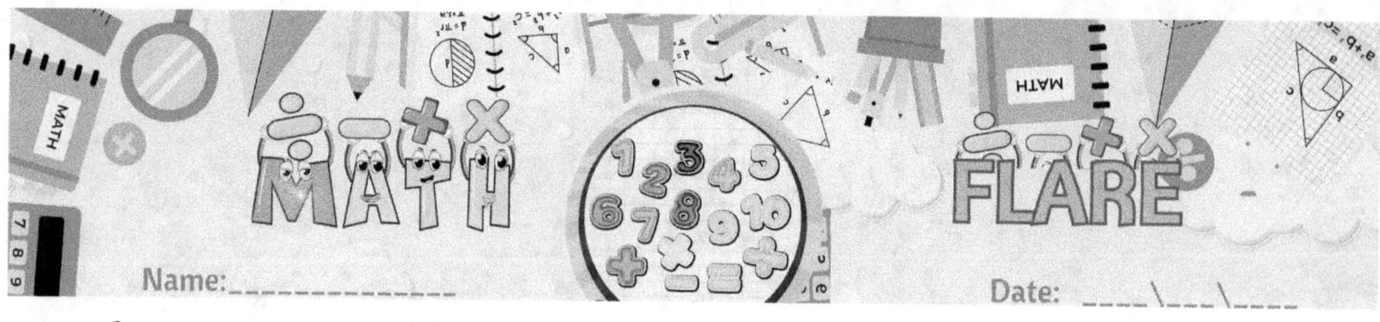

6. $14 + 5z + 3 + 16z$

7. $-k - 19k$

8. $20 - 3(7m - 17)$

9. $-20z + 16 - 16 + 11z$

10. $k - 20k + k + 8 + 18$

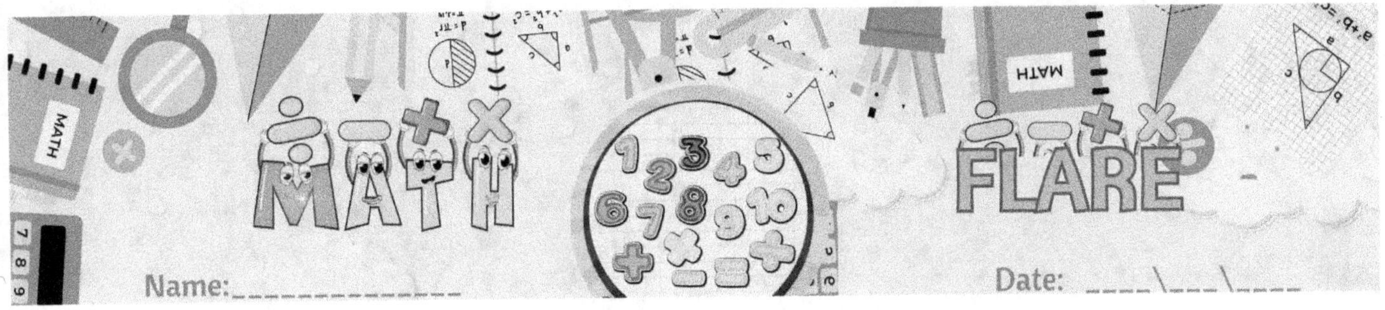

11. $-9m - 8 + 18m$

12. $9k - 16 + 3k - 18 + 20k + 3$

13. $3 + k - 4 + 2k$

14. $-13 + x + 13 - 13x$

15. $-15m + 12 + 6m$

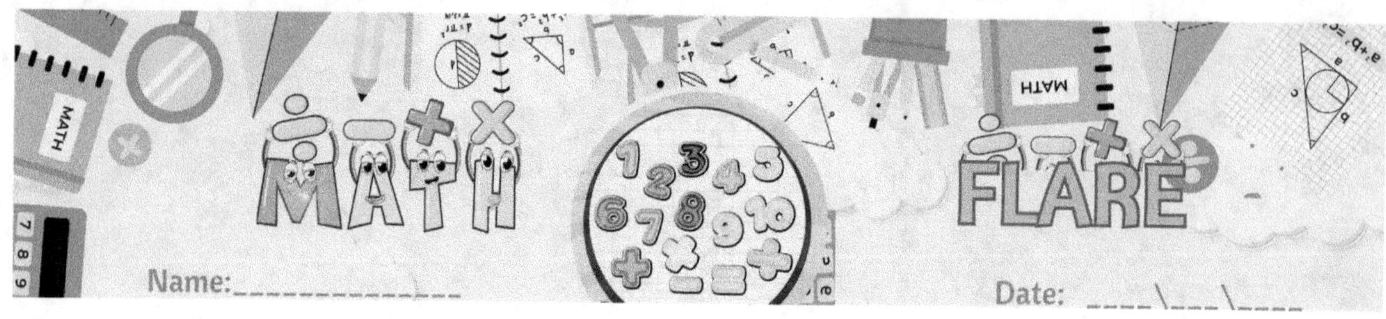

16. $7 + 6(-14z + 15)$

17. $-19k + 12k + 12 - 17k$

18. $-17k + 16 + 19k + 14 + 9k - 5$

19. $-20z - 9z$

20. $15k - 18 - 12k + 14$

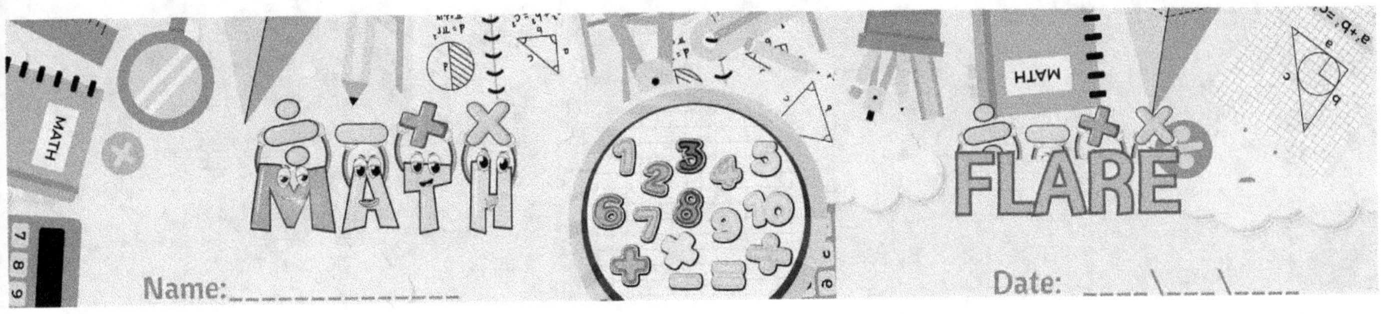

21. $-18x + x$

22. $x - 8x + 16x + 3 + 6$

23. $11y - 12 - 3y + 16 - 17$

24. $9k - k$

25. $7z + 11 - 19 - 8z + 17z$

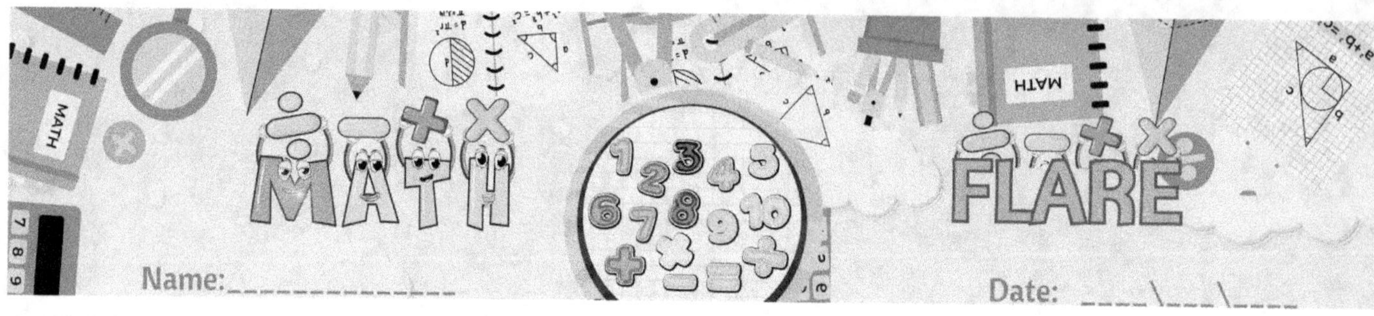

26. $18 - 3y + 4 - 9y + 16 - 14y$

27. $3m + 9 - 8 - 3m + 6m$

28. $17 + 15(-17x + 16)$

29. $-k + 11k$

30. $-16x - x$

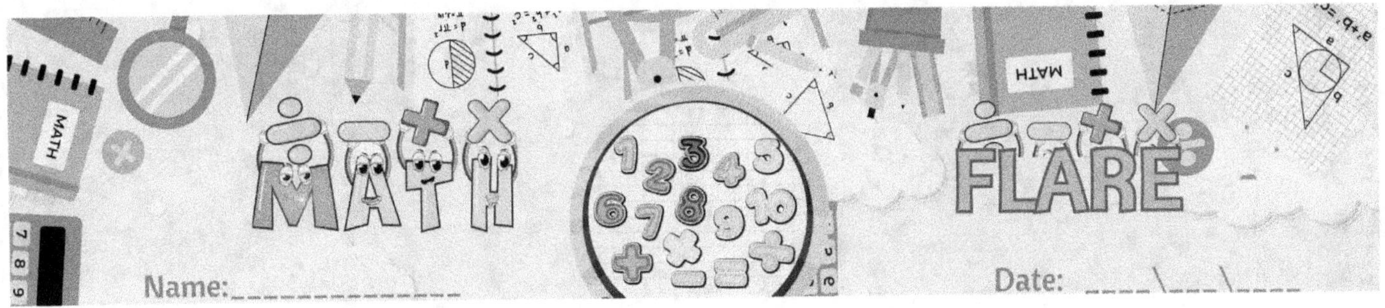

31. $-8 + 11z - 9z - 12 - 10z$

32. $3 + 4(-7y + 4)$

33. $18x - 2x$

34. $-8x + 8 - 8 + 12x$

35. $k - 12k$

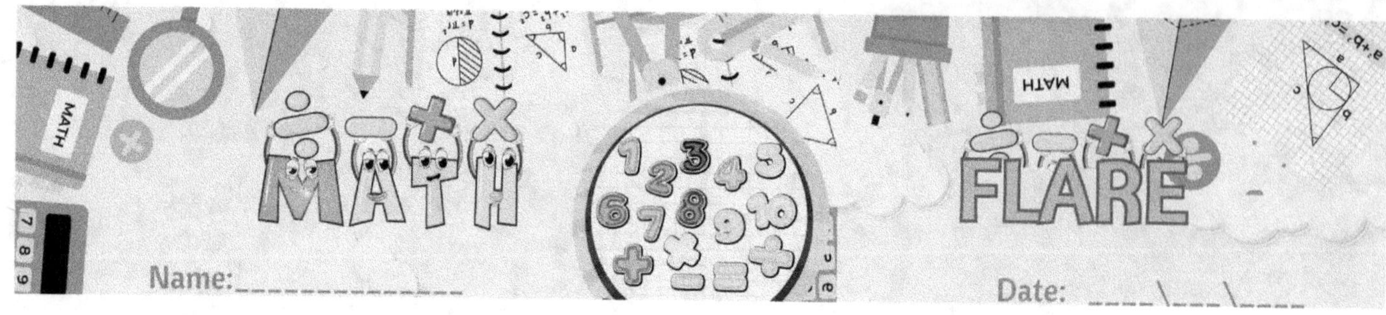

36. $-3x + 14 - 11 + 12x$

37. $-5x - 8 - 16 - 5x$

38. $17 - 2(6m - 19)$

39. $-11 + 20x + 5 - 20x$

40. $8 + 2m - 19m$

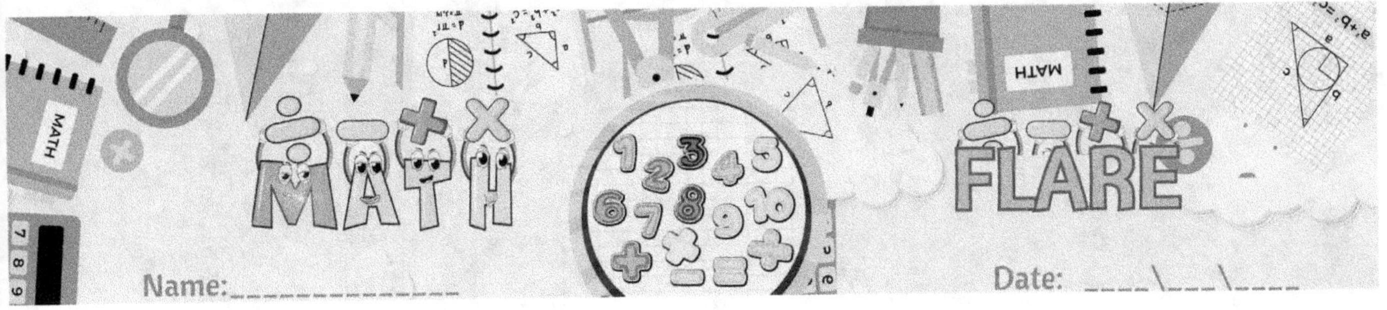

41. $-8 + 17 - 13z + 20z - 9 + 7z$

42. $z + 7z$

43. $2k + 15 + 20k + 18 + 20k + 6$

44. $13x - 12x + 16 + 8$

45. $17 - 16k + 9 - 14k + 8 - 4k$

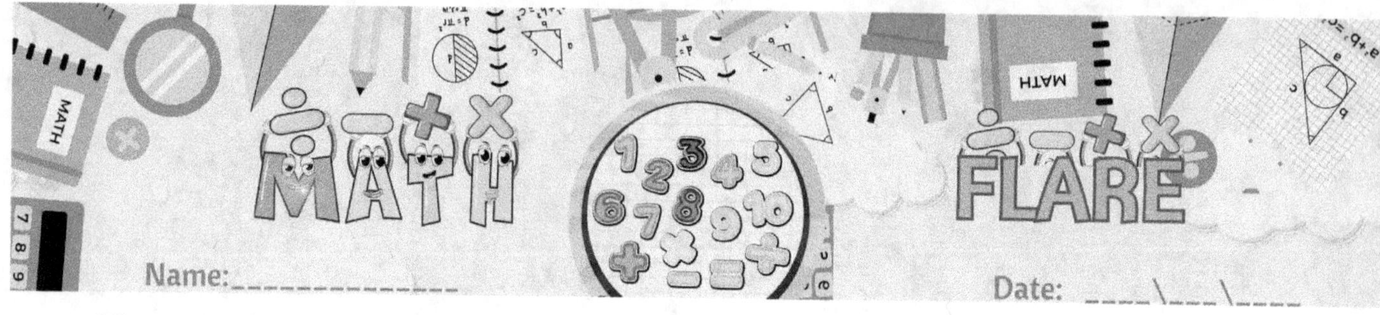

46. $-8 + 9x + 1 - 9x$

47. $15m + 16 + 13m + 2 + 9m + 7$

48. $-19m + 15m + 4 - 12m$

49. $-4m - 3 + 5m$

50. $-19y + y$

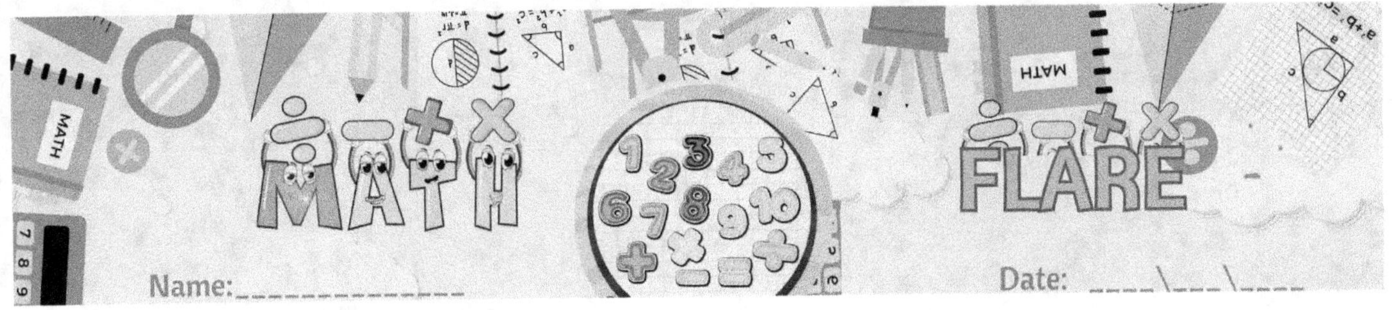

51. $-13 + 11y + 12 - 12y$

52. $2k + 20 - 6k + 2 + 4k + 12$

53. $-19 + 18 - 4m + 5m - 15 + 5m$

54. $13y - 7 - 6y + 18 - 10$

55. $-3m - 15 + 5m$

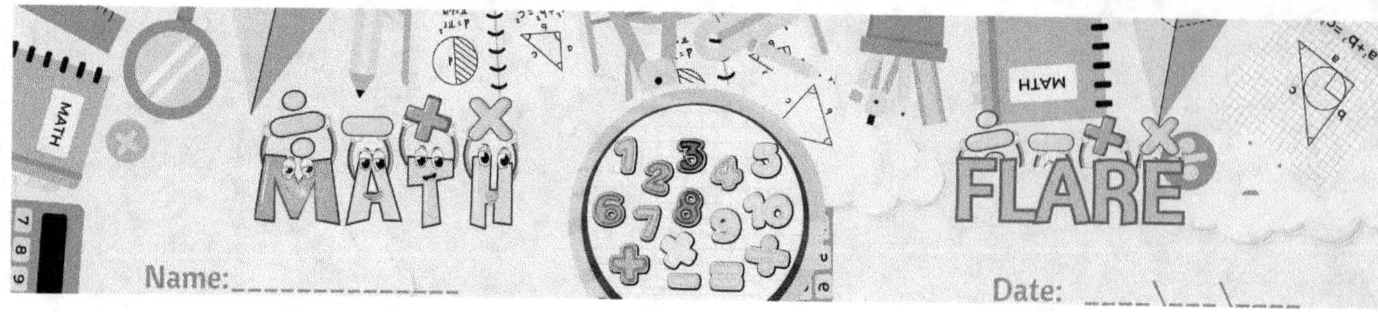

56. $4z - 19 + 10z - 2 + 12z + 11$

57. $-18 - 4z + 15z - 7 + 2z$

58. $4 - 5(-15y + 17)$

59. $-6k - 19 + 6 - 9k$

60. $-k + 17 + 6k$

61. $y - 15y + 3y + 10 + 10$

62. $-12x + 3x$

63. $17 + 5(-3k + 7)$

64. $13 + 9x - 3 + 10x$

65. $k - 10k$

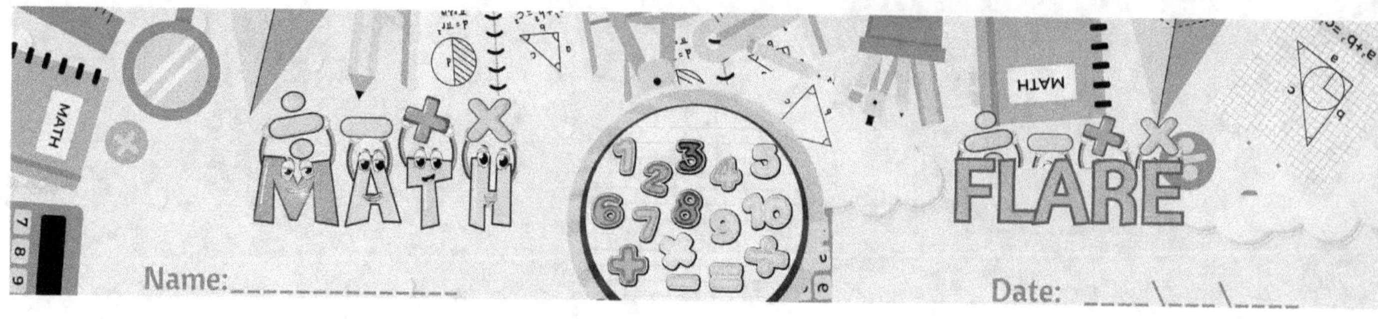

66. $-4 + x + 3 - 6x$

67. $-6 + 7x - 18x - 17 + 19x$

68. $4 + 5(-6x + 4)$

69. $-2m - 5 - 15m$

70. $7y + 9 - 11y + 5 + 20y + 20$

71. $-16x - 5 - 6 - 11x$

72. $-20z + 2z + 5 - 12z$

73. $20 + 4x - 5 + 9x$

74. $6 + 1(-7x + 13)$

75. $-k - 6 + 1 - 20k$

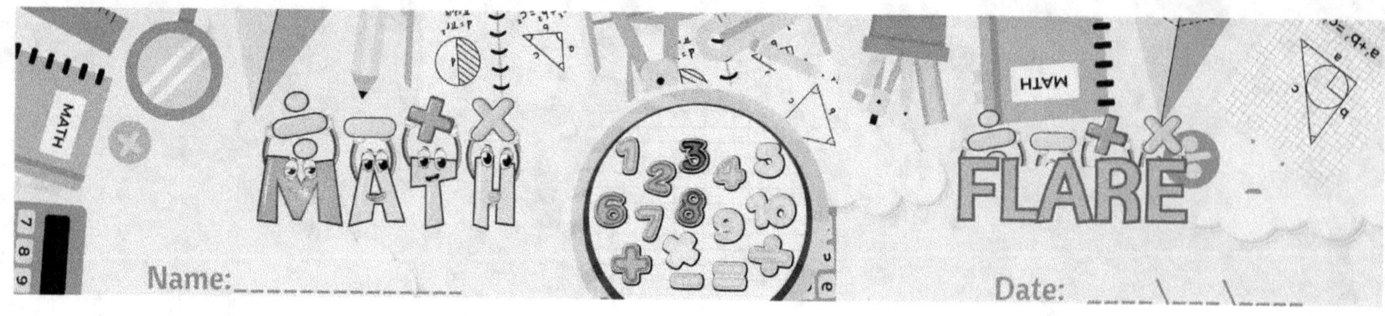

76. $-6x + x$

77. $3 - 3(-13m + 19)$

78. $7k - 11k$

79. $18z + 11 + z$

80. $-8x + 17 - 5x$

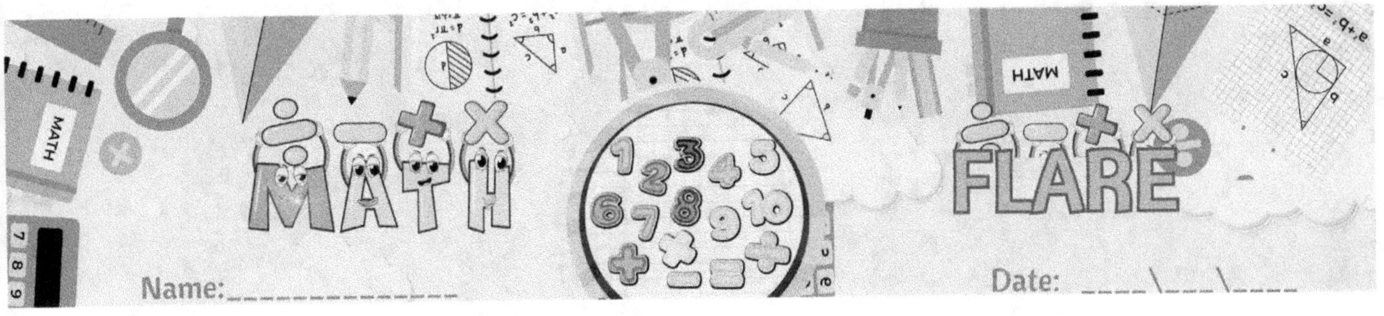

81. $2x - x$

82. $3z + z$

83. $-10m - 16 + 9 - 5m$

84. $6 - 7(20m - 4)$

85. $5y - 6y + 8y - 6 + 20$

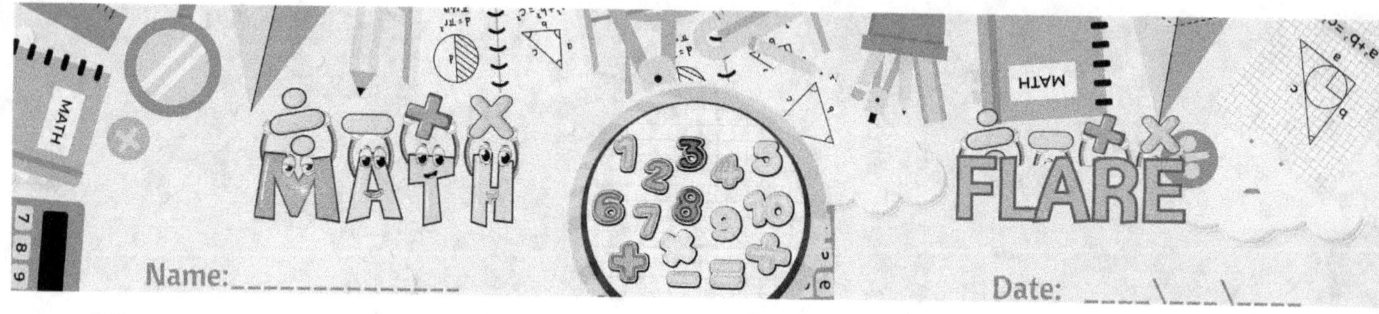

86. $13 + 20z - 17 + 18z - 15 + 12z$

87. $-x + 10x$

88. $19z - 17z + 17 + 5$

89. $15k + k$

90. $5m + 5 + 7m$

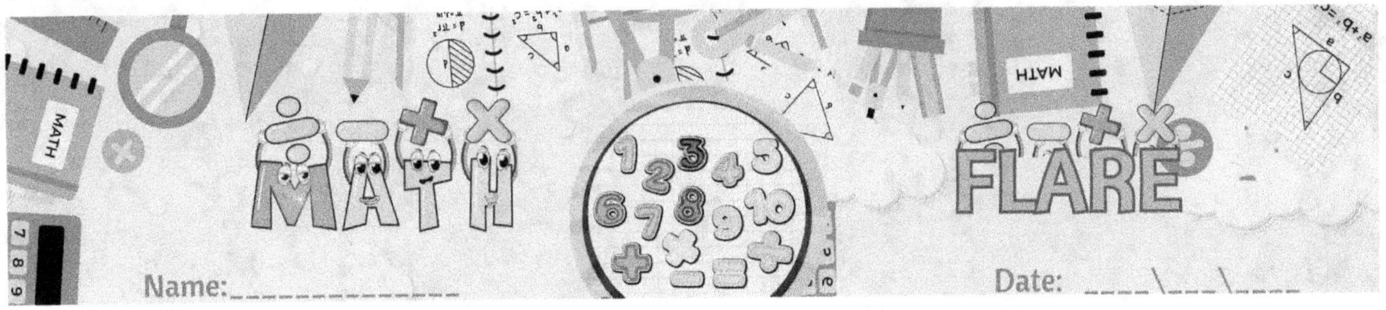

91. $-5 + 8 - 14y + 7y - 2 + 14y$

92. $9y - 3y + 17 + 11$

93. $-5 + 10m + 2 - 3m$

94. $x - 16x$

95. $-7y + 19y + 7 - 11y$

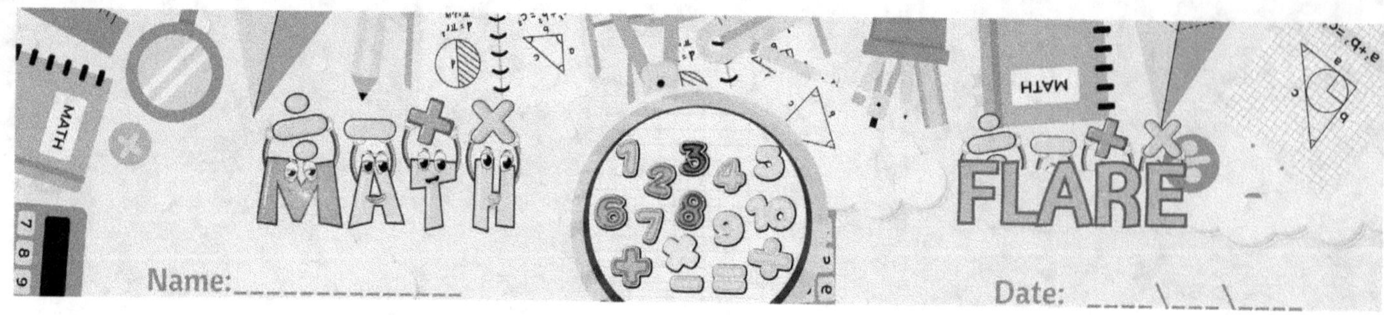

96. $x - 3x + 5x + 10 + 7$

97. $-6z + z$

98. $-6 - y + 8 - 13y$

99. $8 + 18m + 13 + 18m$

100. $4 + x - 16 + 19x$

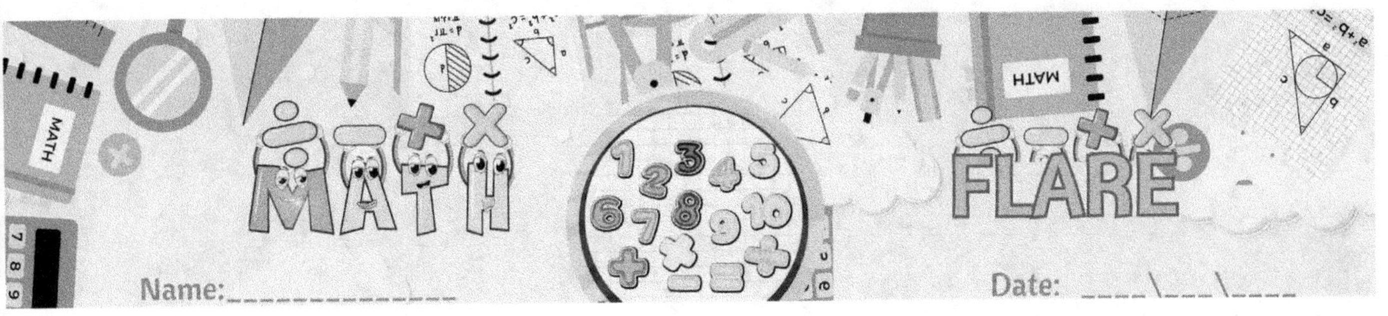

Solving Equations

Evaluate each expression when: $x = 4$

1. $x + 8 =$

2. $8x + 8 =$

3. $x - 6 =$

4. $8 \div x + 3 =$

5. $8x + 7x + 4x =$

6. $\dfrac{2 + 20}{x + 7} =$

7. $(4 + 10x) + (10x - 7) - (7 + 2x) =$

8. $(8x)^1 =$

9. $(8x + 8) + (6x + 10) =$

10. $(x + 6) \div 1 =$

Solving Equations

Evaluate each expression when: x = 1

1. $2 + \dfrac{1+x}{x} - 2 =$

2. $10x + 4x + 4x =$

3. $3(2x) =$

4. $8 + (8x + 3) =$

5. $5x - 10 + 8x =$

6. $1 + \dfrac{11}{x} + 10^1 =$

7. $9 + \dfrac{10}{x} + 3^1 =$

8. $3 - x =$

9. $7 + (9x + 8) - 8 + (8x) =$

10. $\dfrac{45}{x} =$

Solving Equations

Evaluate each expression when: x = 5

1. $\dfrac{x}{1} + 8 =$

2. $(5 + 10x) + (x - 1) - (7 + 8x) =$

3. $8x + 3 =$

4. $x + 7 =$

5. $10 + x =$

6. $7x - 7 =$

7. $4^1 + x^1 =$

8. $10x - 1 =$

9. $9x - x =$

10. $10 \div x + 9 =$

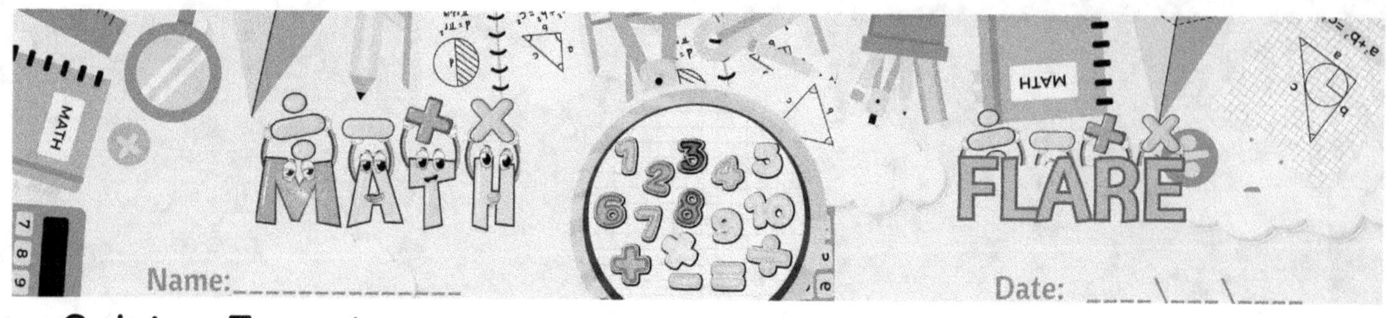

Solving Equations

Evaluate each expression when: x = 4

1. $9 - x =$

2. $2x + 2 =$

3. $10 - x =$

4. $(x^1 + 1) - 9(5 + x) =$

5. $1(1 + x) =$

6. $9x - 7 =$

7. $7x + 1 =$

8. $x + 7 =$

9. $9x + x =$

10. $9x + 5x + 2x =$

Solving Equations

Evaluate each expression when: x = 5

1. $5x - 5 + 10x =$

2. $5x + 2 =$

3. $x + 7 =$

4. $x + 3 =$

5. $2 + \dfrac{x}{1} =$

6. $6 + (9x + 3) =$

7. $(10x)(x) =$

8. $5(6 - x) =$

9. $10x + 6 =$

10. $(5 + 3x) + (4x - 8) - (1 + 10x) =$

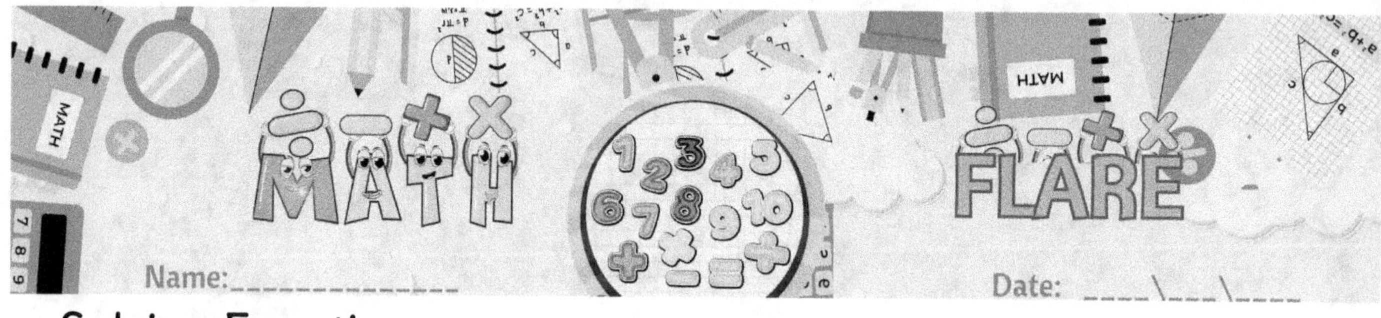

Solving Equations

Evaluate each expression when: $x = 3$

1. $2 + (8x + 7) =$

2. $\dfrac{9 + x}{x + 1} =$

3. $9 + \dfrac{30}{x} + 6^1 =$

4. $3(6 - x) =$

5. $(x^1 + 5) - 9(1 + x) =$

6. $3x - 6 + 9x =$

7. $8(8x) =$

8. $7x + 4 - 4x =$

9. $x^1 + x - 7 =$

10. $5x + 10 - x =$

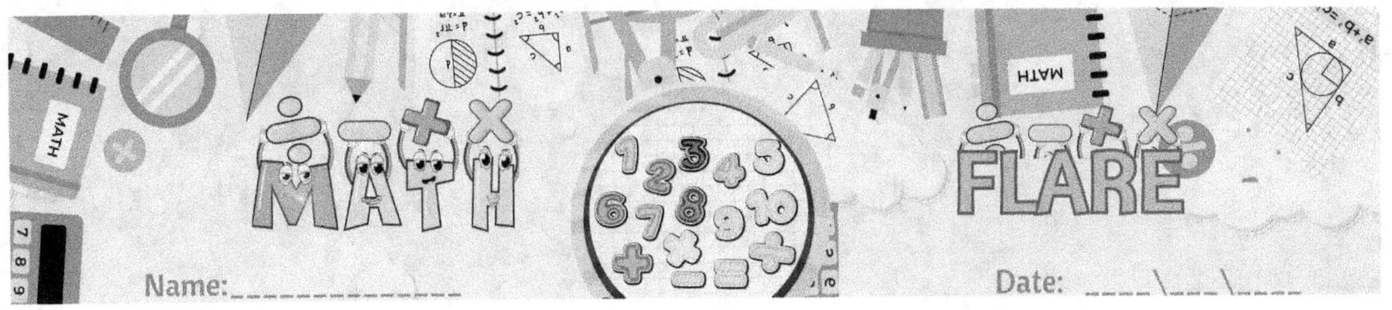

Solving Equations

Evaluate each expression when: $x = 3$

1. $9x + 4x + 7x =$

2. $x \div 3 =$

3. $9 \div (x + 6) =$

4. $6 \div x + 2 =$

5. $10 \div (x + 2) =$

6. $1 + \dfrac{15}{x} + 10^1 =$

7. $4^1 + x^1 =$

8. $(8x)(x) =$

9. $7x + 8 =$

10. $8x + 6 =$

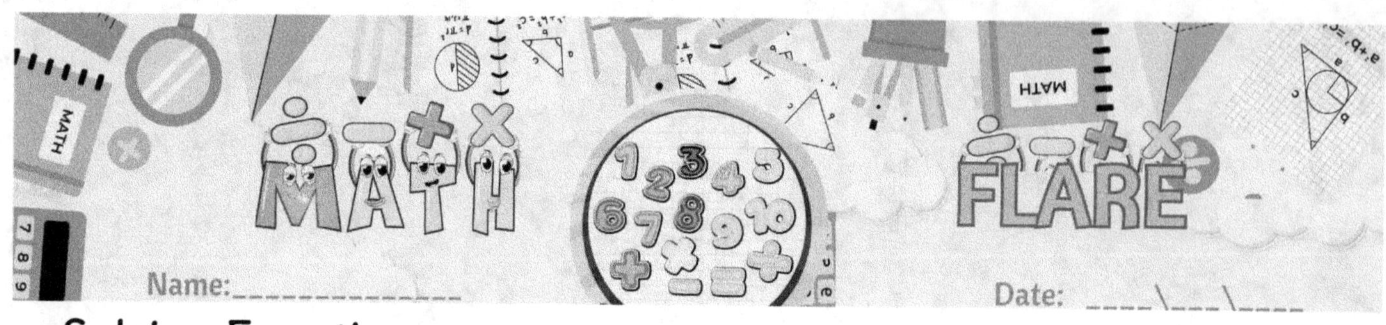

Solving Equations

Evaluate each expression when: x = 2

1. $\dfrac{2}{x} =$

2. $2(6x) =$

3. $\dfrac{x}{2} + 2 =$

4. $10x - 1 =$

5. $(4x)(2x) =$

6. $3(3x) =$

7. $10x + x =$

8. $8 + 7x =$

9. $\dfrac{x}{1} =$

10. $2 - x =$

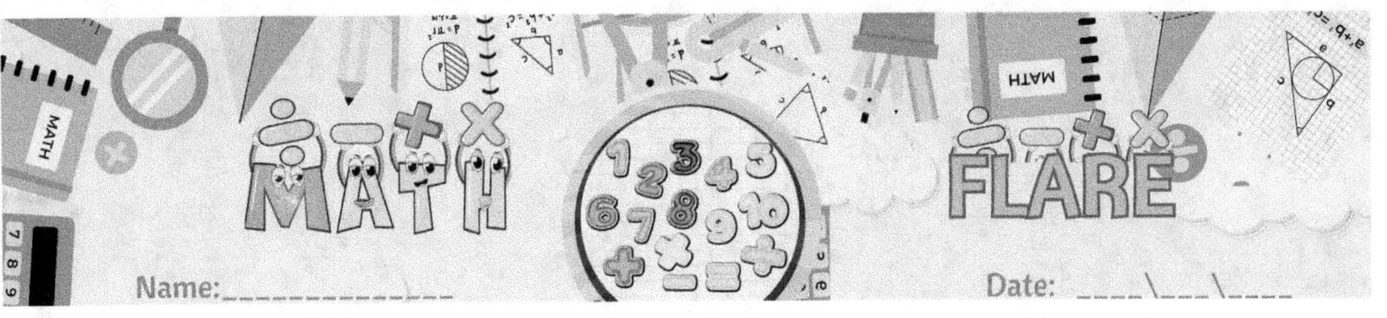

Solving Equations

Evaluate each expression when: $x = 7$

1. $\dfrac{x}{7} + 6 =$

2. $10x + 4 =$

3. $\dfrac{x}{1} =$

4. $x(7 + x) =$

5. $8x + 5 =$

6. $(6x + 4) + (x - 9) =$

7. $(x)^1 =$

8. $5x + 9 =$

9. $5x + 7 =$

10. $x + 8 =$

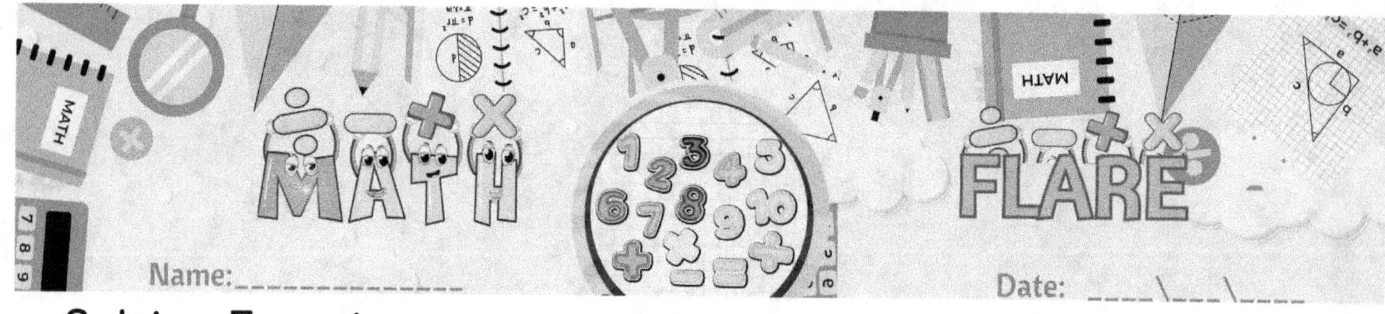

Solving Equations

Evaluate each expression when: $x = 4$

1. $x^1 + x - 1 =$

2. $5 + (4x + 6) - 9 + (6x) =$

3. $(3x + 4) + (x + 1) =$

4. $(6 + 6x) + (9x - 5) - (5 + 7x) =$

5. $4 + 10x =$

6. $x - 9 =$

7. $\dfrac{2 + x}{x + 2} =$

8. $8x + x =$

9. $5(8x - 6) + 1(2 + x) =$

10. $(2x)^1 =$

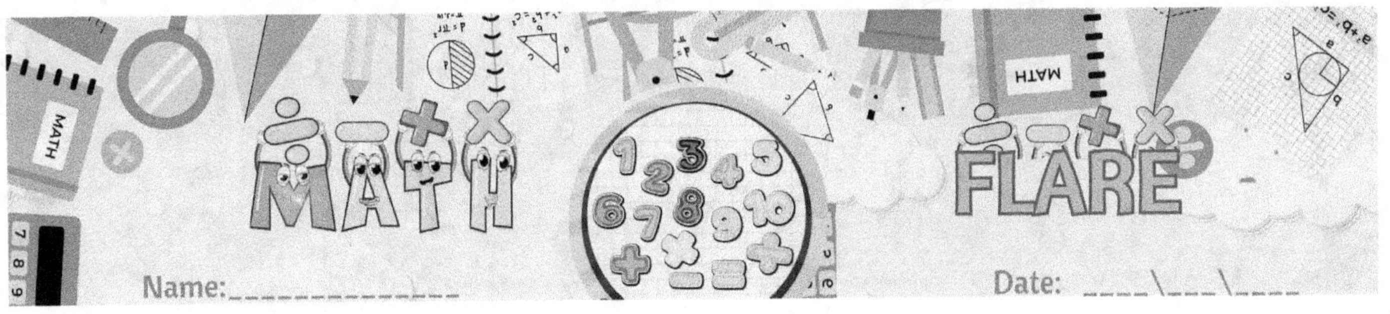

Solving Equations

Evaluate each expression when: x = 5

1. $7 + \dfrac{x}{1} =$

2. $\dfrac{x}{1} =$

3. $(1 + 10x) + (7x - 2) - (8 + 4x) =$

4. $\dfrac{7 + x}{x + 7} =$

5. $x(3 + x) =$

6. $7x + 7 =$

7. $2 + 5x =$

8. $2 + \dfrac{45}{x} + 1^1 =$

9. $6x^1 + 9x^1 =$

10. $1 + x =$

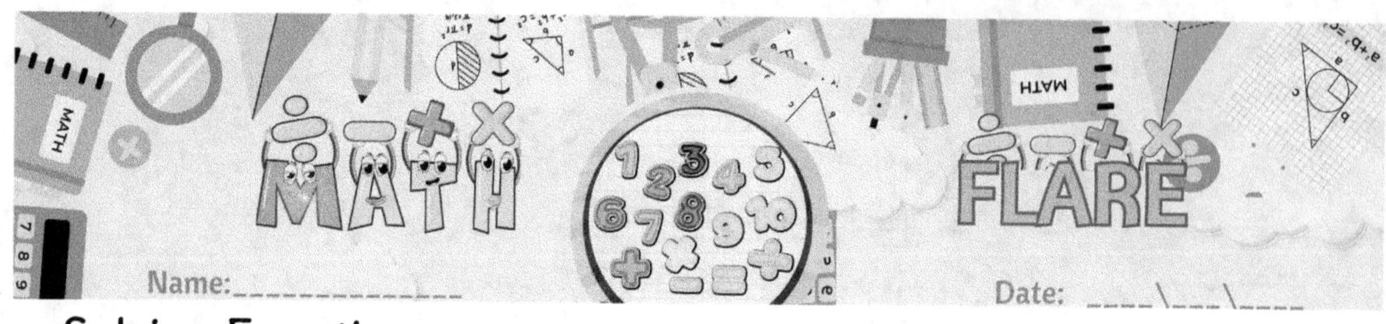

Solving Equations

Evaluate each expression when: $x = 4$

1. $\dfrac{1+x}{x+1} =$

2. $2x + 2 - 4x =$

3. $x^1 + x - 1 =$

4. $2 + \dfrac{6+x}{x} - 10 =$

5. $6 + \dfrac{4}{x} + 4^1 =$

6. $(x^1 + 7) - 9(2 + x) =$

7. $5 + \dfrac{x}{4} =$

8. $9 + x =$

9. $(x + 8) \div 4 =$

10. $\dfrac{16}{x} =$

Name:________________   Date: _______________

Solving Equations

Evaluate each expression when: x = 5

1. $(2x)^1 =$

2. $3x + 9 =$

3. $7x + 6 =$

4. $8 + (5x + 9) =$

5. $(8x + 3) + (3x + 1) =$

6. $5 + (6x + 3) =$

7. $(8x)(x) =$

8. $5x + 10 =$

9. $2x + x =$

10. $3 + \dfrac{4 + x}{5x} - 9 =$

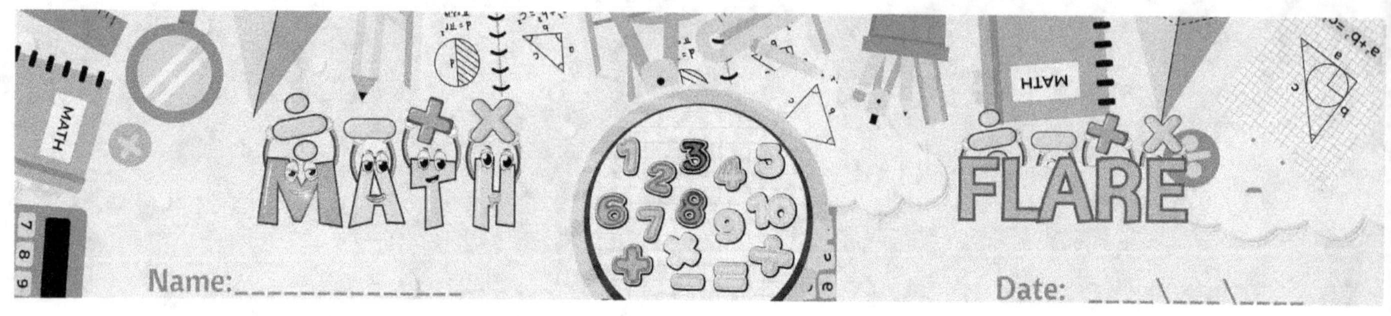

Equations (One Side)

Solve for the variable.

1. $296 = 17m - 3 + 6m$

2. $270 = 9 + \dfrac{20}{z} + 16^2$

3. $361 = 19z + 19$

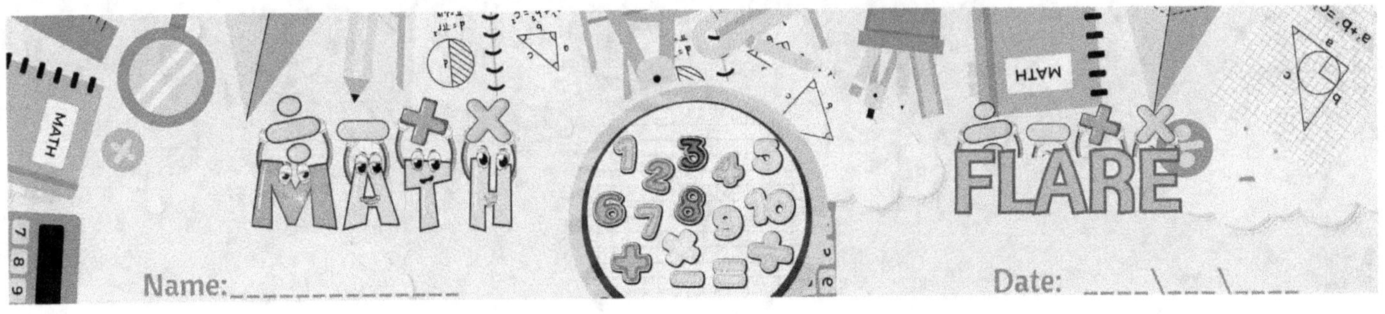

4. $16 + y = 22$

5. $(17k + 15) + (20k - 12) = 669$

6. $23{,}104 = (19y)^2$

7. $198 = 14y + 10y - 18$

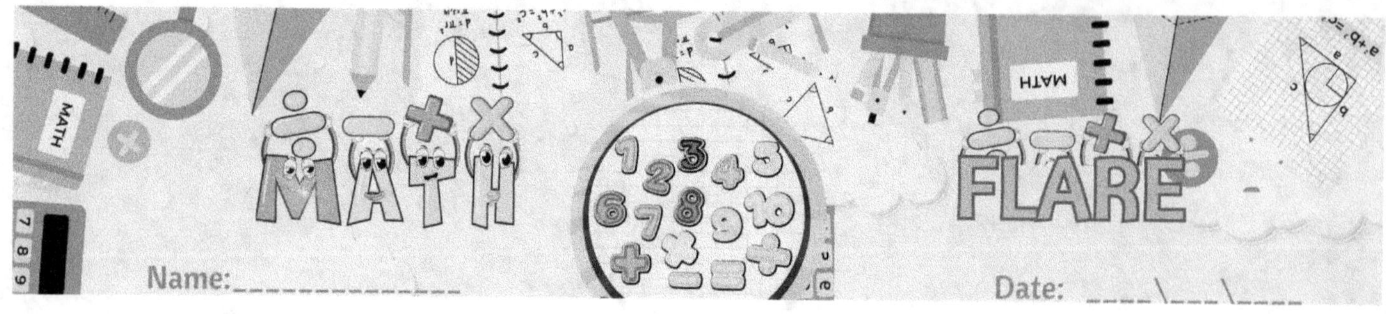

8. $6(18 + m) = 186$

9. $0.6 = 9 \div m$

10. $13 + y = 22$

11. $10 = 14 - z$

12. $5^2 + m^2 = 281$

13. $272 = 17(4y)$

14. $z - 13 = -4$

15. $266 = 9 + \dfrac{1}{m} + 16^2$

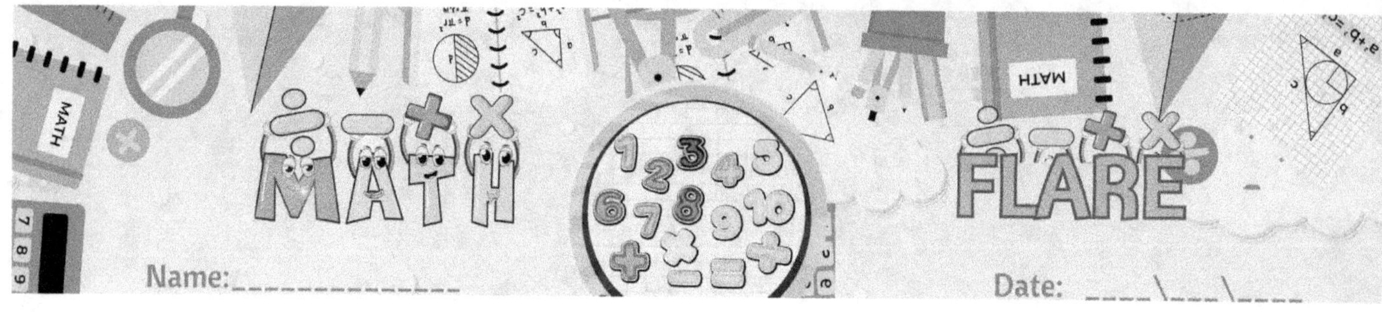

16. $22 = 4y + 6$

17. $6m + 2 = 86$

18. $644 = 12m + 15m + 19m$

19. $4 \div m + 20 = 20.444$

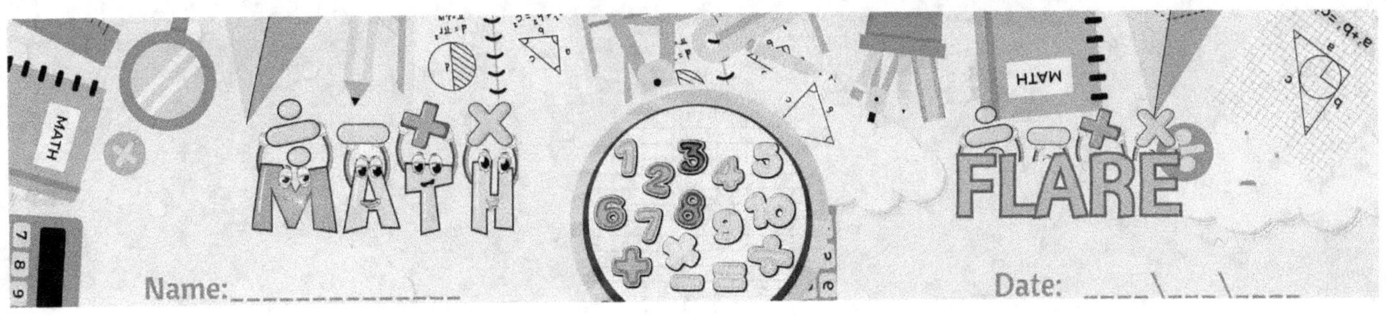

20. $2x - x = 17$

21. $1 = \dfrac{4}{y}$

22. $6k + 2 + (2k - 13) = 77$

23. $38 = 3x - x$

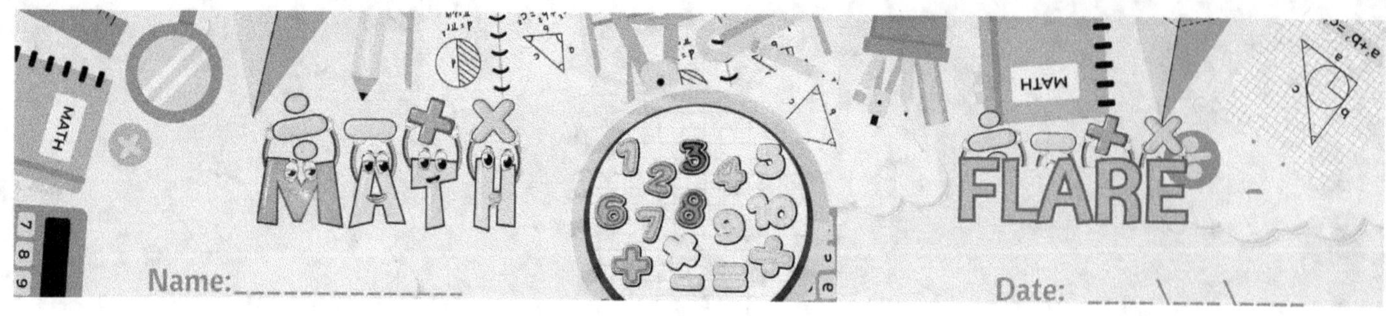

24. $9 \div (y + 15) = 0.36$

25. $6(8 + m) = 132$

26. $15m - m = 28$

27. $19 = 12 + x$

28. $-7.357 = 8 + \dfrac{4+y}{2y} - 16$

29. $530 = (20m + 14) + (12m + 4)$

30. $12 + \dfrac{z}{6} = 14$

31. $2 - z = -16$

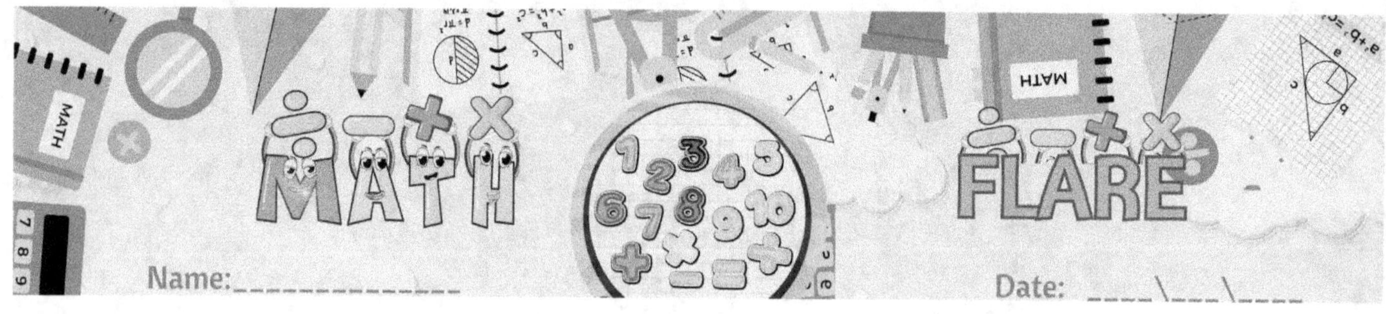

32. $11(13 + y) = 165$

33. $5m + m = 84$

34. $12 + (4k + 6) - 5 + (4k) = 141$

35. $21 = 19 + x$

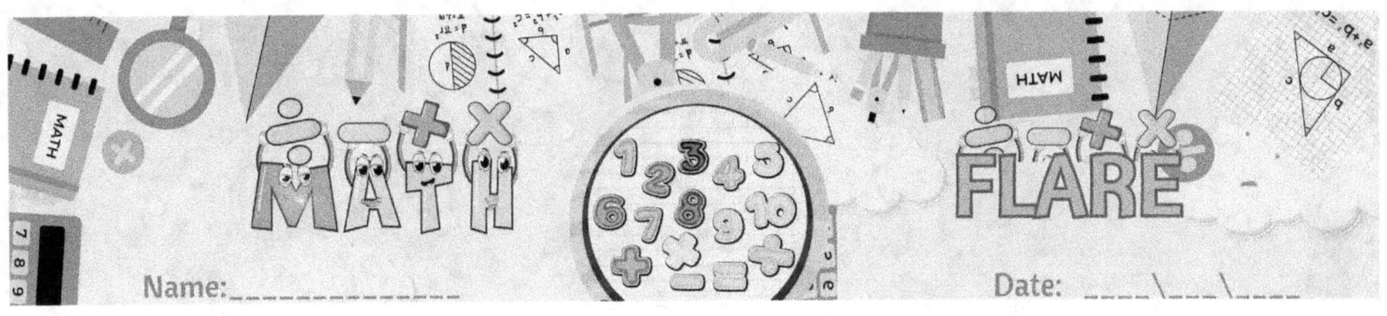

36. $180 = z(11 + z)$

37. $0.667 = \dfrac{10 + m}{m + 20}$

38. $\dfrac{1}{y} = 1$

39. $1.273 = \dfrac{10 + 4}{x + 10}$

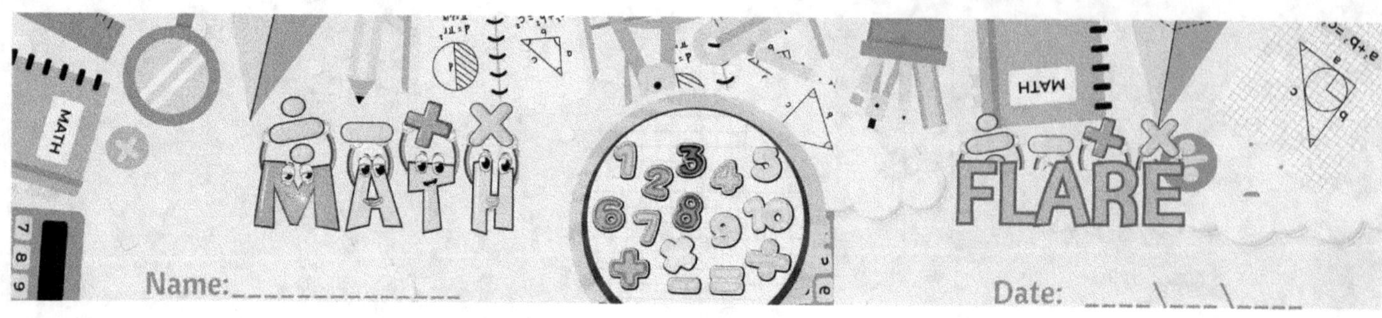

40. $(4y + 20) + (8y + 14) = 58$

41. $2 = \dfrac{14}{k}$

42. $8 + \dfrac{z}{2} = 15$

43. $299 = 10x - 1 + 15x$

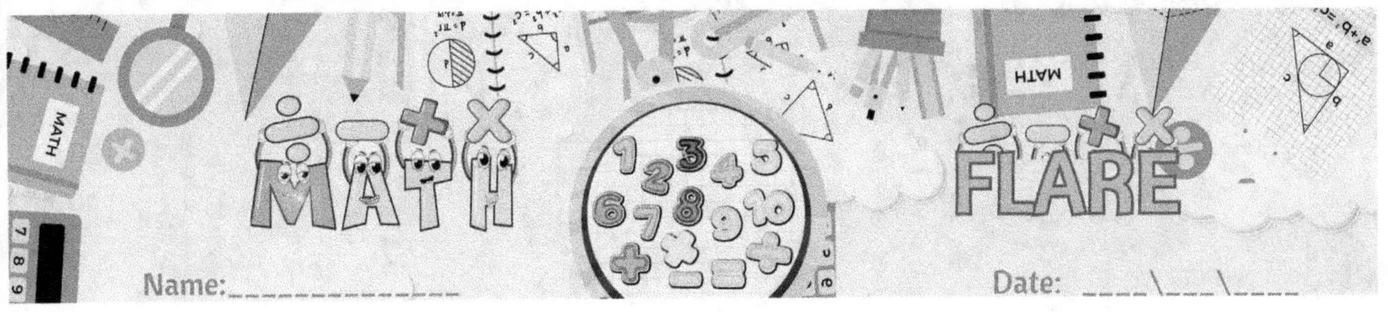

44. $5k + 6 = 11$

45. $1 = 16 \div y$

46. $16k - k = 45$

47. $0.9 = y \div 20$

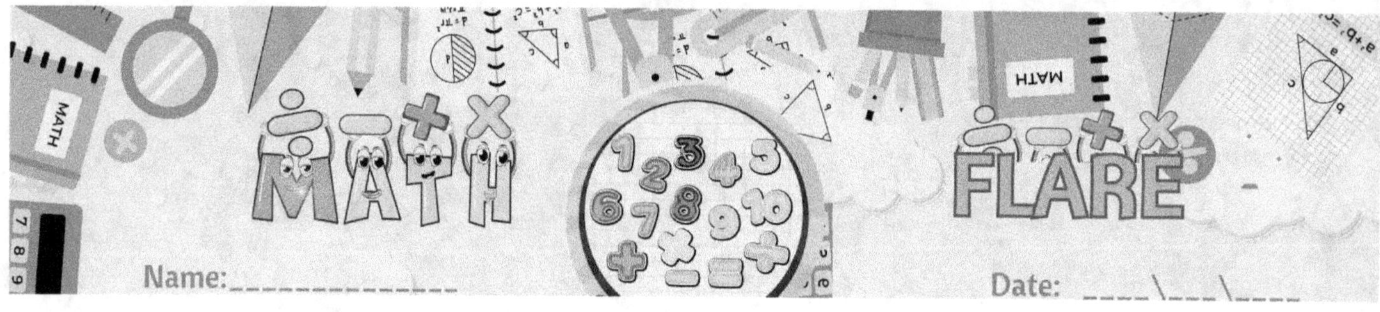

48. $7k + 16 = 30$

49. $259 = 12 + (6k + 19) - 2 + (17k)$

50. $275 = 4k - 13 + 14k$

51. $8 + 16x = 40$

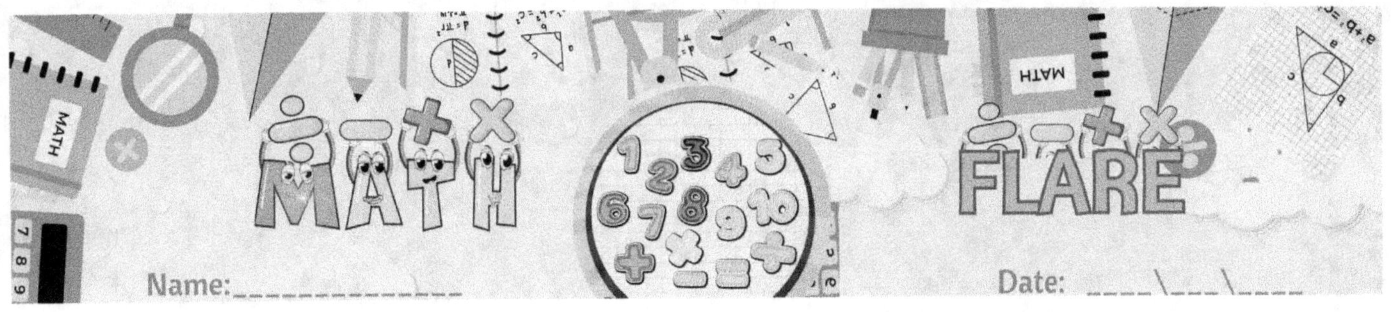

52. $42 = (2x + 6) + (8x - 14)$

53. $24 = m + 8$

54. $14 = 2y - y$

55. $1 = (k + 6) \div 12$

56. $\dfrac{k}{1} + 6 = 14$

57. $1{,}350 = (15k)(10k)$

58. $6z + 20z - 12 = 92$

59. $0.9 = \dfrac{6 + x}{x + 8}$

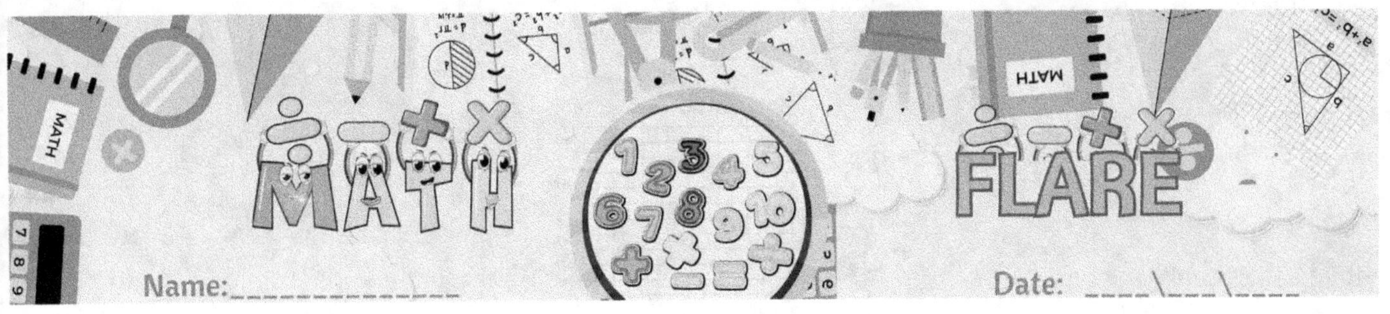

60. $52 = z + 12 + 9z$

61. $64 = (z)(16z)$

62. $216 = 18 + (12x + 6)$

63. $19.071 = 15 \div x + 18$

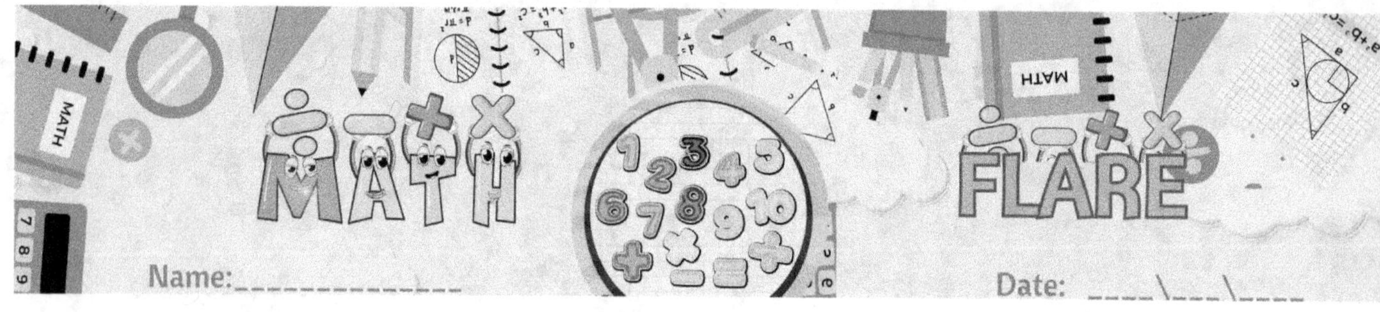

64. $0.286 = 4 \div k$

65. $21 = 20 + \dfrac{x}{8}$

66. $2 = \dfrac{8 + 6}{k + 6}$

67. $16z - 5 + 14z = 535$

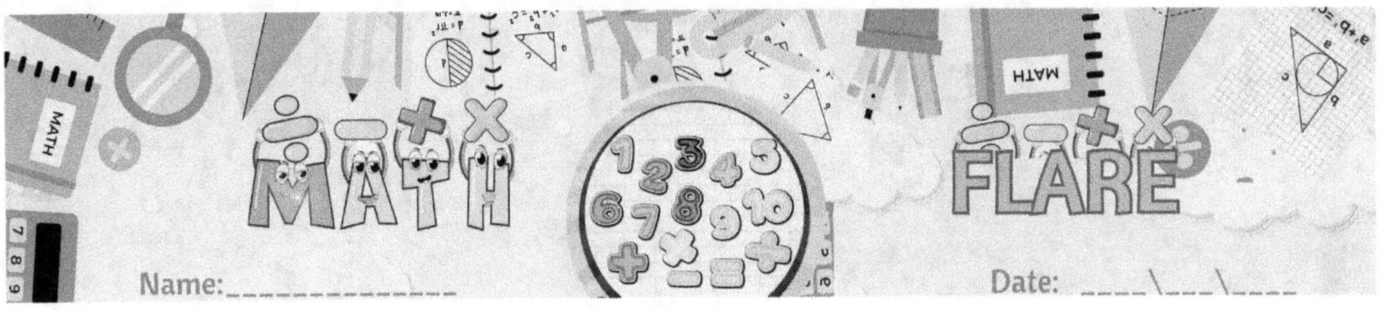

68. $0 = y - y$

69. $\dfrac{m}{5} + 16 = 18$

70. $42 = 14(11 - z)$

71. $18z + 5 + (z - 14) = 86$

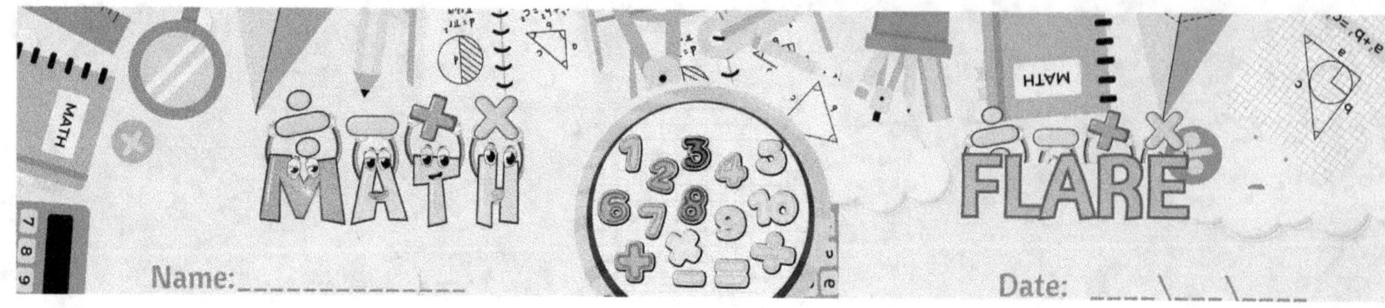

72. $19{,}360 = (16m)(10m)$

73. $318 = 12 + (16x + 7) - 13 + (8x)$

74. $217 = 14m + 7$

75. $20y + 16 = 416$

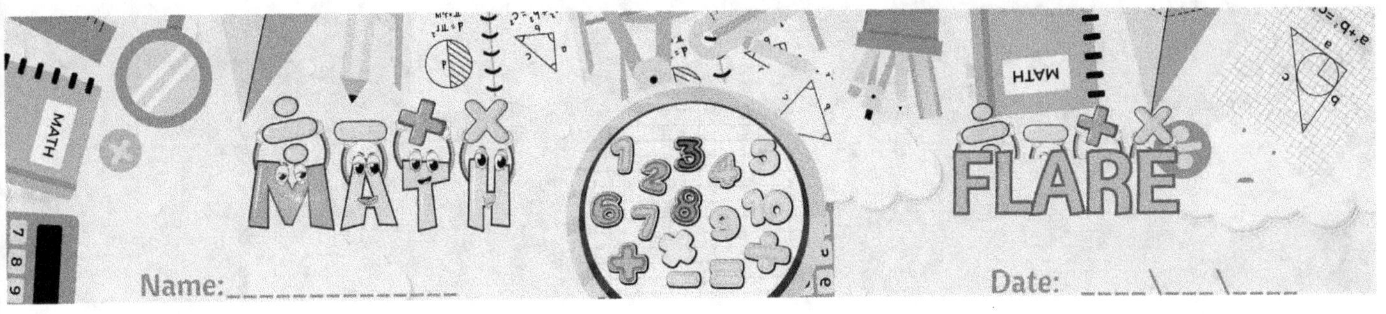

76. $\dfrac{15}{y} = 3$

77. $y - 18 = -12$

78. $9 = \dfrac{y}{2}$

79. $17 = 15 + z$

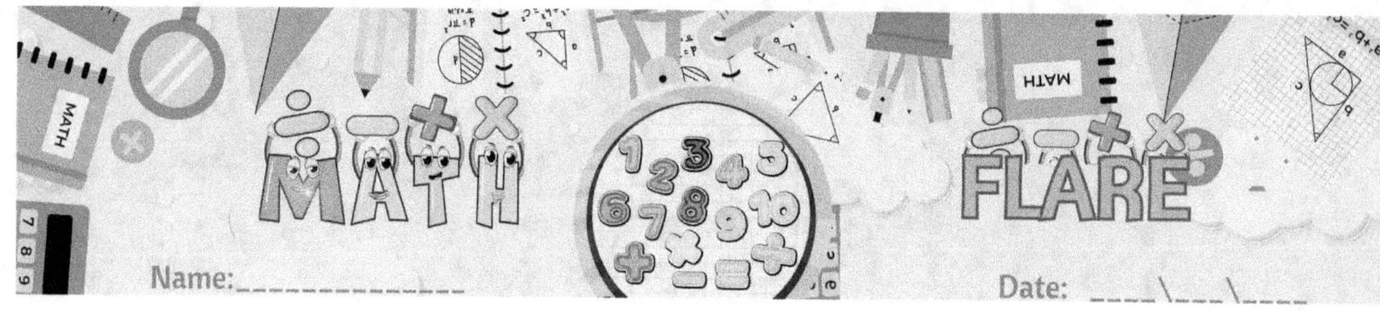

80. $-19 = k - 20$

81. $167 = 20 + (7m + 7)$

82. $1 = \dfrac{x}{10}$

83. $12y + 19 + (13y - 18) = 501$

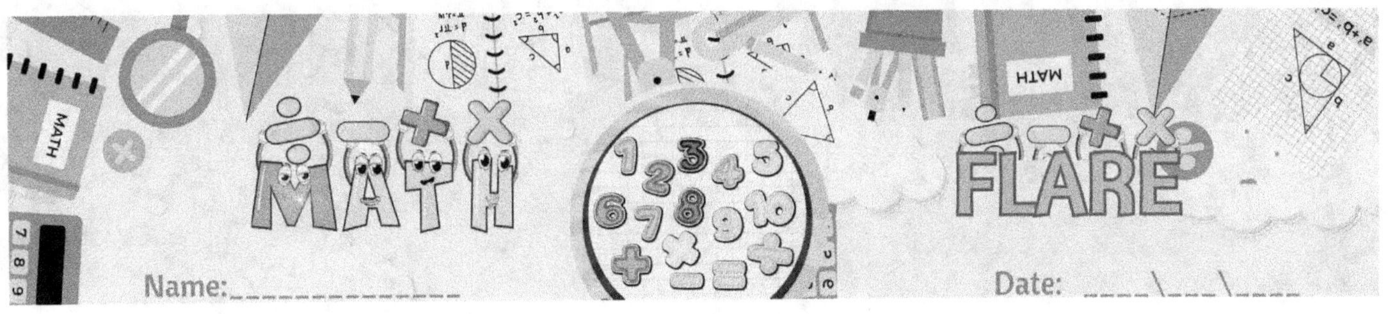

84. $10x - 10 = 130$

85. $\dfrac{12 + 12}{z + 6} = 3$

86. $8z + 4 = 76$

87. $16y - y = 225$

88. $17 = \dfrac{y}{8} + 15$

89. $28{,}500 = (15x)(19x)$

90. $21 = 3m + 18$

91. $\dfrac{m}{4} = 4$

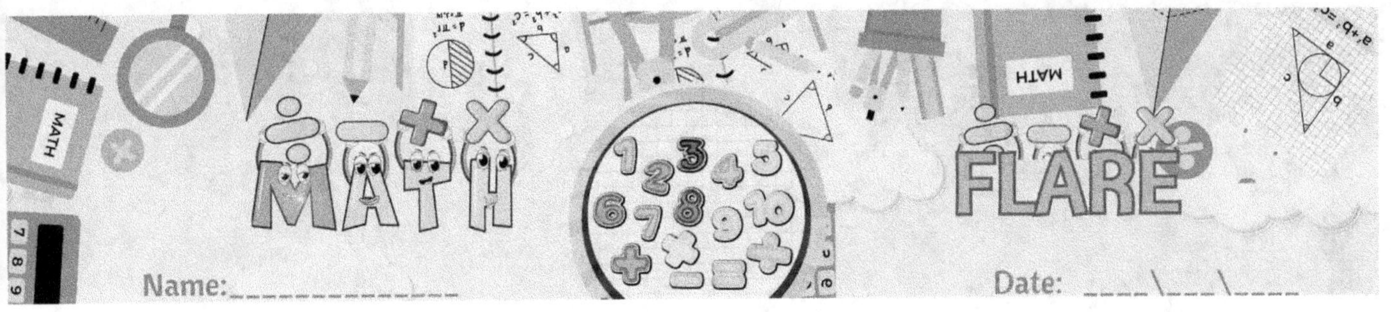

92. $8^2 + k^2 = 208$

93. $241 = 17z + 20$

94. $72 = 14m^2 + 4m^2$

95. $8 \div (m + 8) = 0.889$

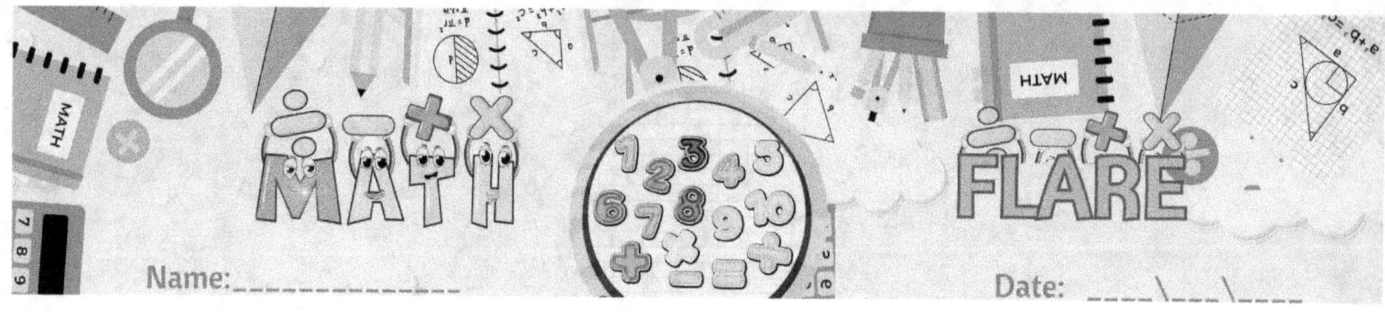

96. $377 = 19^2 + y^2$

97. $k + 6 + 3k = 46$

98. $7x + 12 = 26$

99. $121 = 8z + 17$

100. $4 + \dfrac{6}{m} + 12^2 = 151$

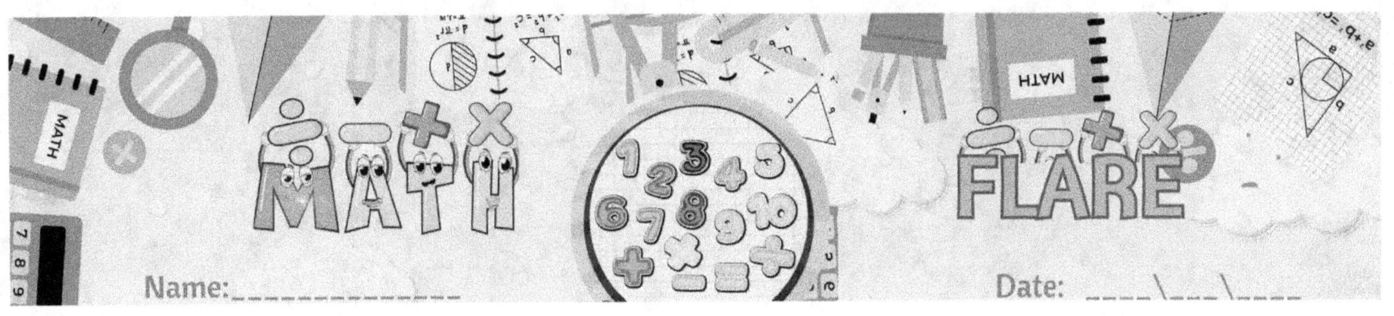

Equations (Two Sides)

Solve for the variable.

1. $20 - x = 4 + 7x + 8$

2. $10 + 7x = 6 + 8x$

3. $7 + 9z = 24 - 8z$

4. $8 + 8k = 5k + 20$

5. $4 + 6y = 14 + y$

6. $4 + 5k = 20 + 3k$

7. $7 + 4k = 27 - k$

8. $13 + x = 1 + 2x + 9$

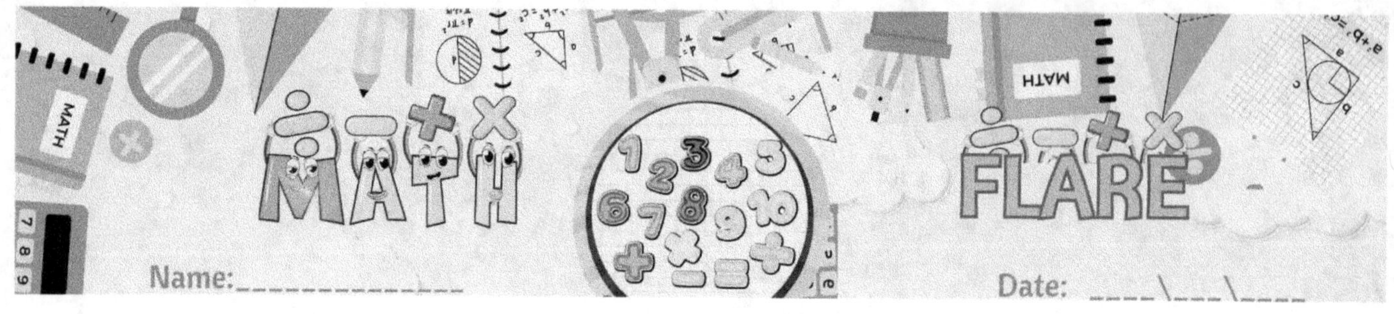

9. $2m + 9 = 36 - m$

10. $8x + 1 = 2 + 7x$

11. $9 + 4z + 8 = 32 + z + 3$

12. $21 - x = 8 + 2x + 4$

13. $13 + k = 8k + 6$

14. $9x + 1 = 86 - 8x$

15. $22 - k = 1 + 2k$

16. $15 + x + 0 = 1 + 6x + 9$

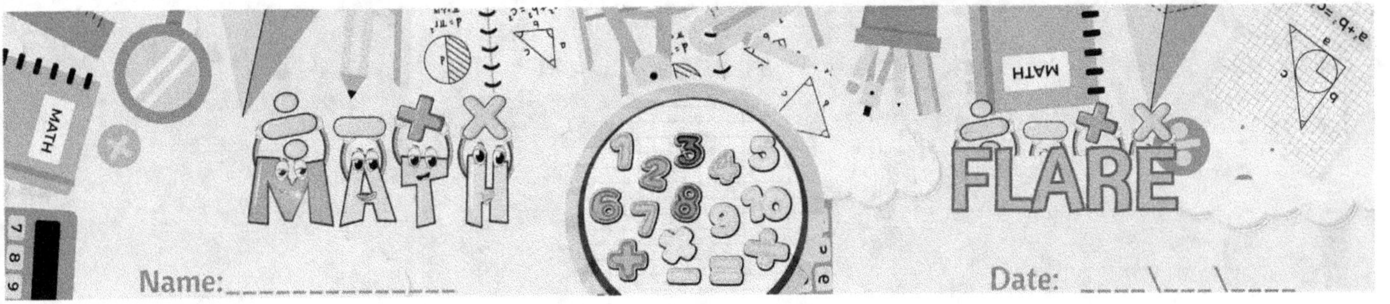

17. $93 - 8k = 9k + 8$

18. $27 - m = 8m + 9$

19. $8y + 6 = 30 - 4y$

20. $1 + 7k = 25 - 5k$

21. $1 + 2k = 9 + k$

22. $14 - x = 3x + 2$

23. $9m + 8 = 127 - 8m$

24. $6 + m = 3 + 2m$

25. $21 - x + 7 = 9 + 2x + 1$

26. $7 + 2y + 7 = 23 - y + 15$

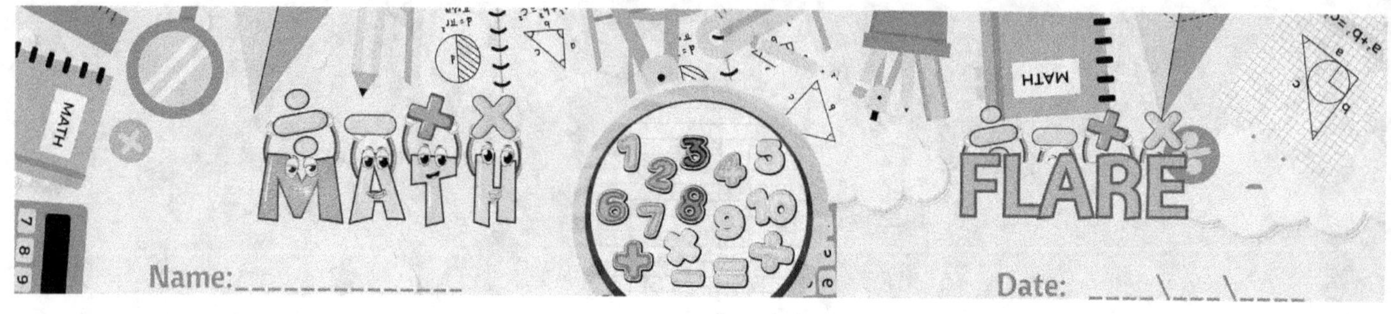

27. $8 + z = 2z + 5$

28. $22 - 2z = 8 + 5z$

29. $81 - m = 8 + 7m + 1$

30. $9m + 4 = 37 - 2m$

31. $9 + 9y = 121 - 7y$

32. $8 + 8k + 2 = 42 + k + 3$

33. $13 + m = 1 + 3m + 4$

34. $21 + m = 4 + 3m + 5$

35. $1 + 8m = 22 + m$

36. $56 + k = 2 + 8k + 5$

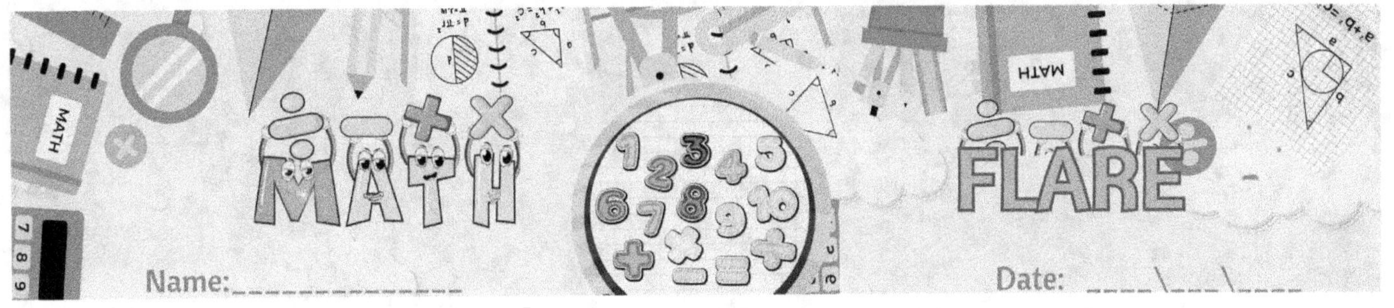

37. $14 + y = 2y + 6$

38. $10 - k + 3 = 2 + 7k + 3$

39. $7 + 6y + 2 = 51 - y$

40. $5m + 19 = 1 + 8m$

41. $4m + 41 = 9 + 8m$

42. $2 + 6x + 8 = 73 - x$

43. $19 + x + 2 = 9 + 2x + 7$

44. $6m + 5 = 2m + 9$

45. $30 - z + 5 = 2 + 7z + 1$

46. $32 + 4m = 4 + 8m$

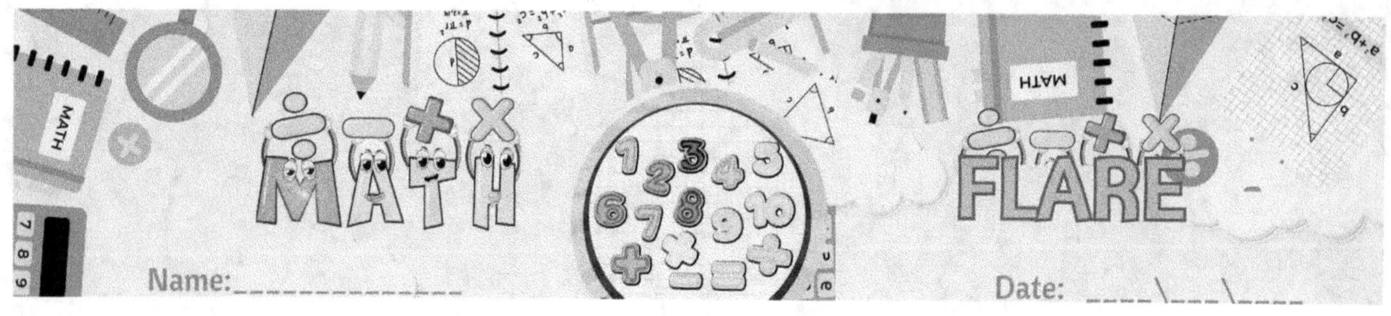

47. $49 - 2k = 7k + 4$

48. $56 + y + -2 = 7 + 7y + 5$

49. $5 + 2m = 7 + m$

50. $6 + 9k = 61 - 2k$

51. $9m + 5 = 6m + 17$

52. $4k + 33 = 6 + 7k$

53. $6 + 7m + 4 = 64 + m$

54. $11 + k = 3 + 2k$

55. $2x + 1 = 5 + x$

56. $5 + 8k + 2 = 25 - k$

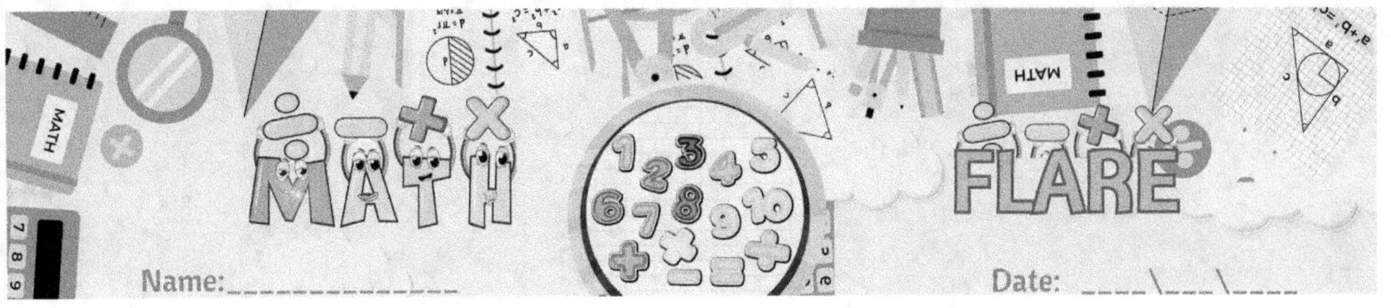

57. $7 + 7m = 73 - 4m$

58. $3x + 7 = 27 - x$

59. $47 - 4x = 3 + 7x$

60. $22 - z = 7 + 4z$

61. $41 - 2k = 6 + 3k$

62. $8 + 6m = 13 + m$

63. $4 + 9k = 10 + 8k$

64. $52 + z + 0 = 3 + 7z + 7$

65. $2 + 5y + 4 = 7 + y + 3$

66. $8z + 9 = 9z + 6$

67. $45 - m = 5 + 4m$

68. $6 + 8z = 12 + 7z$

69. $7 + 7k + 4 = 83 - k$

70. $2z + 8 = 17 + z$

71. $3 + 9z = 8z + 5$

72. $2z + 5 = 20 - z$

73. $50 - y + 13 = 4 + 5y + 5$

74. $3 + 3x + 8 = 47 - x$

75. $43 - y = 3 + 7y$

76. $136 - 7y = 9y + 8$

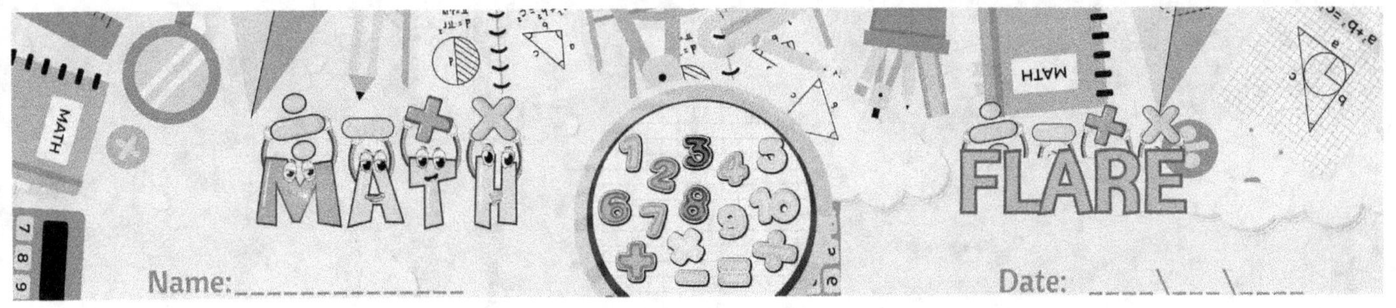

77. $23 - z + 7 = 5 + 8z + 7$

78. $2 + 2k + 2 = 25 - k$

79. $73 - 7x = 9x + 9$

80. $60 + k = 2 + 8k + 2$

81. $39 + x = 3 + 7x$

82. $66 - m = 2 + 6m + 1$

83. $9x + 8 = 63 - 2x$

84. $6m + 7 = 73 - 5m$

85. $2 + 8k = 52 - 2k$

86. $23 - x = 9 + 2x + 2$

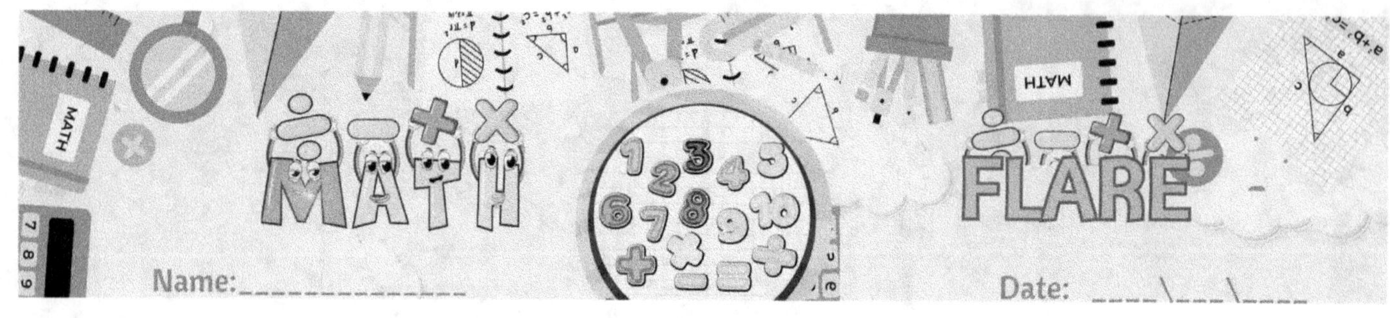

87. $140 - 8z = 4 + 9z$

88. $13 + m = 2m + 9$

89. $3 + 3z = 19 + z$

90. $59 - k = 6 + 4k + 8$

91. $2z + 1 = 7 + z$

92. $1 + 2m + 9 = 3 - m + 10$

93. $7x + 1 = 13 + x$

94. $6 + 2y + 8 = 15 + y$

95. $23 - k + 13 = 8 + 3k + 8$

96. $4 + 2k + 3 = 5 + k + 3$

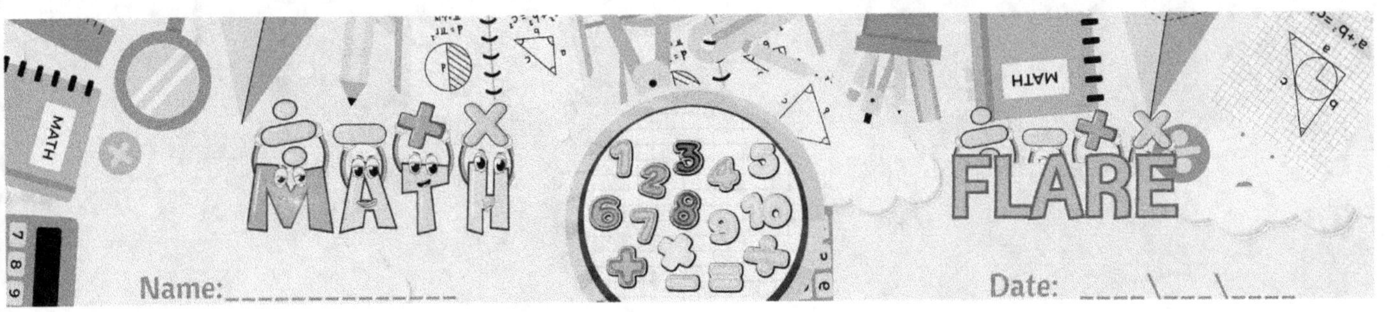

Name:_____________________   Date: _______________

Verbal Algebra Expressions

1. Eight is equal to the quotient of a number and 8. Find the number.

2. The sum of two consecutive numbers is 15. What are the numbers?

3. Six more than seven times a number is equal to the number increased by 66. What is the number?

4. 10 is equal to the product of five and some number. Find the number.

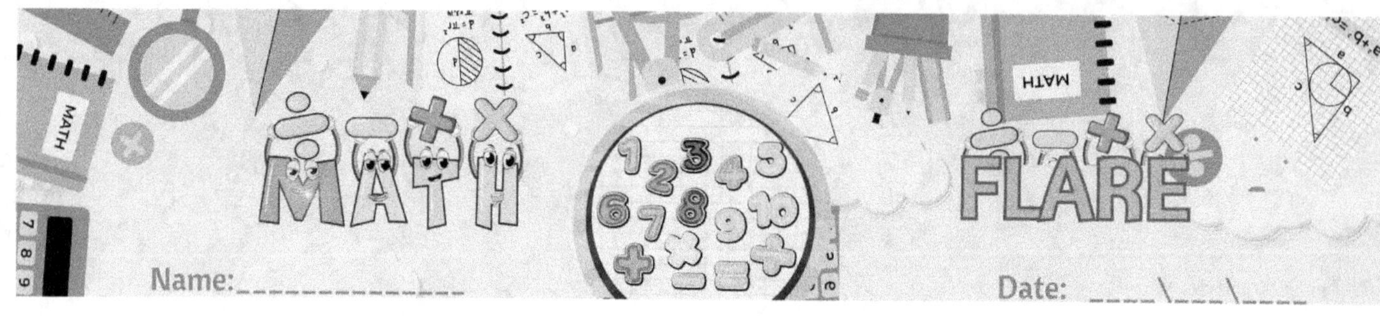

5. The quotient of a number and four increased by 8 is 17. What is the number?

6. Find two consecutive odd integers such that eight times the larger decreased by the smaller is 65.

7. The greater of two numbers is 9 less than eight times the smaller number. Their sum is 45. Find the numbers.

8. One number is five times another. Their sum is 6. Find the numbers.

9. The sum of two consecutive numbers is 3. What are the numbers?

10. The sum of two numbers is 6. The difference of the same two numbers is two. Find the numbers.

11. A number diminished by 7 is 4. Find the number.

12. The quotient of a number and ten is 8. Find the number.

13. One of two numbers is eight more than the other. The sum of the numbers is 26. Find the numbers.

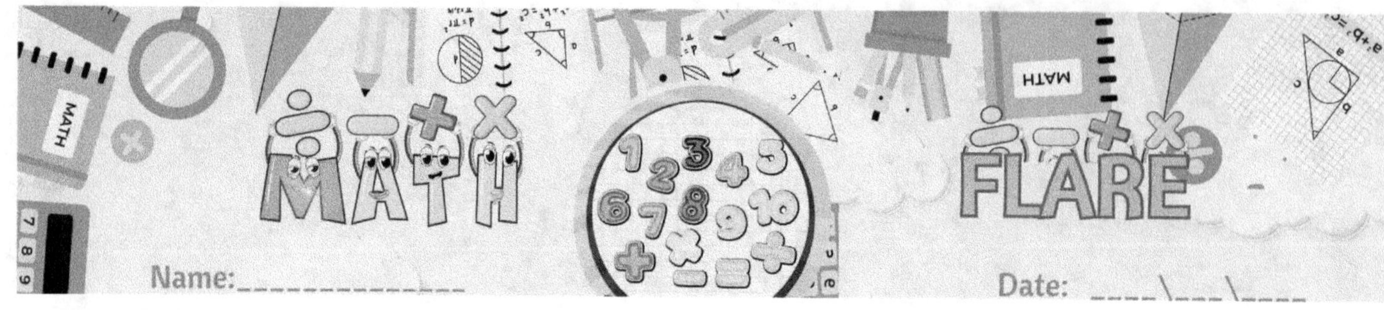

14. The sum of two consecutive numbers is 11. What are the numbers?

15. Two times a number equals 18 less than four times the number. What is the number?

16. Four times the sum of a number and seven times the number is 64. Find the number.

17. One number is ten times another. Their sum is 55. Find the numbers.

18.   The quotient of a number and three is 8. Find the number.

19.   Four times a number is 8. What is the number?

20.   Ten times the difference of 12 minus a number is 80. What is the number?

21.   The product of nine and some number is equal to the sum of that number and 16. What is the number?

22.   If the product of seven and a number is increased by 4, the result is 32. Find the number?

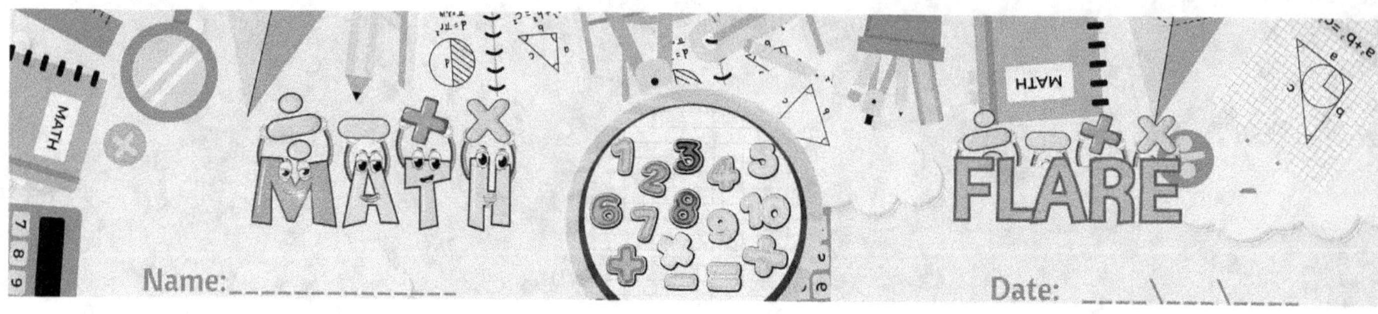

23. A number diminished by 1 is 5. Find the number.

24. Three times the difference of 16 minus a number is 27. What is the number?

25. The sum of two numbers is 24. One number is six less than the other. Find the numbers.

26. If the product of two and a number is increased by 5, the result is 15. Find the number?

27. Find two consecutive odd integers such that five times the larger decreased by the smaller is 22.

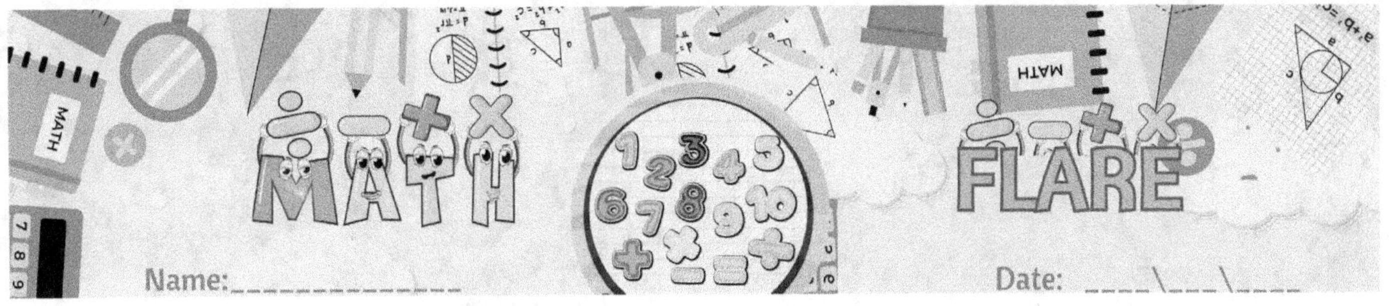

28. One number is three more than another number. The sum of the larger number and twice the smaller number is 30. Find the numbers?

29. One less than seven times a number is 55. Find the number.

30. The sum of four consecutive even numbers is 28. What are the numbers?

31. The difference of two numbers is 38. The larger number is 10 more than five times the smaller number. What are the numbers?

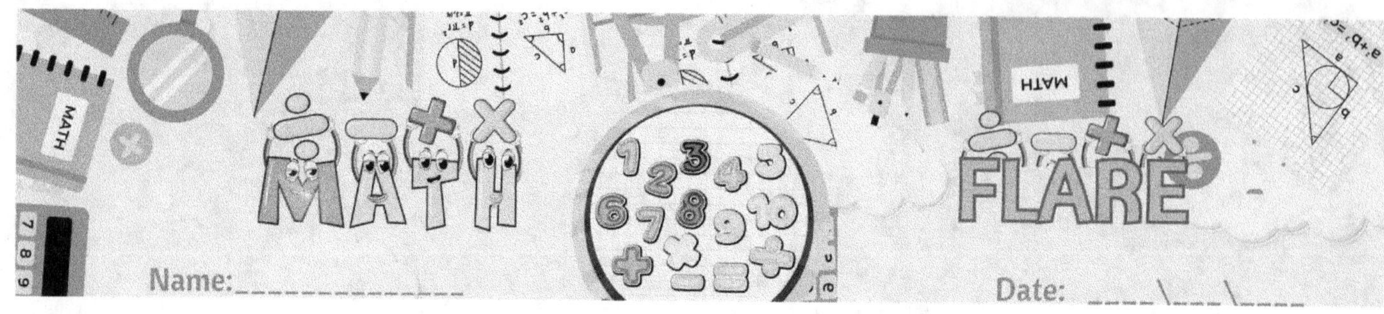

32.   The quotient of a number and three is 9. Find the number.

33.   Nine less than a number is 7. Find the number.

34.   The greater of two numbers is 6 less than six times the smaller number. Their sum is 15. Find the numbers.

35.   The sum of two numbers is 15. The larger number is four times the smaller number. What are the numbers?

36.   Five times a number is 0. What is the number?

37.   If the product of ten and a number is increased by 4, the result is 34. Find the number?

38.   The sum of a number and nine is 15. Find the number.

39.   Three is equal to the quotient of a number and 4. Find the number.

40.   If the product of ten and a number is increased by 2, the result is 62. Find the number?

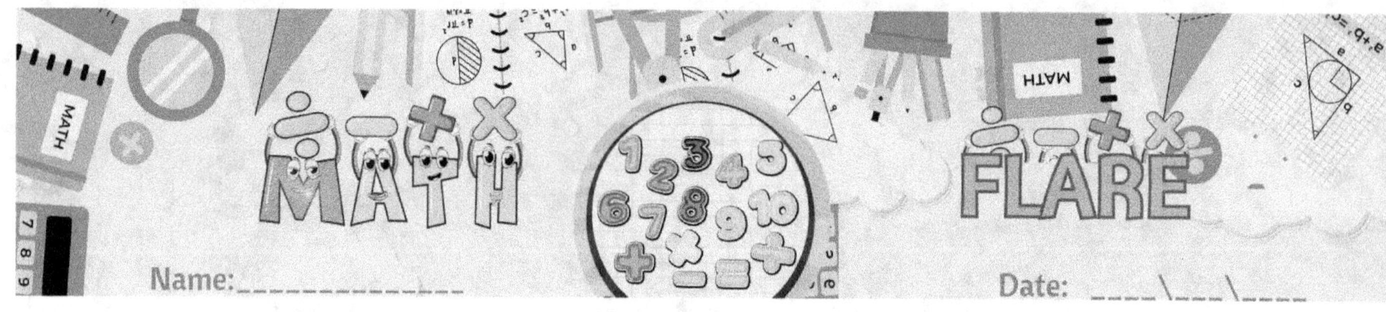

41. Four times the difference of 19 minus a number is 36. What is the number?

42. The sum of two numbers is 42. The larger number is five times the smaller number. What are the numbers?

43. The product of two numbers is 77. One number is four less than the other. What are the numbers?

44. One-third of a number is 0. Find the number.

45. The product of nine and a number is 45. What is the number?

46. The greater of two numbers is 2 less than eight times the smaller number. Their sum is 43. Find the numbers.

47. One more than a number is 9. What is the number?

48. When a number is divided by five, the result is 3. What is the number?

49. A number diminished by 8 is 6. Find the number.

50. One-fourth of a number increased by 2 is 3. What is the number?

51. The sum of two numbers is 9. The larger number is eight times the smaller number. What are the numbers?

52. The quotient of a number and seven increased by 9 is 12. What is the number?

53. Three-fourths of a number diminished by 2 is 1. Find the number.

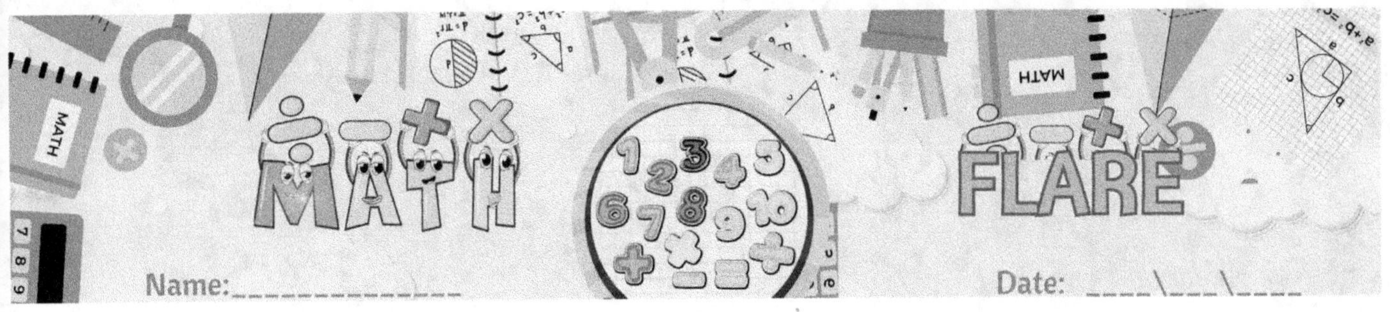

54. The sum of two numbers is 40. The larger number is nine times the smaller number. What are the numbers?

55. The sum of two numbers is 28. The difference of the same two numbers is ten. Find the numbers.

56. Six times a number diminished by 27 is 45. Find the number.

57. The quotient of a number and ten is 2. Find the number.

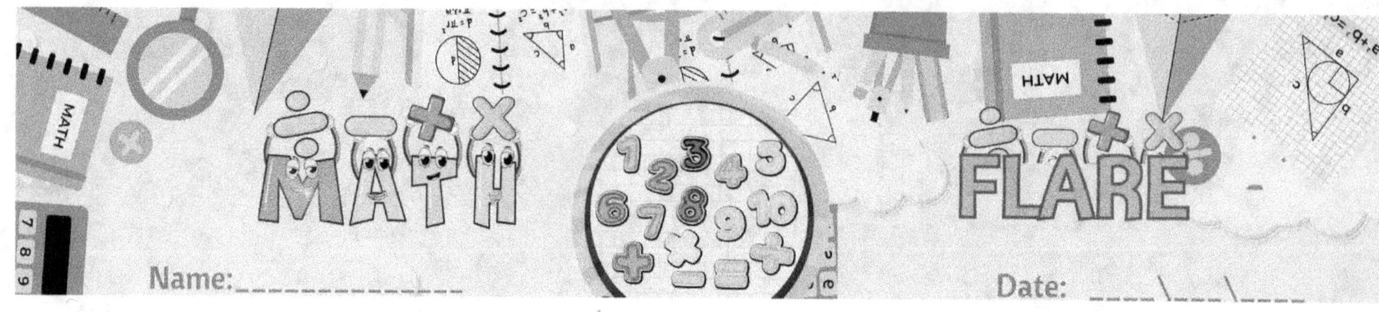

58.   Five times a number decreased by 14 is 31. Find the number.

59.   One-half of a number decreased by 1 is 0. Find the number.

60.   Eight times a number diminished by 39 is 9. Find the number.

61.   Find two consecutive odd integers such that six times the larger decreased by the smaller is 17.

Chapter. 02

Linear Equation

<u>Understanding Linear Functions</u>

A linear equation is an algebraic equation that represents a straight line when graphed on a coordinate plane. It consists of variables raised to the power of 1 (i.e., no exponents higher than 1) and constant coefficients.

The general form of a linear equation in one variable x is:

$$ax + b = 0$$

Where a and b are constants, and x is the variable.

Let's solve the linear equation:

$$-2x + 9 = 5$$

- **Isolate the variable term:** We want to isolate the term containing x on one side of the equation. To do this, we'll move the constant term to the other side. Subtract 9 from both sides:

$$-2x + 9 - 9 = 5 - 9$$

$$-2x = -4$$

- **Divide by the coefficient of the variable:** To solve for x, divide both sides by the coefficient of x, which is -2:

$$\frac{-2x}{-2} = \frac{-4}{-2}$$

$$x = 2$$

<u>Slop from Two Points</u>

The slope between two points on a Cartesian coordinate system is a measure of the steepness of the line connecting those points. It's calculated by finding the change in the y-coordinates divided by the change in the x-coordinates.

- The coordinates of the first point as $(x_1 , y_1) = (2, -30)$.

- The coordinates of the second point as $(x_2 , y_2) = (-5, 40)$.

The formula to calculate the slope (m) between two points:

$$\frac{y2 - y1}{x2 - x1}$$

$$= \frac{40 - (-30)}{-5 - 2} = \frac{70}{-7}$$

$$\text{Slope} = -10$$

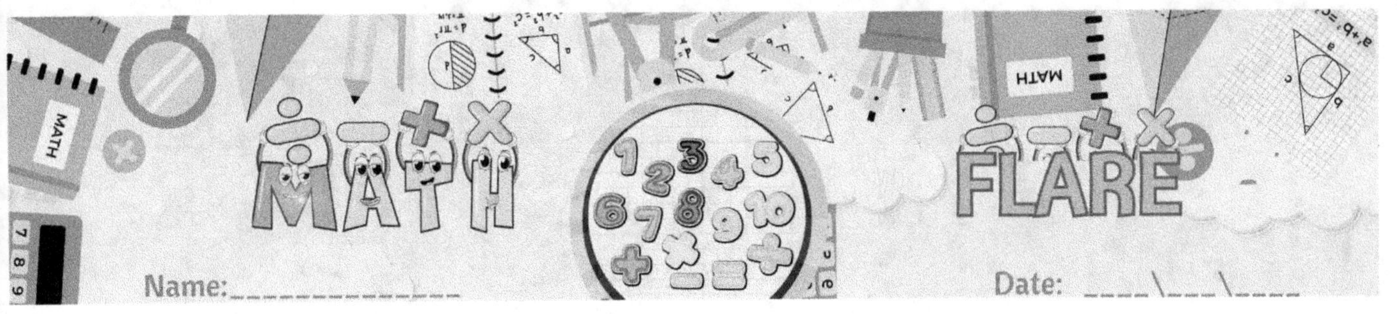

Standard Linear Equations

1. $3x + 3 = -21$

2. $-3x + 7 = 13$

3. $2x + -6 = 6$

4. $-2x + 0 = -2$

5. $1x + 9 = 16$

6. $10x + 1 = 41$

7. $-3x + -6 = 6$

8. $-5x + 3 = -7$

9. $6x + 10 = -2$

10. $-3x + 7 = 4$

11. $5x + 3 = 28$

12. $3x + -3 = 18$

13. -7x + -5 = -12

19. -10x + 5 = 45

14. -2x + -5 = -11

20. -8x + 4 = 44

15. -5x + -7 = -17

21. -6x + 9 = -21

16. -4x + -4 = -24

22. 2x + 9 = 9

17. -10x + 4 = 84

23. 6x + -7 = 35

18. 7x + -3 = 53

24. 4x + -10 = -6

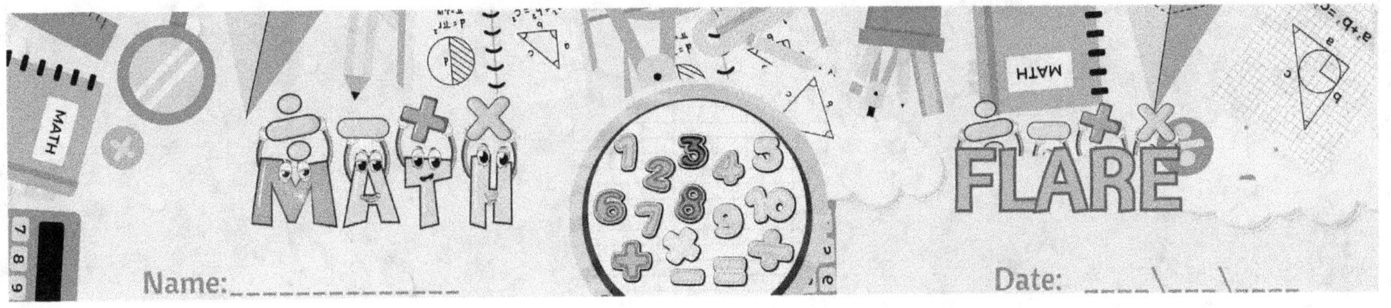

25. 7x + 1 = -69

26. -3x + -1 = -4

27. 8x + -4 = 76

28. 7x + -1 = -71

29. -2x + 9 = 7

30. -3x + -7 = 2

31. -2x + -3 = -13

32. 7x + 2 = 58

33. -8x + 5 = -59

34. 6x + -2 = -38

35. 7x + -8 = 41

36. -2x + -10 = -12

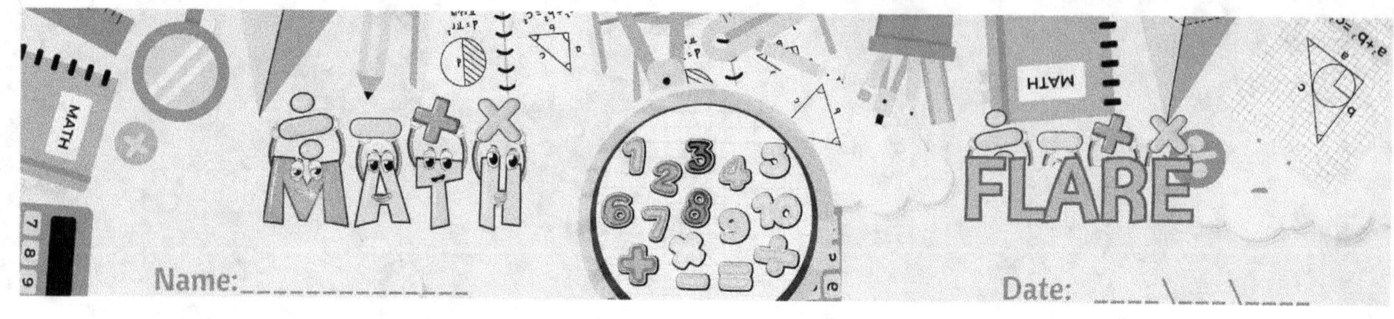

37. $-6x + -6 = 18$

43. $7x + 3 = -25$

38. $1x + -1 = 0$

44. $-7x + -6 = 8$

39. $9x + 7 = 16$

45. $8x + -4 = -84$

40. $7x + 9 = 79$

46. $3x + 1 = -8$

41. $2x + 8 = -12$

47. $-2x + 8 = -6$

42. $2x + 6 = 18$

48. $3x + -3 = 24$

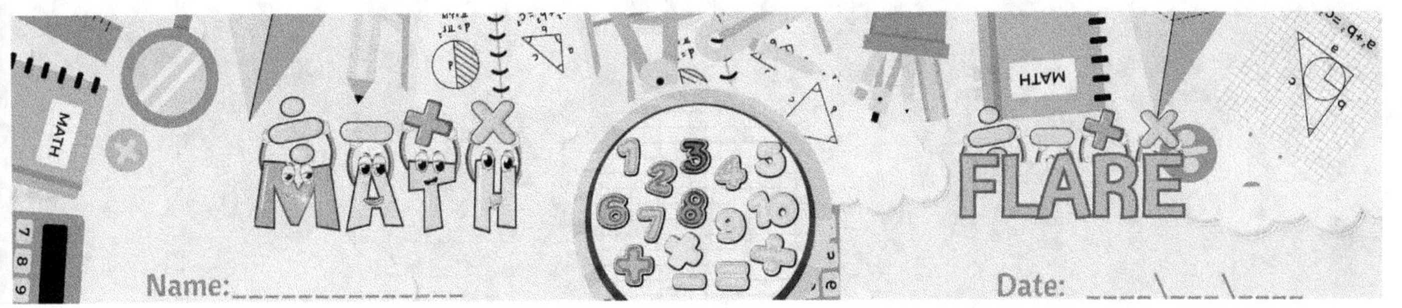

Find Slope from Two Points

1. (4, -19) and (-8, 41)

2. (-10, -59) and (8, 49)

3. (2, -10) and (6, -30)

4. (9, -19) and (7, -13)

5. (4, -9) and (-10, 5)

6. (9, 53) and (6, 35)

7. (3, 15) and (-5, -33)

8. (3, 26) and (3, 26)

9. (-2, 14) and (-3, 18)

10. (1, 0) and (8, 63)

11. (-1, -8) and (1, 0)

12. (-7, -10) and (2, 8)

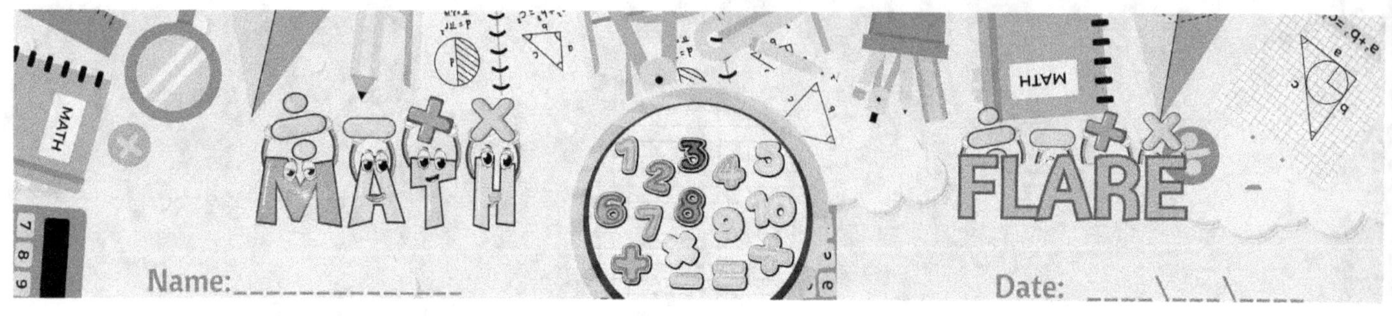

13. (0, 0) and (-3, 9)

14. (6, -57) and (0, 3)

15. (-9, -96) and (-2, -26)

16. (9, -39) and (-3, 21)

17. (7, 63) and (1, 9)

18. (7, -6) and (-1, 2)

19. (3, -3) and (5, -9)

20. (10, -13) and (-9, 25)

21. (-2, 22) and (-4, 42)

22. (10, 34) and (0, 4)

23. (1, -8) and (7, -8)

24. (-8, -47) and (10, 79)

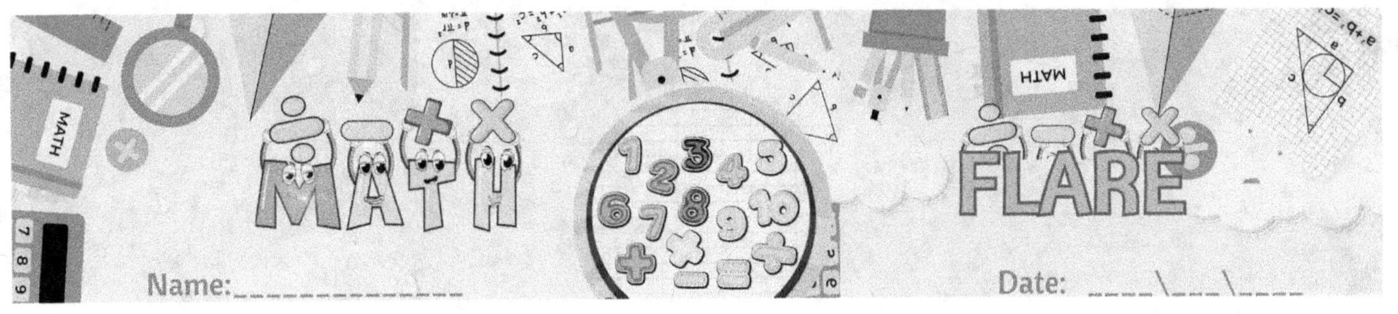

25. (-4, 11) and (-2, 5)

26. (2, -1) and (-4, -13)

27. (-4, 30) and (8, -54)

28. (6, 50) and (9, 71)

29. (-2, -22) and (-7, -57)

30. (1, 7) and (-7, -17)

31. (-9, -63) and (-5, -35)

32. (-7, 53) and (3, -37)

33. (1, -11) and (10, -83)

34. (-10, -32) and (-7, -23)

35. (10, -94) and (-10, 106)

36. (1, -11) and (-7, 13)

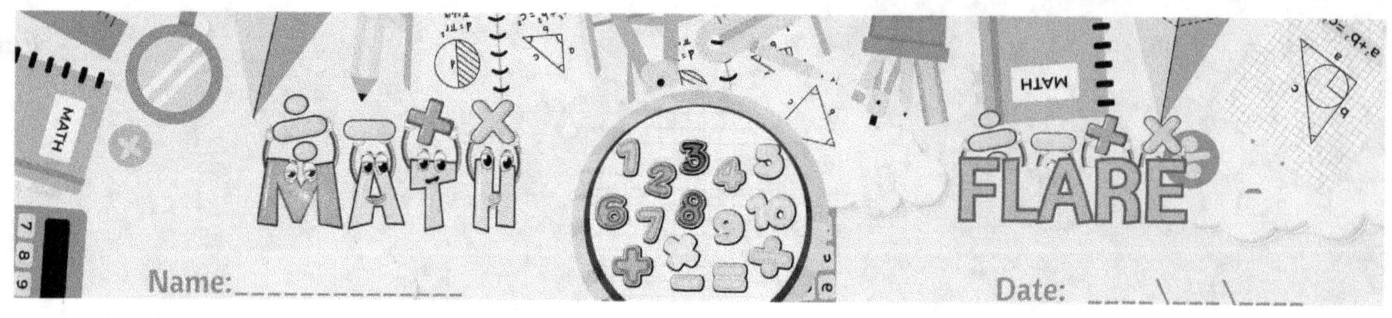

37. (9, 70) and (0, 7)

38. (0, 0) and (2, 10)

39. (-8, -21) and (-3, -11)

40. (-8, -64) and (5, 53)

41. (-8, 61) and (2, -9)

42. (6, 55) and (5, 46)

43. (9, 53) and (-9, -55)

44. (-10, 79) and (-6, 47)

45. (8, 36) and (6, 26)

46. (10, -26) and (2, -10)

47. (-5, 11) and (7, -1)

48. (-8, 47) and (10, -43)

Chapter. 03

System of Equations

A system of equations is a collection of two or more equations involving the same set of variables. The solution to a system of equations is the set of values for the variables that satisfy all the equations simultaneously.

Solving by Elimination:

To solve a system of equations by elimination, we manipulate the equations to eliminate one of the variables.

Given the system:

$$4x + 5y = 6$$

$$10x + 6y = 8$$

Step 1: Multiply each equation by a constant such that the coefficients of one of the variables become equal or multiples of each other.

Let's try to eliminate the variable x.

- Multiply the first equation by 5 and the second equation by -2:

$$20x + 25y = 30$$

$$-20x - 12y = -16$$

Step 2: Add the two equations together to eliminate the variable x.

$$(20x - 20x) + (25y - 12y) = 30 - 16$$

$$13y = 14$$

Step 3: Solve for y:

$$y = \frac{14}{13} = 1.077$$

Step 4: Substitute the value of y into one of the original equations to solve for x. Let's use the first equation:

$$4x + 5\left(\frac{14}{13}\right) = 6$$

$$4x + \frac{70}{13} = 6$$

$$4x = 6 - \frac{70}{13}$$

$$4x = \frac{78 - 70}{13}$$

$$4x = \frac{8}{13}$$

$$x = \frac{2}{13} = 0.154$$

the solution to the system of equations is x = 0.154 and y = 1.077.

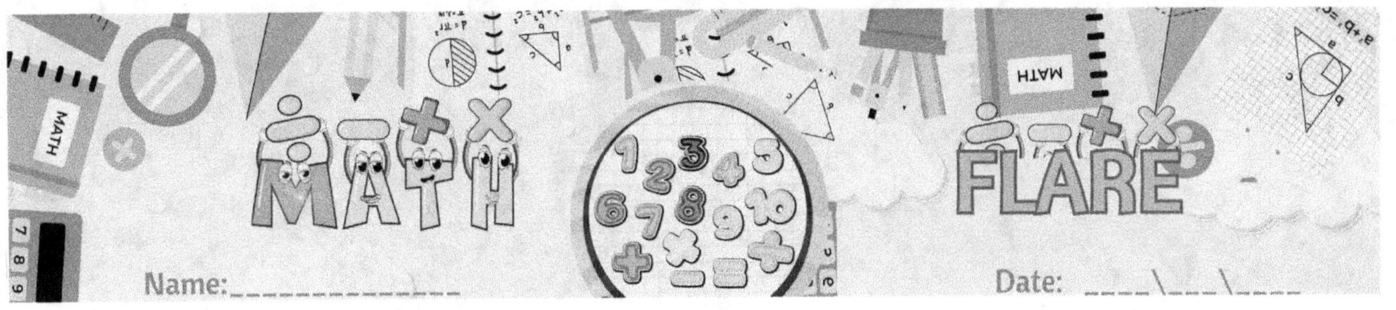

System of Equations

1. $2x + 1y = 5$

   $5x + 5y = 2$

2. $10x + 10y = 1$

   $10x + 2y = 6$

3. $5x + 9y = 2$

   $8x + 4y = 7$

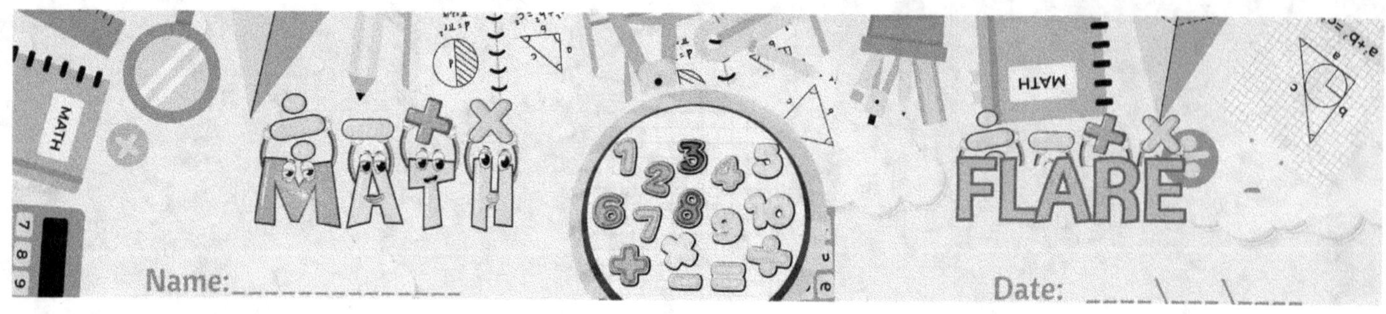

4. $6x + 1y = 9$

$3x + 3y = 3$

5. $3x + 4y = 10$

$1x + 10y = 3$

6. $6x + 1y = 6$

$4x + 6y = 5$

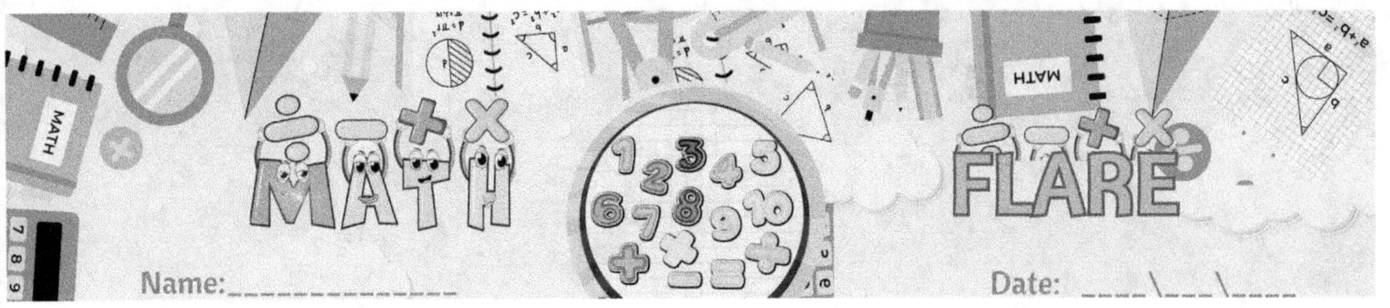

7. $3x + 10y = 3$

   $7x + 7y = 3$

8. $10x + 6y = 8$

   $10x + 3y = 2$

9. $4x + 9y = 4$

   $3x + 9y = 5$

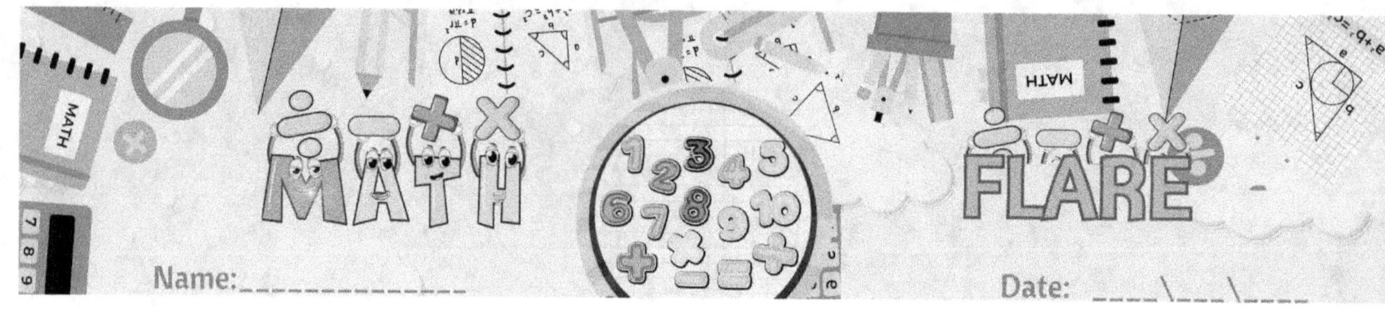

10. 5x + 8y = 2

    4x + 4y = 3

11. 6x + 10y = 7

    4x + 8y = 1

12. 1x + 9y = 7

    3x + 5y = 8

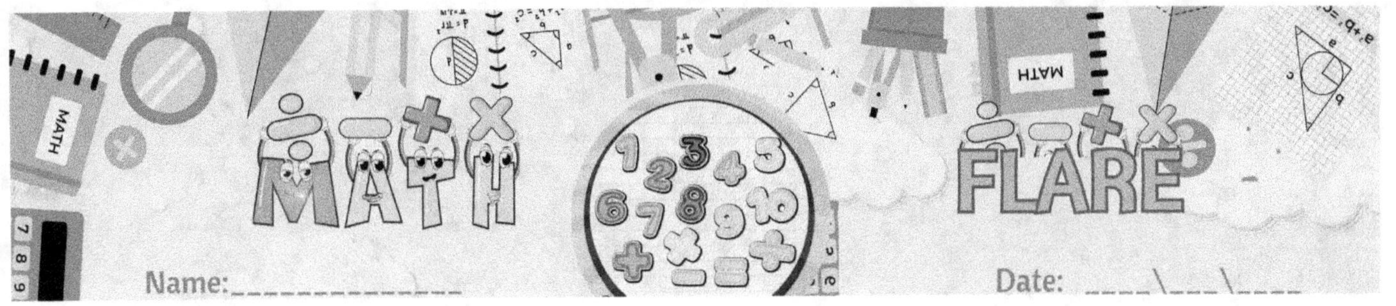

13. $3x + 2y = 3$

   $8x + 9y = 9$

14. $7x + 4y = 4$

   $8x + 5y = 3$

15. $3x + 4y = 3$

   $3x + 2y = 8$

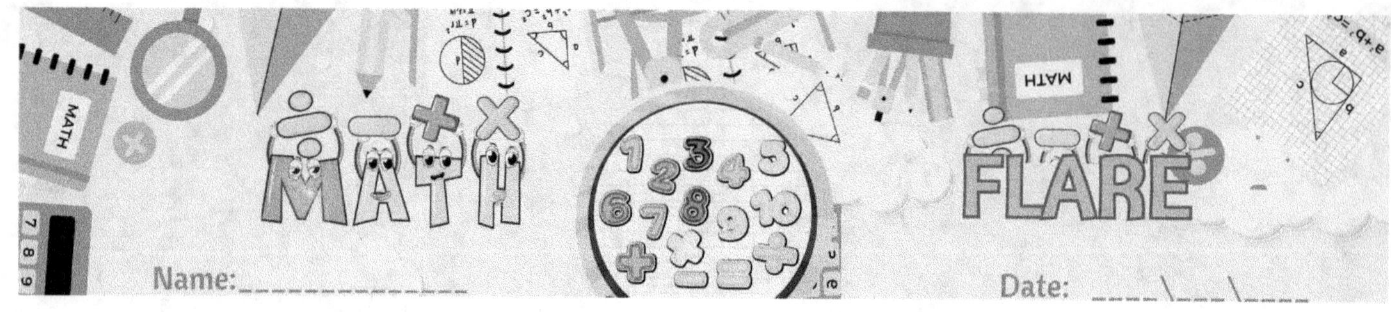

16. $5x + 7y = 4$

$4x + 4y = 7$

17. $1x + 3y = 1$

$6x + 2y = 6$

18. $6x + 8y = 3$

$8x + 2y = 10$

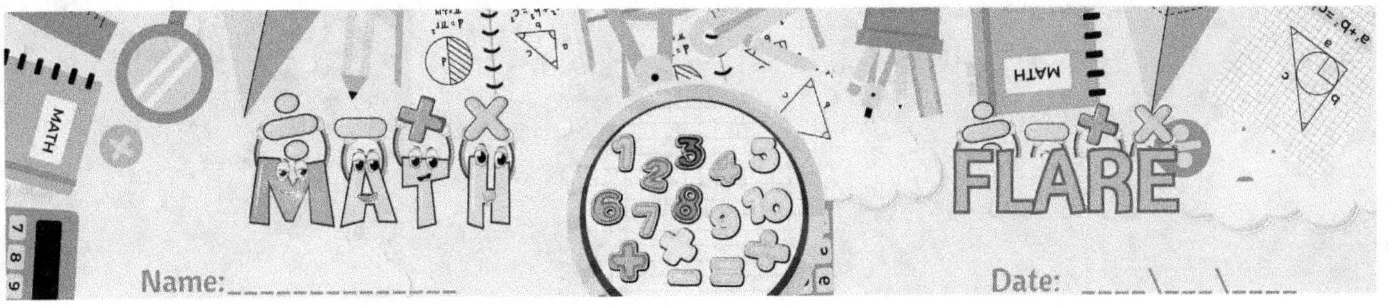

19. $9x + 7y = 7$

    $2x + 8y = 9$

20. $5x + 6y = 6$

    $7x + 1y = 7$

21. $4x + 6y = 4$

    $9x + 5y = 3$

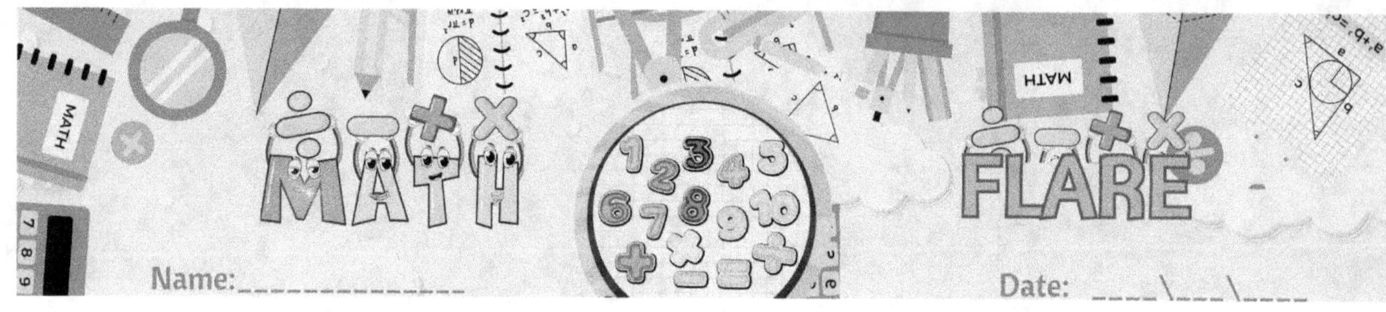

22. $6x + 8y = 2$

$5x + 10y = 7$

23. $9x + 6y = 3$

$7x + 10y = 7$

24. $4x + 5y = 4$

$2x + 2y = 6$

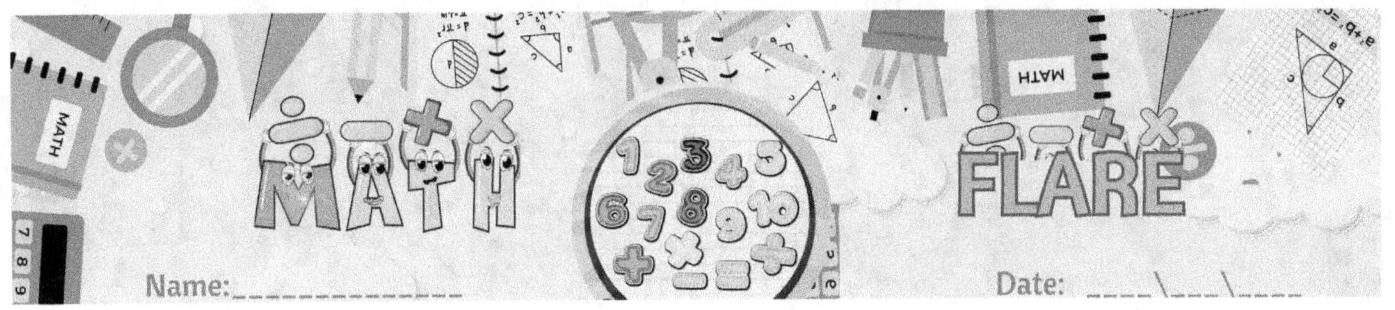

25. $10x + 9y = 2$

   $9x + 5y = 8$

26. $7x + 3y = 5$

   $7x + 7y = 3$

27. $3x + 10y = 7$

   $7x + 2y = 7$

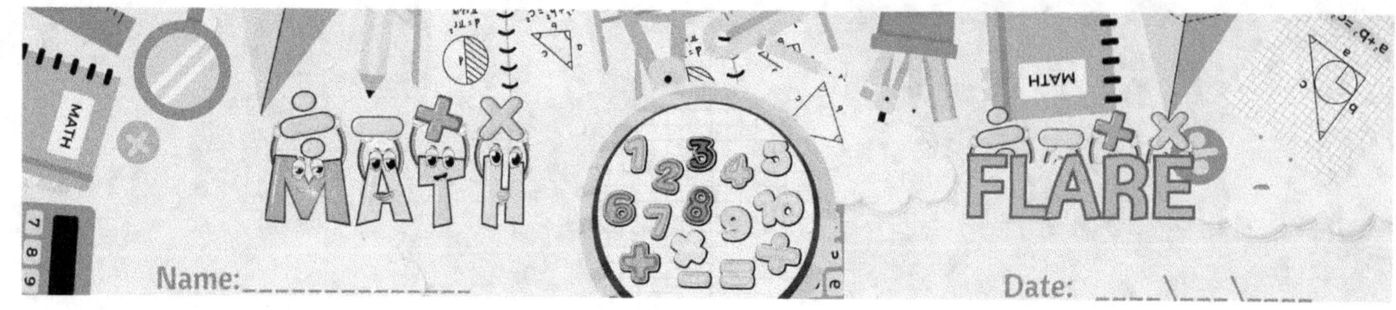

28. $6x + 2y = 7$

$8x + 3y = 8$

29. $10x + 6y = 10$

$3x + 8y = 1$

30. $8x + 10y = 5$

$3x + 7y = 7$

Chapter. 04

Quadratic Equations

A quadratic equation is a polynomial equation of the second degree, meaning it can be written in the form:

$$ax^2 + bx + c = 0$$

where a, b, and c are constants, and x is the variable being solved for. The solutions to a quadratic equation are the values of x that make the equation true.

Now, let's solve the quadratic equation $11x^2 - 1 = 0$ and understand it step by step using quadratic formula.

1. **Identify the coefficients:**

   In the equation $11x^2 - 1 = 0$,

   $$a=11, b=0, \text{ and } c=-1.$$

2. **Apply the quadratic formula:**

   The quadratic formula states that for an equation $ax^2 + bx + c = 0$, the solutions for x are given by:

   $$x = \frac{-b \pm \sqrt{b^2 - 4ac}}{2a}$$

   Plugging in the values a=11, b=0, and c=−1 into the quadratic formula, we get:

   $$x = \frac{-0 \pm \sqrt{0 - 4(11)(-1)}}{2(11)}$$

3. Simplify inside the square root:

$$0^2 - 4(11)(-1) = 0 - (-44) = 44$$

4. Plug in the simplified values:

$$X = \frac{\pm \sqrt{44}}{22}$$

5. Simplify the square root:

Since 44 is not a perfect square, we can write it as $\sqrt[2]{11}$

$$X = \frac{\pm \sqrt[2]{11}}{22}$$

6. Simplify further if possible:

We can simplify $\sqrt[2]{11}$ to $\sqrt{11}$ by canceling out the common factor:

$$X = \frac{\pm \sqrt{11}}{11}$$

7. Final solution:

So, the solutions to the equation are:

$$X = \frac{\sqrt{11}}{11} \text{ and } X = \frac{-\sqrt{11}}{11}$$

or

$$(x = 0.302, \text{ and } x = -0.302)$$

These are the roots of the quadratic equation. They represent the points where the graph of the quadratic equation intersects the x-axis.

Let's solve another equation:

$$-4p^2 + 6p - 6 = 0$$

$$p = \frac{-b \pm \sqrt{b^2 - 4ac}}{2a}$$

where $a = -4$, $b = 6$, and $c = -6$.

Let's plug these values into the quadratic formula:

$$p = \frac{-6 \pm \sqrt{6^2 - 4(-4)(-6)}}{2(-4)}$$

First, let's simplify inside the square root:

$$6^2 - 4(-4)(-6)$$

$$= 36 - 96 = -60$$

So, we have:

$$p = \frac{-6 \pm \sqrt{-60}}{-8}$$

We can simplify the square root of −60 by factoring out −1:

$$\sqrt{-60}$$

$$= \sqrt{-1 \times 60}$$

$$= \sqrt{-1} \times \sqrt{60}$$

$$= i\sqrt{60}$$

So, we have:

$$p = \frac{-6 \pm i\sqrt{60}}{-8}$$

Simplify:

$$\sqrt{60} \text{ to } \sqrt{4 \times 15} = 2\sqrt{15}$$

$$p = \frac{-6 \pm i \times 2\sqrt{15}}{-8}$$

Now, divide both the numerator and denominator by −2 to simplify:

$$p = \frac{3 \pm i\sqrt{15}}{4}$$

So, the solutions to the equation are:

$$p = \frac{3 + i\sqrt{15}}{4} \text{ and } p = \frac{3 - i\sqrt{15}}{4}$$

This equation -4p² + 6p - 6 = 0 has no real solutions.

When a quadratic equation has no real solutions, it means that the solutions are not real numbers, but rather complex numbers. In this case, the solutions involve the imaginary unit i because the discriminant ($b^2 - 4ac$) is negative, which results in taking the square root of a negative number when applying the quadratic formula.

In mathematics, such equations are said to have "no real roots" or "no real solutions." They are also sometimes referred to as having "complex roots" or "complex solutions." Complex numbers include a real part and an imaginary part, and they are often written in the form $a + bi$, where a and b are real numbers and i is the imaginary unit, defined as $i = \sqrt{-1}$.

Let's solve another equation:

$$12x^2 + 6x - 2 = 0$$

$$X = \frac{-b \pm \sqrt{b^2 - 4ac}}{2a}$$

where $a = 12$, $b = 6$, and $c = -2$.

Let's plug these values into the quadratic formula:

$$X = \frac{-6 \pm \sqrt{6^2 - 4(12)(-2)}}{2(12)}$$

First, let's simplify inside the square root:

$$6^2 - 4(12)(-2)$$

$$= 36 - (-96)$$

$$= 36 + 96$$

$$= 132$$

So, we have:

$$X = \frac{-6 \pm \sqrt{132}}{24}$$

Now, let's simplify the square root of 132:

$$X = \frac{-6 \pm \sqrt{4 \times 33}}{24}$$

$$X = \frac{-6 \pm 2\sqrt{33}}{24}$$

$$X = \frac{-6 \pm \sqrt{33}}{12}$$

So, the solutions to the equation are:

$$X = \frac{-6 + \sqrt{33}}{12} \text{ and } X = \frac{-6 - \sqrt{33}}{12}$$

or (x = 0.229, and x = -0.729)

Let's solve a Quadratic Equation where the right side is a number instead of 0.

$$-8n^2 + 6n + 30 = 7$$

To solve the equation, we first need to bring all terms to one side to set the equation equal to zero:

$$-8n^2 + 6n + 30 - 7 = 0$$

Simplify:

$$-8n^2 + 6n + 23 = 0$$

Now, to solve for n, we can use the quadratic formula:

$$n = \frac{-b \pm \sqrt{b^2 - 4ac}}{2a}$$

where $a = -8$, $b = 6$, and $c = 23$.

Plugging these values into the formula, we get:

$$n = \frac{-6 \pm \sqrt{6^2 - 4(-8)(23)}}{2(-8)}$$

$$n = \frac{-6 \pm \sqrt{36 + 736}}{-16}$$

$$n = \frac{-6 \pm \sqrt{772}}{-16}$$

Now, let's simplify the square root of 772. We can factor out 4:

$$\sqrt{772} = \sqrt{4 \times 193} = 2\sqrt{193}$$

So, our equation becomes:

$$n = \frac{-6 \pm 2\sqrt{193}}{-8}$$

So, the solutions to the equation are:

$$n = \frac{-3 + \sqrt{193}}{-8} \text{ and } n = \frac{-3 - \sqrt{193}}{-8}$$

or

$$(n = -1.362, \text{ and } n = 2.112)$$

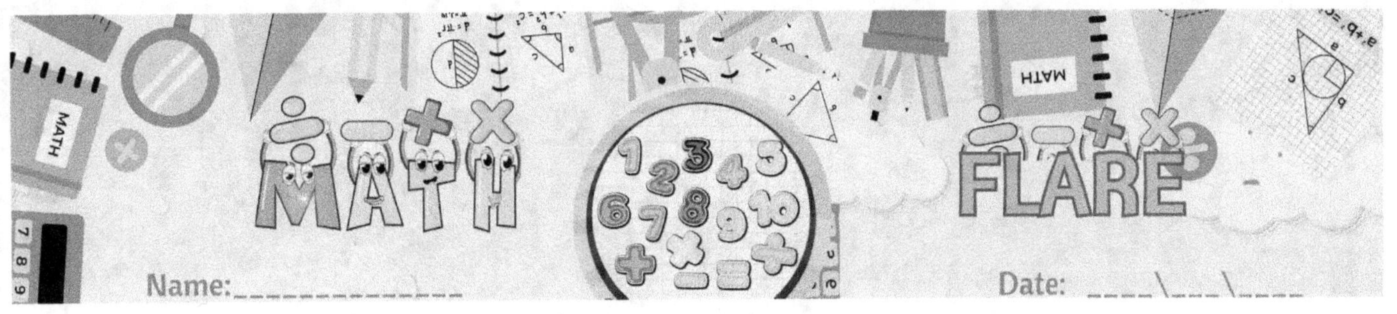

Quadratic Equations

1. $11r^2 - r - 8 = 0$

2. $3a^2 + a - 10 = 0$

3. $4a^2 + 7a - 24 = 0$

4. $5r^2 - 9r - 80 = 0$

9. $3n^2 + 9n - 12 = 0$

5. $9x^2 - 5x - 2 = 0$

6. $8n^2 - 6n - 1 = 0$

7. $4n^2 - 6n - 11 = 0$

8. $4n^2 + 4n - 143 = 0$

14. $3x^2 - 5x + 2 = 0$

10. $10m^2 + 3m - 19 = 0$

15. $3m^2 + 5m - 12 = 0$

11. $9v^2 - 2v - 6 = 0$

16. $2r^2 + 9r + 10 = 0$

12. $n^2 + 10n + 16 = 0$

17. $8x^2 + 12x - 15 = 0$

13. $6k^2 - 5k - 6 = 0$

18. $2k^2 - k - 5 = 0$

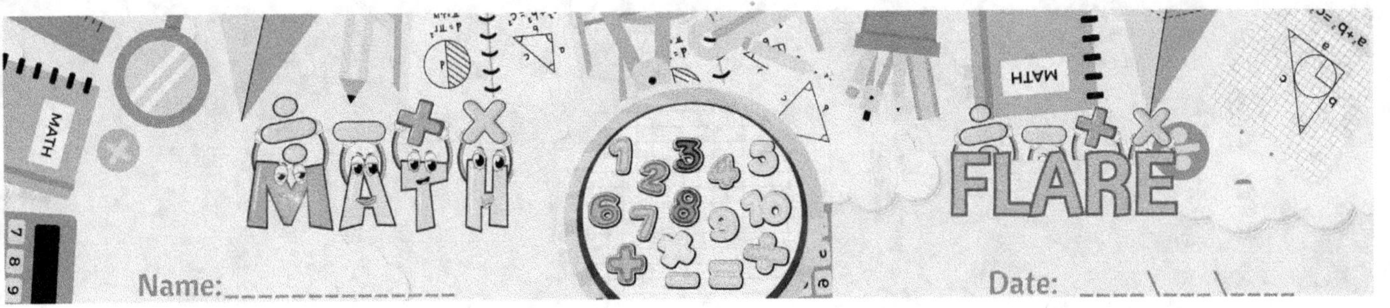

19. $5m^2 + m - 10 = 0$

24. $6x^2 + 9x - 27 = 0$

20. $5a^2 + 9a - 14 = 0$

25. $3n^2 + 9n + 6 = 0$

21. $9k^2 - 3k - 24 = 0$

26. $2m^2 - 8m + 6 = 0$

22. $8m^2 - m - 23 = 0$

27. $3x^2 - 10x - 6 = 0$

23. $n^2 + n - 2 = 0$

28. $5p^2 + 11p - 36 = 0$

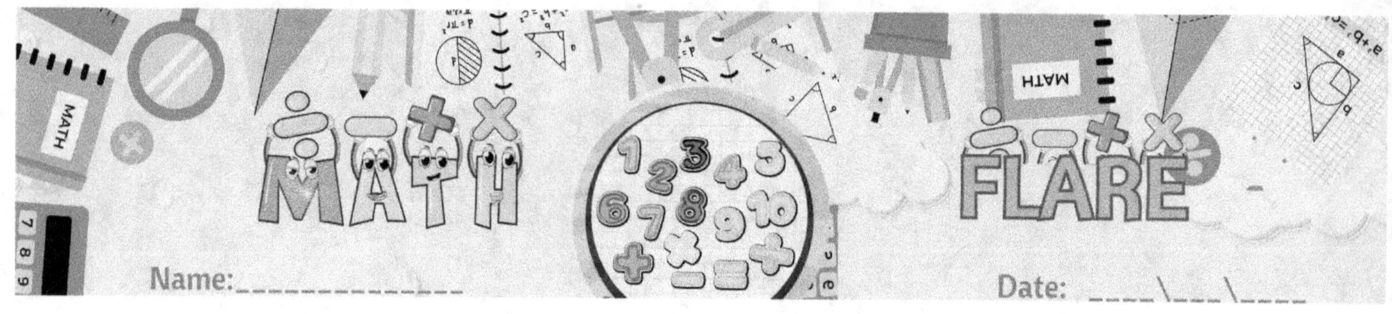

29. $4x^2 + 4x - 17 = 0$

34. $x^2 + 9x - 16 = -6$

30. $6x^2 + 10x - 8 = 0$

35. $7x^2 - 10x - 26 = -12$

31. $n^2 - 10n - 90 = 6$

36. $11k^2 - 8k + 12 = 7$

32. $5n^2 + 8n - 43 = 5$

37. $11r^2 - 7r + 21 = 10$

33. $n^2 - 8n + 23 = 8$

38. $2k^2 - 11k - 37 = -7$

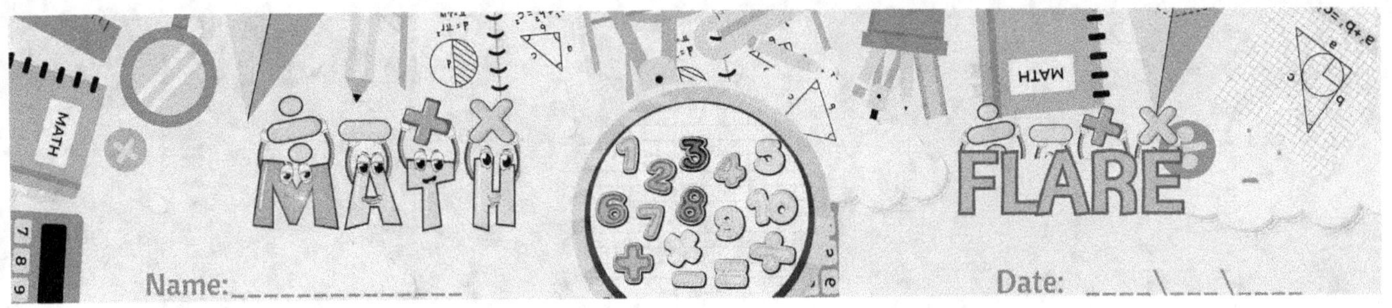

39. $6m^2 + 10m - 17 = -7$

44. $5x^2 - 6x - 18 = 3$

40. $4r^2 + 3r - 16 = 11$

45. $3b^2 + b - 7 = 3$

41. $2r^2 - 12r - 43 = 11$

46. $n^2 + 12n - 18 = -11$

42. $5m^2 - 3m + 2 = 10$

47. $3x^2 + 11x - 82 = 10$

43. $v^2 - 5v = -11$

48. $5p^2 - 8p - 1 = -11$

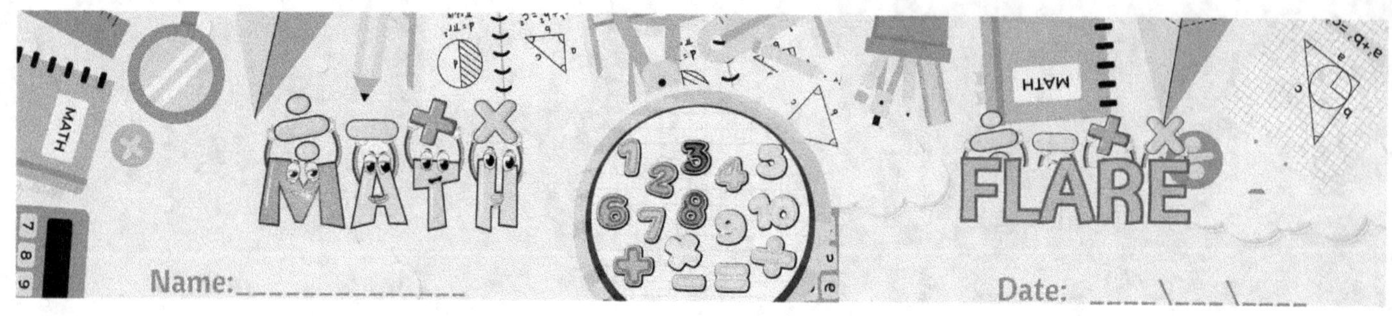

49. $8n^2 - 7n + 21 = 11$

54. $4r^2 + 6r - 35 = 5$

50. $6r^2 + 5r - 2 = 9$

55. $n^2 - 4n - 114 = 3$

51. $10k^2 + 4k - 23 = -6$

56. $8a^2 - 11a + 6 = 10$

52. $3x^2 - 9x + 6 = -6$

57. $9x^2 - 9x + 1 = -7$

53. $5v^2 - 11v + 14 = 12$

58. $2m^2 - 6m - 91 = -11$

Chapter. 05

Polynomials

A polynomial is an algebraic expression consisting of one or more terms, where each term is a constant, a variable, or a product of constants and variables raised to whole number exponents.

Examples of polynomials include:

- $(7v^2 + 2v^4) + (8v^2 + 4v^4)$
- $(2v + 4v^2 + 2) - (5v - 4v^4 - 6v^2)$
- $(7x - 5\,y)(2x - 6\,y)$
- $(6x^2 + 4xy + 6\,y^2)(8x^2 + 3xy + 3\,y^2)$
- $\dfrac{2x^3 + 8x^2 + 2x}{2x^2}$

Operations on Polynomials

Addition of Polynomials:

- To add polynomials, simply combine like terms.
- Like terms are terms that have the same variable(s) raised to the same power(s).
- For example, to add $3x^2 + 2x$ and $5x^2 - 7x$, group the like terms: $3x^2 + 5x^2$ and $2x -7x$, then add each group separately.

Subtraction of Polynomials:

- To subtract polynomials, distribute the negative sign and then add.

- For example, to subtract $x^2 - 2x$ from $4x^2 + 3x$, distribute the negative sign to each term in the second polynomial: $-(x^2 - 2x)$, then add each term separately.

<u>Multiplication of Polynomials:</u>

- To multiply polynomials, use the distributive property and then combine like terms.

- For example, to multiply $(x + 2)(3x - 4)$, distribute each term in the first polynomial to each term in the second polynomial, then combine like terms.

<u>Division of Polynomials:</u>

- Division of polynomials involves dividing one polynomial by another. It can be done using long division or synthetic division.

Let's solve the expression:

$$(7x^2 - 7x) - (x - 2x^2)$$

Step 1: Distribute the Negative Sign:

Distribute the negative sign in the second polynomial:

$$(7x^2 - 7x) - x + 2x^2$$

Step 2: Combine Like Terms:

$$(7x^2 + 2x^2) + (-7x - x)$$

Step 3: Perform addition and subtraction of coefficients:

$$9x^2 - 8x$$

Let's perform the multiplication of polynomials:

$$(5u + 2v)(8u^2 - uv - 3v^2)$$

We can distribute each term in the first polynomial $(5u+2v)$ to every term in the second polynomial $(8u2 - uv - 3v2)$.

1. Multiply $5u$ by each term in the second polynomial:

$$5u \cdot 8u^2 = 40u^3$$

$$5u \cdot (-uv) = -5u^2v$$

$$5u \cdot (-3v^2) = -15uv^2$$

2. Multiply $2v$ by each term in the second polynomial:

$$2v \cdot 8u^2 = 16u^2v$$

$$2v \cdot (-uv) = -2uv^2$$

$$2v \cdot (-3v^2) = -6v^3$$

Combine the like terms:

$$40u^3 - 5u^2v - 15uv^2 + 16u^2v - 2uv^2 - 6v^3$$

Combine the like terms involving u and v.

$$40u^3 + (16u^2v - 5u^2v) + (-15uv^2 - 2uv^2) - 6v^3$$

$$40u^3 + 11u^2v - 17uv^2 - 6v^3$$

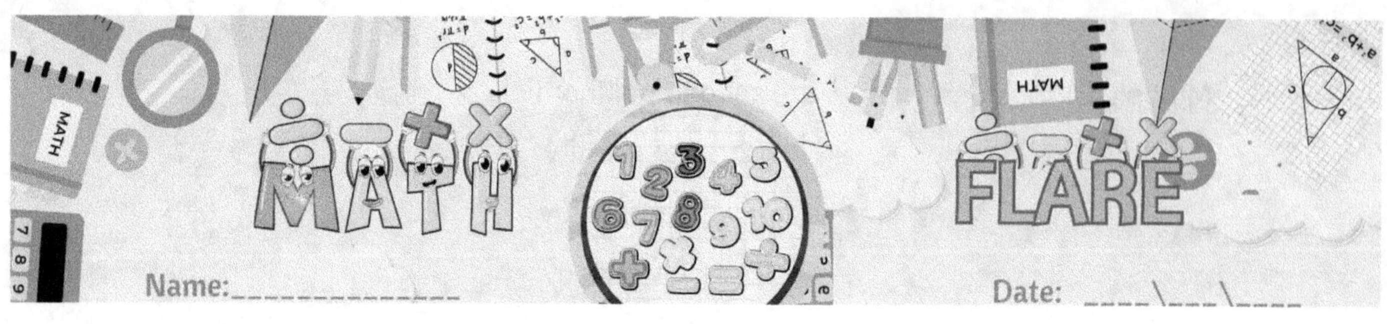

Polynomials: Addition and Subtraction

1. $(7x^2 - 7x) - (x - 2x^2)$

2. $(x^2 + 2x^3) + (2x^3 + 6x^2)$

3. $(2n^4 - 4) - (4 - 8n^4)$

4. $(2n^2 - 6) + (3 + 2n^2)$

5. $(7v^2 + 2v^4) + (8v^2 + 4v^4)$

6. $(6n^2 - 4n) + (n^2 - 2n^3)$

7. $(6r^4 - 3) - (4r^4 - 6)$

8. $(8 + 4n^4) + (6 + 8n^4)$

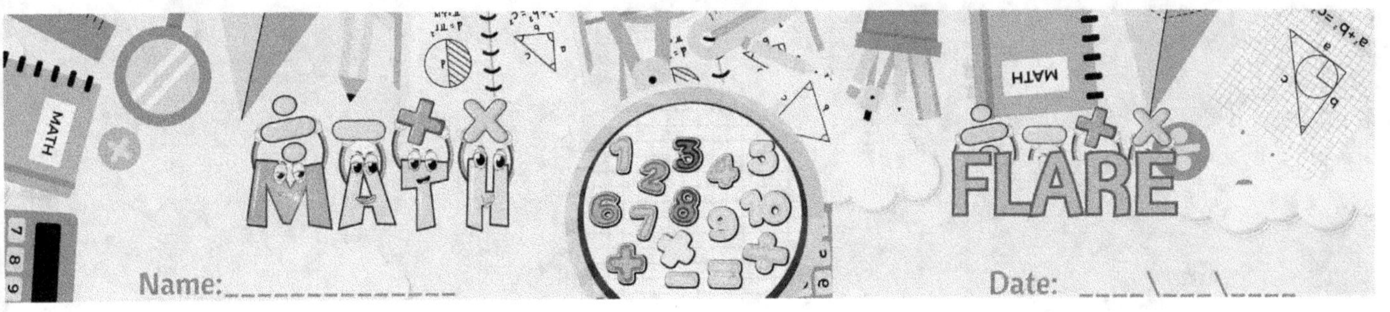

9. $(5v + 5v^2) - (5v^2 + v)$

14. $(5n + 7n^4) - (7n^4 - 2n^2)$

10. $(7m^2 - 5m) + (3m^2 + 8m)$

15. $(8n^2 + 4n^4) - (2n^4 - 4n^2)$

11. $(4 - m^3) + (8m^3 - 4)$

16. $(5r^2 - 5r^3) + (5r^3 - 5r^2)$

12. $(8 - 8n^2) + (2 - n^2)$

17. $(6x + 8x^2) + (2x + 7x^2)$

13. $(4v^3 + 2v^4) + (5v^4 - v^3)$

18. $(8v^3 + 5) - (2 + 7v^3)$

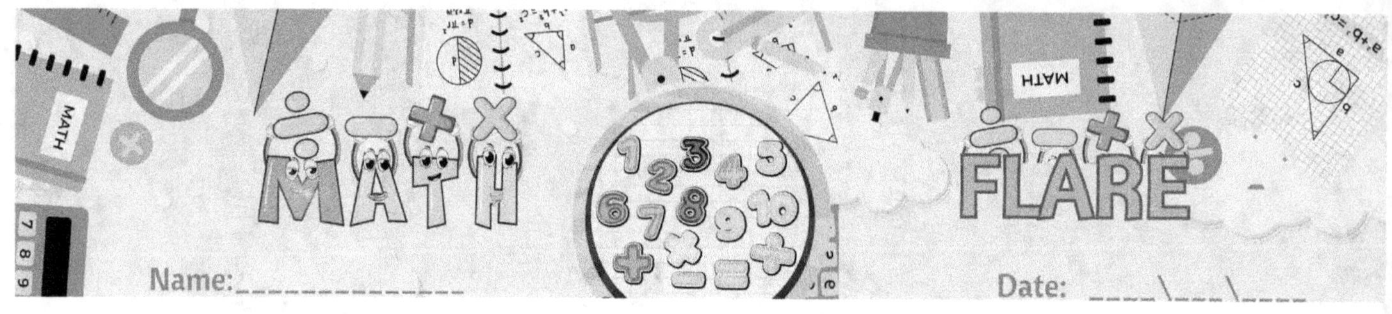

19. $(8n^4 - 2) - (3n^4 + 1)$

24. $(n^2 - 3n) + (2n - 2n^2)$

20. $(8p^3 - 3p^4) + (7p^4 - 7p^3)$

25. $(4r^3 + 6r) - (7r + 5r^3)$

21. $(n + 1) - (4 + 8n)$

26. $(7 + 3x^2) - (6x^2 - 1)$

22. $(7r^4 - 1) + (3 - 7r^4)$

27. $(4p^3 + p) - (2p^3 + 4p)$

23. $(4n^3 - 2n) + (6n^3 + 8n)$

28. $(6 - 5n) - (4n - 2)$

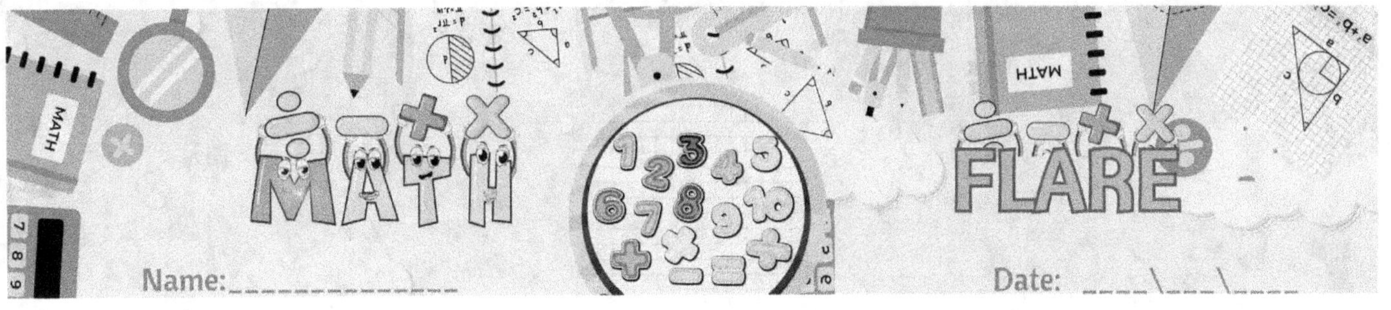

29. $(4x^2 - 6x^3) + (6x^3 - 7x^2)$

30. $(7x^4 - 8) - (2x^4 - 8)$

31. $(4 + b^3) + (4b^2 + 5b^3 + 8)$

32. $(8b - 1) + (5 + 2b + 4b^4)$

33. $(5x^3 + 4x^4) - (2x^3 + 2x^4 + 6x^2)$

34. $(3 - 6n) - (4n^4 + 3n + 3)$

35. $(8a - 7a^4) + (7a^4 - a - 8a^3)$

36. $(4x^3 - 8x^2) - (6 + 6x^3 + 7x^2)$

37. $(8r^4 - 7r^3) - (4r^2 + 8r^3 - 6r^4)$

38. $(5x - 6x^4) + (5 - 8x^4 - 3x)$

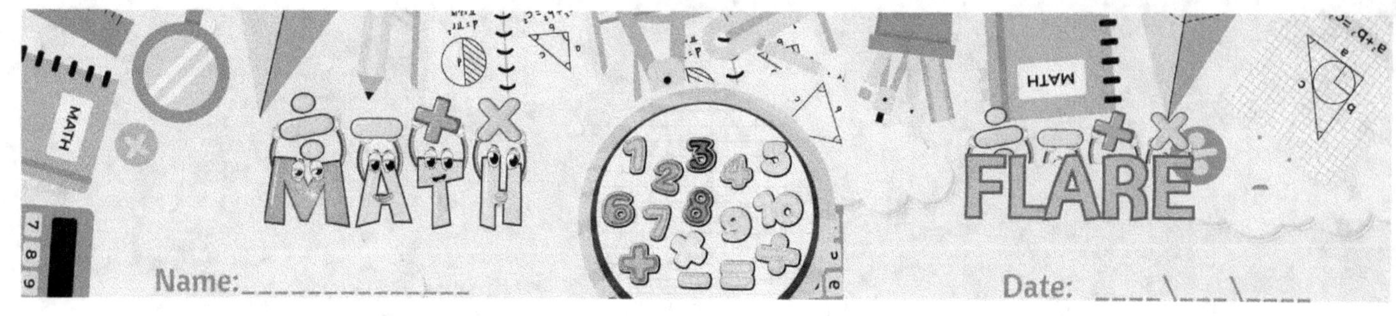

39. $(8n^3 - n^4) + (n^4 + 4n - 6n^3)$

44. $(6p^4 + 5) - (6 + 6p^3 - 3p^4)$

40. $(3 + 6n^4) + (8 - 8n^4 - 6n^3)$

45. $(6x^3 - 6x^2) - (6x^3 + 7x + 4x^2)$

41. $(r^3 - 5r) + (5r - r^3 + 4r^2)$

46. $(5k - 3k^2) + (4k + 6k^2 - 4k^3)$

42. $(8 - 2n^2) - (4 + 2n^3 + 7n^2)$

47. $(2x^3 - 7x^4) + (6x^4 + 5x^3 + 1)$

43. $(7x + 6) + (4x^4 + 6x + 6)$

48. $(3n - 6) + (6n + 1 + 6n^4)$

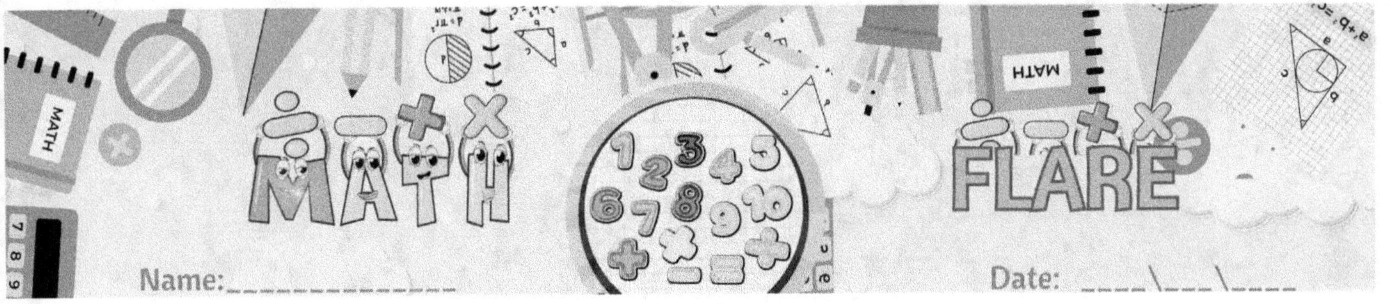

49. $(6v^3 + 5v^2) - (8v - v^3 + 5v^2)$

50. $(4x + 5x^2) - (x + 5x^2 + 8)$

51. $(1 - 2n^4) + (2n^4 - 6 + 2n)$

52. $(x^4 - 8x) + (2x - 6x^3 + 7x^4)$

53. $(8 - 7v^2) + (6 + 8v + 4v^2)$

54. $(2a^3 - 4) - (2 - 5a^3 + 2a^2)$

55. $(7x^4 + 2) - (1 - 3x + 2x^4)$

56. $(2k^2 - 5k^3) + (5k^2 - 3 + 7k^3)$

57. $(7m^2 - 5m) - (8m + m^2 - 6m^3)$

58. $(3p^4 - 8) - (2p^4 + 7 - 8p^2)$

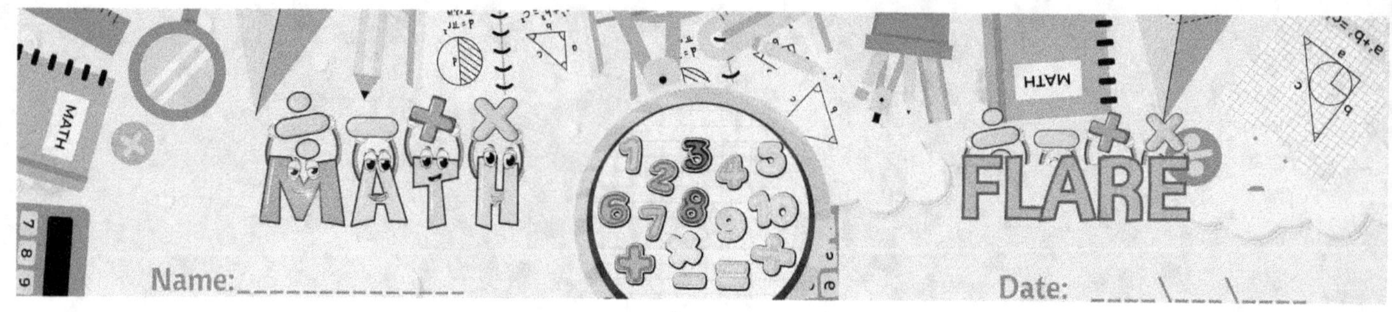

59. $(2x^2 + 6x^3) + (5 - 8x^2 - 8x^3)$

64. $(8n^4 + 8n - 2n^2) + (4n - 6n^4 - 2n^2)$

60. $(6v^3 + 4v) + (v^3 - 7v - 4v^4)$

65. $(5n^3 - 7n + 3n^4) + (n + 4 + 3n^3)$

61. $(2v + 4v^2 + 2) - (5v - 4v^4 - 6v^2)$

66. $(7x - 7x^3 + 2x^4) + (6x^4 - x^2 + 4x)$

62. $(5x^2 + 3x^4 + 8x) - (2x + 4x^4 + 7x^2)$

67. $(3p^3 + 5p - 7p^4) - (6 + 2p^4 + p^3)$

63. $(7n^2 + 6 - 3n) - (4n - 6n^2 - 3n^3)$

68. $(2 + 3x^4 + 4x^3) + (2x^3 - 5 - 8x^4)$

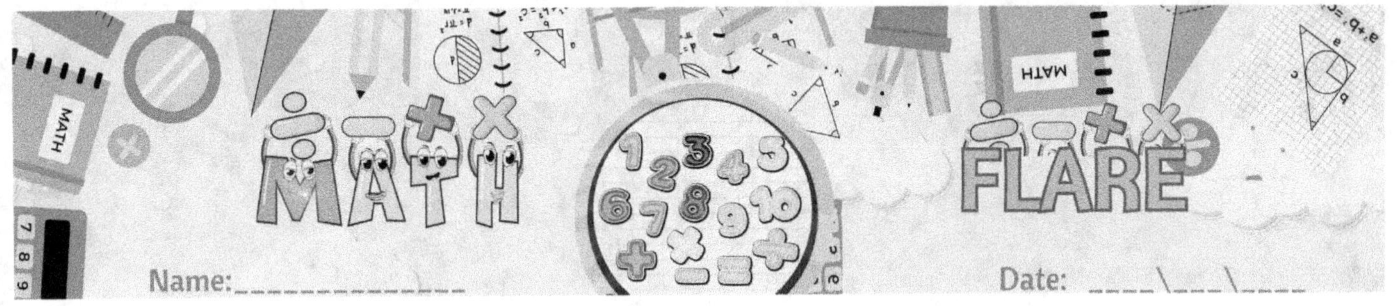

Name:_____________________   Date: _______________

69. $(4 - 4n^3 - 5n^2) + (7 + 5n^2 - 8n^3)$

74. $(2 - 3k^3 - 5k^2) + (k^2 - k^3 + 7)$

70. $(8 - 8n + 4n^4) - (n^4 - 6n + 7)$

75. $(7r + 6r^3 - 5r^4) + (6r^4 - 5r^2 + 4r)$

71. $(3m - 3m^3 - 2m^4) + (m^4 + m^2 + 6m^3)$

76. $(v^4 - 3v + 1) - (4v - v^3 - 6)$

72. $(6m^2 - 2m^4 + 5m^3) + (7m^3 + 5m^2 + 3)$

77. $(p^3 + 7p - 6p^2) + (2p^3 + 6p^2 + 5p)$

73. $(3x^4 + 8x^2 + 3x) + (2x^2 + 7x - 4x^4)$

78. $(5r - 8r^2 - 1) + (1 + 5r^2 - r)$

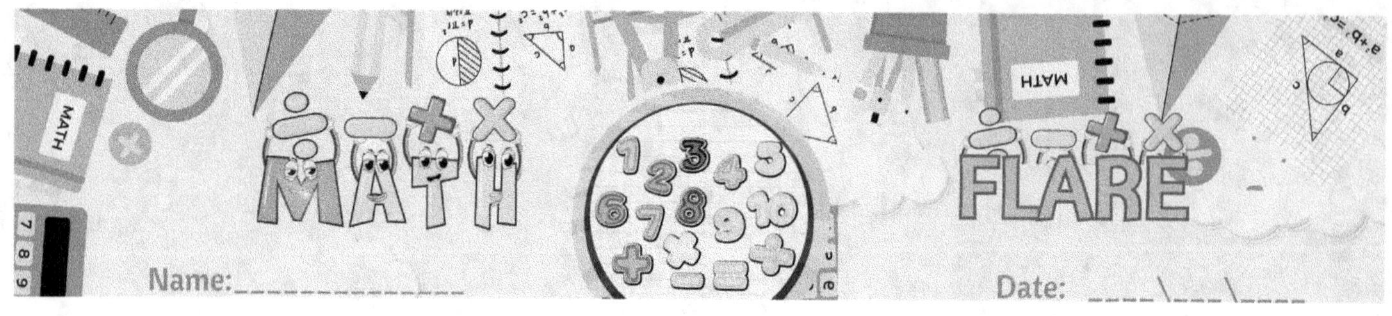

79. $(3 - 7b^4 - 5b^3) - (7 - b^3 - b^2)$

84. $(8m - 6 - m^3) - (5m^4 - 6 - 7m)$

80. $(7 + 8m^2 - 4m^4) + (3m^4 - 6 + 5m)$

85. $(5 - n^2 + n^4) - (2n^3 + 2 - 7n^4)$

81. $(a - 4 - 8a^2) + (2a + 5 + 5a^2)$

86. $(3n + 6n^4 - 7n^2) + (7n^2 - 8n^4 - n)$

82. $(5x^4 - x^2 - 4x^3) - (5x^2 - 8x^4 + 5x^3)$

87. $(2p^4 - 8p + 3p^3) - (5p^3 - p^4 - 8p)$

83. $(7v^2 - 4v^4 + 2) + (7v^2 + 3v + 5)$

88. $(x^3 - 2x^2 - 1) - (1 + 5x^2 + 3x^4)$

Polynomials: Multiplication

1. $(7x - 5y)(2x - 6y)$

2. $(6x - 7y)(3x - 4y)$

3. $(7x - 8y)(3x - 2y)$

4. $(2m + 6n)(6m + 7n)$

5. $(2x + 4y)(3x - y)$

6. $(5a - 3b)(8a - 8b)$

7. $(8x - 3y)(7x + 3y)$

8. $(3x - 2y)(6x + 8y)$

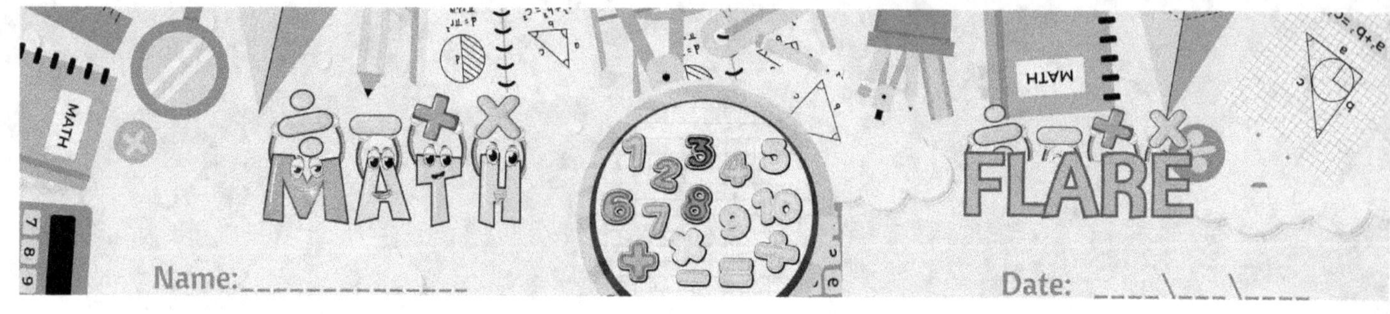

9. (7m - 2n)(6m - 4n)

10. (5x - 7 y)(3x + y)

11. (6x - 5 y)(2x + 3 y)

12. (4x - 4 y)(2x + 7 y)

13. (5x - 8 y)(8x + 2 y)

14. (a + 8b)(3a + 8b)

15. (2m - 6n)(8m - 6n)

16. (2u - v)(4u + v)

17. (7m + 7n)(8m + 3n)

18. (8u - 5v)(4u - 4v)

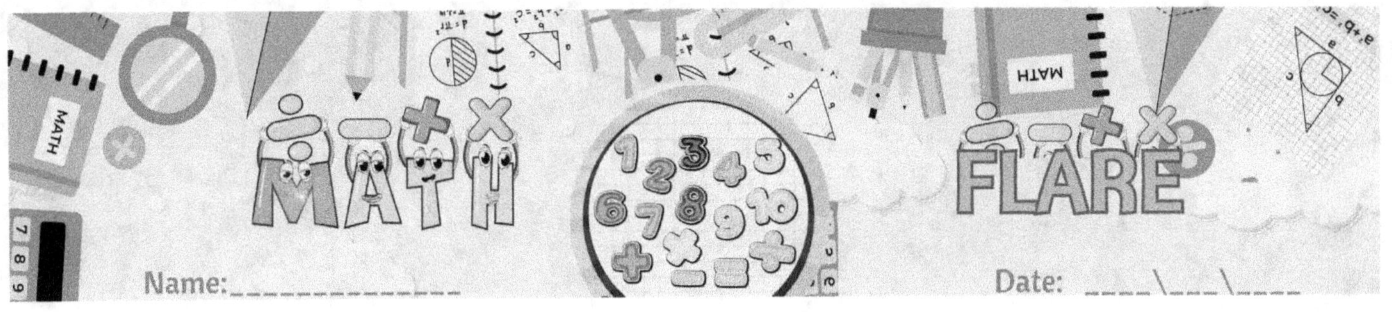

19. $(3x - 5y)(8x + 7y)$

24. $(x + y)(7x + 2y)$

20. $(5x - 8y)(2x + 6y)$

25. $(8x - 5y)(6x - 2y)$

21. $(2m + 4n)(5m - 3n)$

26. $(6m - 5n)(2m + 8n)$

22. $(a + 7b)(6a - b)$

27. $(4x - 2y)(2x - y)$

23. $(2u + 3v)(6u - 8v)$

28. $(4x - 3y)(8x + y)$

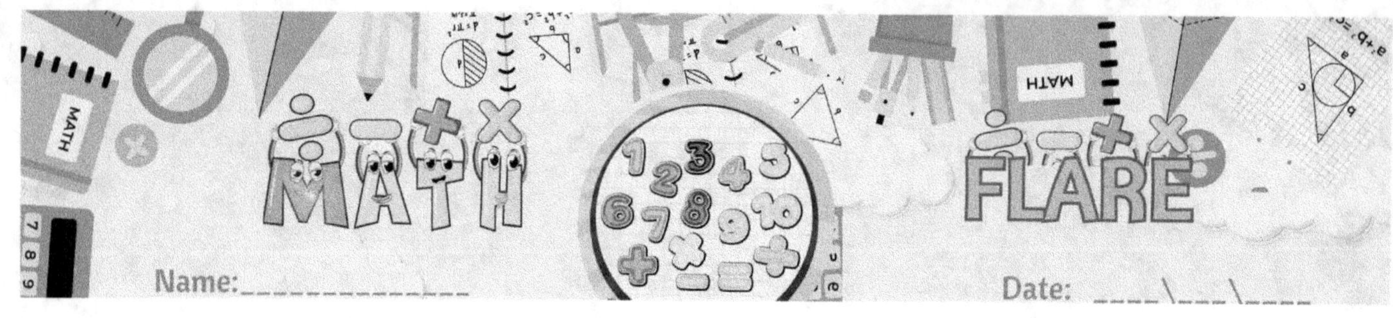

29. $(3x - 4y)(8x + 3y)$

30. $(2u + 2v)(5u + 8v)$

31. $(6x + 5y)(x^2 - 2xy - y^2)$

32. $(5u + 2v)(8u^2 - uv - 3v^2)$

33. $(5x - 5y)(4x^2 - 4xy + 2y^2)$

34. $(8m + 2n)(3m^2 - mn - 6n^2)$

35. $(x + 3y)(4x^2 + 6xy + 5y^2)$

36. $(8x + y)(2x^2 + xy + 2y^2)$

37. $(5m - 8n)(6m^2 - 3mn - 7n^2)$

38. $(6x - 4y)(8x^2 + 8xy - y^2)$

39. $(2m - 4n)(2m^2 + 8mn + 5n^2)$

40. $(8a + 8b)(a^2 - 4ab - 3b^2)$

41. $(3x - 5y)(5x^2 + 6xy - 6y^2)$

42. $(8x + 2y)(7x^2 + 8xy - 5y^2)$

43. $(7m - 2n)(3m^2 - mn + 2n^2)$

44. $(8x - 8y)(x^2 - 4xy - 8y^2)$

45. $(3x + 4y)(3x^2 + 8xy - 6y^2)$

46. $(8x + y)(3x^2 - 8xy + 6y^2)$

47. $(6x - 6y)(8x^2 - 3xy - 8y^2)$

48. $(3u + 4v)(3u^2 + uv + 8v^2)$

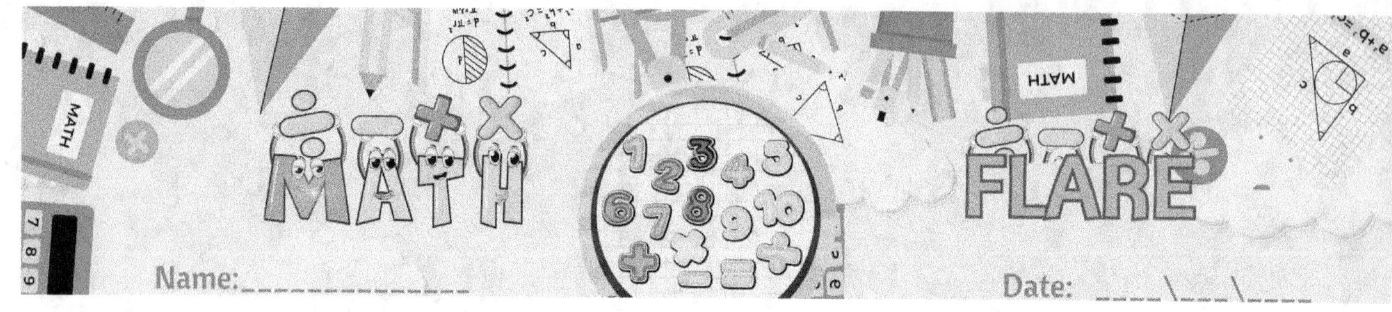

49. $(x + 8y)(7x^2 + xy + 7y^2)$

54. $(x - 6y)(6x^2 - 3xy + 4y^2)$

50. $(7u + 3v)(2u^2 - 8uv - 5v^2)$

55. $(2u - 3v)(6u^2 + 5uv - 6v^2)$

51. $(3x + y)(2x^2 - 4xy + y^2)$

56. $(7x + y)(5x^2 - 8xy - 6y^2)$

52. $(5m + 2n)(7m^2 - 6mn - 8n^2)$

57. $(6x + 7y)(3x^2 - xy - 7y^2)$

53. $(u - 3v)(8u^2 - 2uv - 3v^2)$

58. $(2x - 2y)(x^2 + xy + 4y^2)$

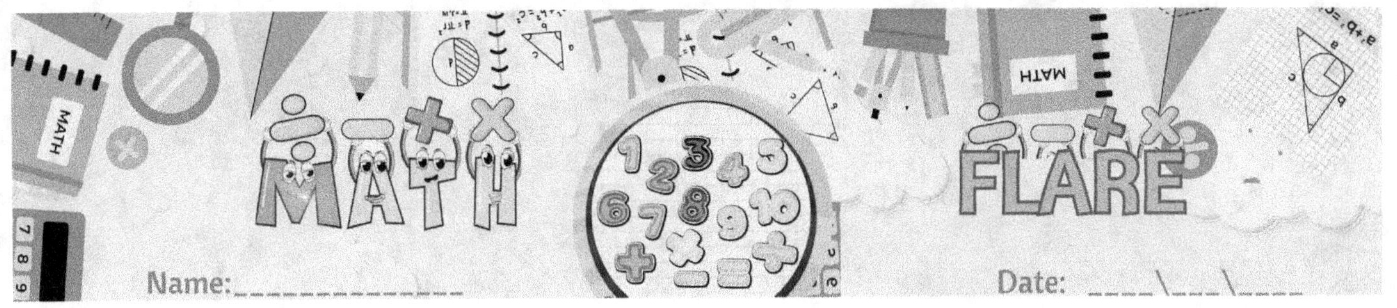

59. $(m - 6n)(m^2 - 2mn - 7n^2)$

60. $(x + 7y)(8x^2 - 3xy + 6y^2)$

61. $(6x^2 + 4xy + 6y^2)(8x^2 + 3xy + 3y^2)$

62. $(6x^2 + 2xy + 2y^2)(x^2 - 7xy - 4y^2)$

63. $(7x^2 + 3xy - 8y^2)(2x^2 - 6xy + y^2)$

64. $(6x^2 + 5xy + 2y^2)(8x^2 - 6xy + 6y^2)$

65. $(a^2 - 2ab + 8b^2)(6a^2 - 7ab - 5b^2)$

66. $(u^2 - 4uv + 7v^2)(3u^2 + 8uv - 7v^2)$

67. $(5x^2 + 6xy - 6y^2)(7x^2 + 8xy - 7y^2)$

68. $(5x^2 + 6xy + 6y^2)(4x^2 - 7xy - 3y^2)$

69. $(5u^2 + 5uv + 8v^2)(8u^2 + 4uv - 8v^2)$

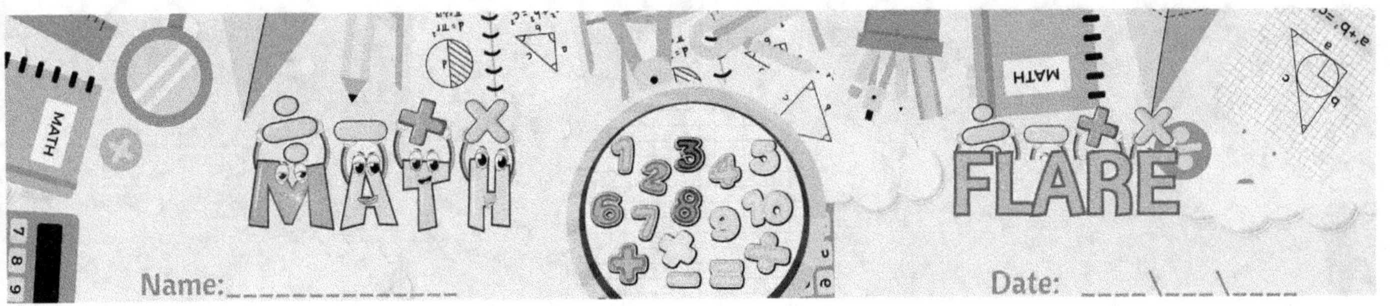

70. $(8a^2 + 6ab + 4b^2)(a^2 + ab + 5b^2)$

71. $(8x^2 - 7xy + 2y^2)(5x^2 + 7xy + 2y^2)$

72. $(7x^2 + 4xy - 3y^2)(2x^2 + 2xy - 2y^2)$

73. $(2x^2 + 8xy - 8y^2)(6x^2 - 7xy + y^2)$

74. $(2x^2 + 7xy + 2y^2)(7x^2 - 4xy + 2y^2)$

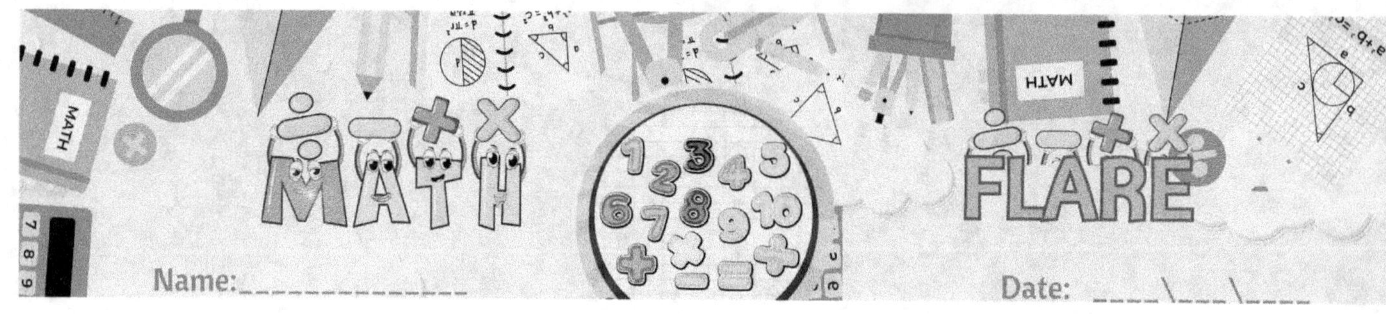

75. $(a^2 + 4ab - 3b^2)(4a^2 - 7ab + 2b^2)$

76. $(7x^2 - 6xy + 5y^2)(2x^2 - 6xy + 5y^2)$

77. $(6x^2 + 8xy + 2y^2)(7x^2 + 8xy - y^2)$

78. $(x^2 - 7xy + y^2)(6x^2 - 3xy - y^2)$

79. $(2x^2 - 5xy - 8y^2)(8x^2 - 6xy + 5y^2)$

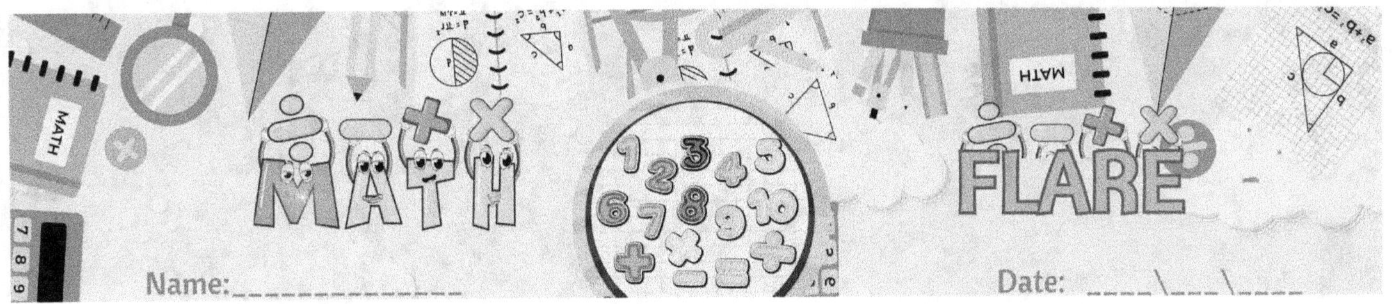

Name:_________________   Date: _______________

80. $(8u^2 - 5uv - 5v^2)(6u^2 + 8uv + 8v^2)$

81. $(x^2 - 8xy - 3y^2)(2x^2 + 5xy + 2y^2)$

82. $(3x^2 + 4xy - 8y^2)(8x^2 - 2xy - 4y^2)$

83. $(3a^2 - 3ab - 2b^2)(8a^2 - ab + b^2)$

84. $(a^2 + 8ab - 6b^2)(5a^2 - 3ab + 8b^2)$

85. $(2x^2 + 4xy + 4y^2)(7x^2 + 4xy - 8y^2)$

86. $(6a^2 - 2ab - 6b^2)(8a^2 + 2ab + 8b^2)$

87. $(x^2 - 3xy + 8y^2)(3x^2 - 7xy - 5y^2)$

88. $(8a^2 - 2ab + 4b^2)(5a^2 - 7ab - b^2)$

89. $(2a^2 - 6ab - 8b^2)(8a^2 - 4ab - 6b^2)$

Chapter. 06

Geometry

Area and Perimeter

The area of a shape represents the amount of space it occupies. The perimeter of a shape is the total distance around its outer edge.

Area of Rectangle

For a square, since all four sides are equal, we only need to know the length of one side to find its area. We can calculate the area of a square by multiplying the length of one side by itself (squared). So, if the length of one side of the square is 's', then the area (A) is given by:

$$A = s \times s$$

4 in

4 in

$$A = 4 \times 4$$

$$A = 16$$

Perimeter of Rectangle

For a square, since all four sides are equal, we can find the perimeter by adding up the lengths of all four sides. If 's' represents the length of one side, then the perimeter (P) is given by:

$$P = 4 \times s$$

$$P = 4 \times 4$$

$$P = 16$$

Area of Triangle:

The area of a triangle represents the amount of space enclosed within its three sides. The formula for calculating the area of a triangle depends on the type of triangle. For a general triangle, we use the formula:

$$A = \frac{1}{2} \times \text{base} \times \text{height}$$

Where:

- A represents the area of the triangle.

- The base is the length of any one side of the triangle.

- The height is the perpendicular distance from the base to the opposite vertex.

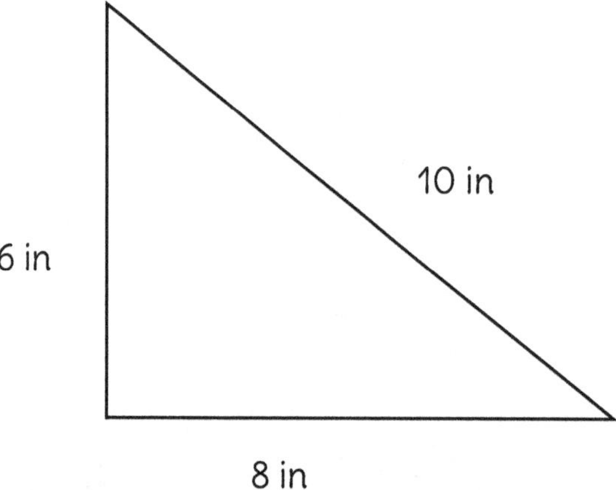

$$A = \frac{1}{2} \times base \times height$$

$$A = \frac{1}{2} \times 6 \times 8$$

$$A = \frac{1}{2} \times 48$$

$$A = 24$$

Perimeter of Triangle:

The perimeter of a triangle is the total length of its three sides. To find the perimeter, we simply add the lengths of all three sides together:

$$P = side1 + side2 + side3$$

$$P = 6 + 8 + 10$$

$$P = 24$$

Equilateral Triangle

An equilateral triangle is a triangle in which all three sides are equal in length. To find the area and perimeter of an equilateral triangle, we can use the following formulas:

- Area (A): $\frac{\sqrt{3}}{4} \times a^2$ where a is the length of one side of the equilateral triangle.
- Perimeter (P): $P = 3a$ where a is the length of one side of the equilateral triangle.

Let's solve a problem:

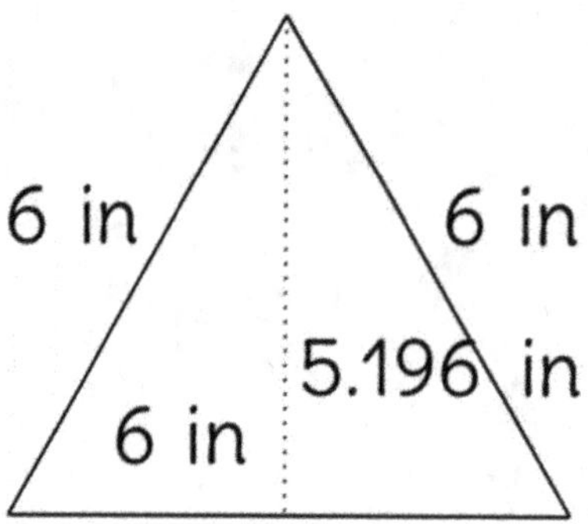

Area of Equilateral Triangle:

$$\text{Area (A): } \frac{\sqrt{3}}{4} \times (6)^2$$

$$\text{Area (A): } \frac{\sqrt{3}}{4} \times 36$$

$$\text{Area (A): } \frac{36\sqrt{3}}{4}$$

$$\text{Area (A): } \frac{36(1.73)}{4}$$

$$\text{Area (A): } \frac{62.35}{4}$$

$$\text{Area (A): } 15.59 \text{ in}^2$$

Perimeter of Equilateral Triangle:

$$P = 3a$$

$$P = 3(6) = 18$$

<u>Isosceles Triangle</u>

An isosceles triangle is a triangle with at least two sides of equal length. The angles opposite the equal sides are also equal.

Area of Isosceles Triangle

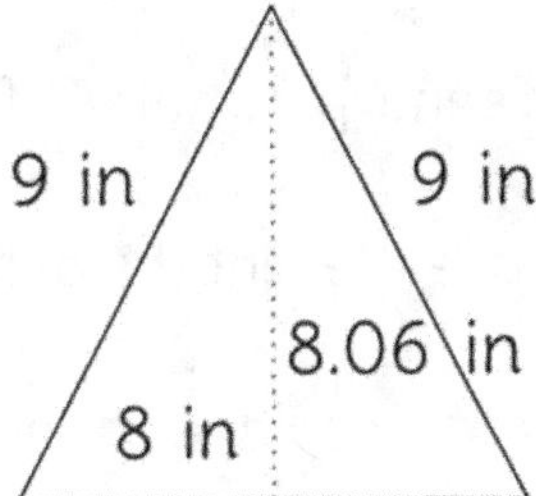

$$A = \frac{1}{2} \times \text{base} \times \text{height}$$

$$A = \frac{1}{2} \times 8 \times 8$$

$$A = \frac{1}{2} \times 64$$

$$A = 32$$

Perimeter of Isosceles Triangle

The perimeter of a triangle is the total length of its three sides. To find the perimeter, we simply add the lengths of all three sides together:

$$P = \text{side1} + \text{side2} + \text{side3}$$

$$P = 9 + 9 + 8$$

$$P = 26$$

<u>Scalene Triangle</u>

A scalene triangle is a triangle with no equal sides and no equal angles. The formula for finding various properties of a scalene triangle is as follows:

Area (A): The area of a scalene triangle can be calculated using Heron's formula, which is given by:

$$A = \sqrt{s(s-a)(s-b)(s-c)}$$

where s is the semi-perimeter of the triangle,

and a, b, and c are the lengths of its three sides.

Perimeter (P): The perimeter of a scalene triangle is the sum of the lengths of its three sides.

$$P = side1 + side2 + side3$$

Let's find the Area and Perimeter of a Scalene Triangle:

15.6 cm   16.6 cm

15.52 cm

7.7 cm

Area (A): First, we calculate the semi-perimeter (s):

$$S = \frac{a+b+c}{2} = \frac{15.6+16.6+7.7}{2} = \frac{39.8}{2} = 19.9 \text{ cm}$$

Heron's formula to find the area:

$$A = \sqrt{s(s-a)(s-b)(s-c)}$$

$$A = \sqrt{19.9\,(19.9-15.6)(19.9-16.6)(19.9-7.7)}$$

$$A = \sqrt{19.9 \times 4.3 \times 3.3 \times 12.2}$$

$$A = \sqrt{3445} \approx 59$$

Perimeter (P):

$$P = side1 + side2 + side3$$

$$P = 15.6 + 16.6 + 7.7$$

$$P = 39.8$$

Area and Perimeter of an L-shape

The L-shaped figure typically consists of two rectangles joined together to form an L-shape. To find the area and perimeter of an L-shaped figure, we will need to calculate the areas and perimeters of each rectangle and then combine them.

Area=Area of Rectangle 1 + Area of Rectangle 2

Perimeter=Perimeter of Rectangle 1 + Perimeter of Rectangle 2

Let's find the Area and Perimeter of an L-shape:

Area of L-Shape

$$\text{Area 1} = 4.38 \times 4.5 = 19.7 \text{ cm}^2$$

$$\text{Area 2} = 11.28 \times 6.54 = 73.7 \text{ cm}^2$$

$$\text{Area} = 19.7 + 73.7$$

$$\text{Area} = 93.481 \text{ cm}^2$$

Perimeter of L-Shape

$$P = 11.28 + 6.54 + 6.78 + 4.38 + 4.5 + 10.92$$

$$P = 44.4 \text{ cm}$$

Area and Perimeter of U-shape

U-shape is basically composed of three rectangles, we'll need to calculate the area and perimeter of each rectangle separately and then sum them up.

Area of the U-shape:

The total area (A) of the U-shape is the sum of the areas of the three rectangles:

$$A = A1 + A2 + A3$$

Perimeter of the U-shape: The total perimeter (P) of the U-shape is the sum of the perimeters of the three rectangles:

$$P = P1 + P2 + P3$$

Let's find the area and perimeter of the following U-shape:

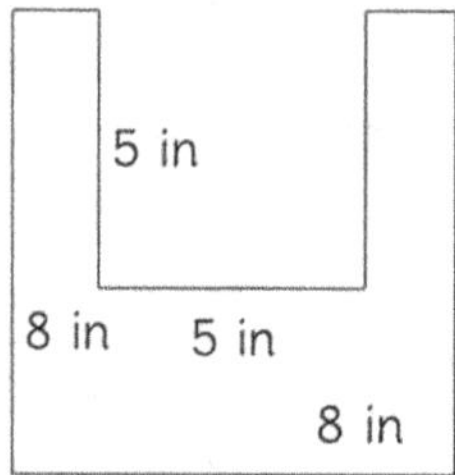

Area:

$$A1 = 8 \times 1.5 = 12 + A2 = 3 \times 5 = 15 + A3 = 8 \times 1.5 = 12$$

$$= 12 + 15 + 12$$

$$= 39 \text{ in}^2$$

Perimeter:

$$2 \times 8 + 2 \times 5 + 2 \times 8$$

$$= 16 + 10 + 16$$

$$= 42$$

Area and Perimeter of T-shape

The T-shape consists of two rectangles joined together to form a T-like structure.

Area of the T-shape:

To find the total area of the T-shape, we need to calculate the areas of both rectangles and then add them together.

$$\text{Area of Rectangle 1} = \text{Length} \times \text{Width}$$

$$\text{Area of Rectangle 2} = \text{Length} \times \text{Width}$$

$$\text{Total Area} = \text{Area of Rectangle 1} + \text{Area of Rectangle 2}$$

The perimeter of the T-shape is the sum of the perimeters of the two rectangles, minus the length of the overlapping side:

$$\text{Perimeter} = 2(l1 + w1) + 2(l2 + w2) - (w1 - w2)$$

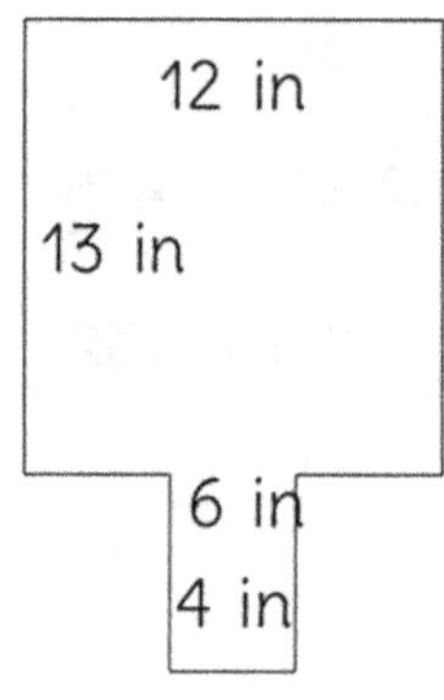

Area= 12 × 13 + 6 × 4

Area= 156 + 24

Area= 180 in²

Perimeter= 2(12+13) +2(6+4) – (12-4)

Perimeter=2(25) + 2(10) – 8

Perimeter= 50 + 20 – 8

Perimeter= 62 in²

Area and Perimeter of Parallelogram

A parallelogram is a four-sided polygon with opposite sides that are parallel and equal in length. To find the area and perimeter of a parallelogram, we use specific formulas based on its dimensions.

For example:

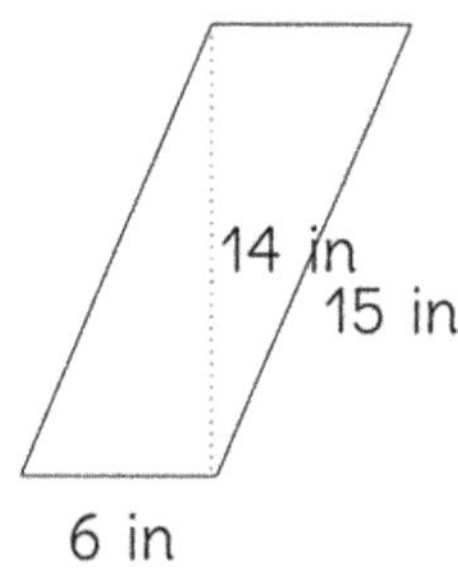

Let's denote:

- The length of one side of the parallelogram as $a = 15$.

- The length of an adjacent side (parallel to a) $b = 6$.

- The height of the parallelogram (perpendicular distance between the two parallel sides) as $h=14$

Area of Parallelogram

$$\text{Area} = \text{Base} \times \text{Height}$$

$$\text{Area} = 6 \times 14$$

$$\text{Area} = 84$$

Perimeter of Parallelogram

$$2(a + b)$$

$$= 2(15+6)$$

$$= 2(21)$$

$$= 42$$

Area and Perimeter of Trapezoids

A trapezoid is a quadrilateral with at least one pair of parallel sides. To find the area and perimeter of a trapezoid, we use specific formulas based on its dimensions.

For example:

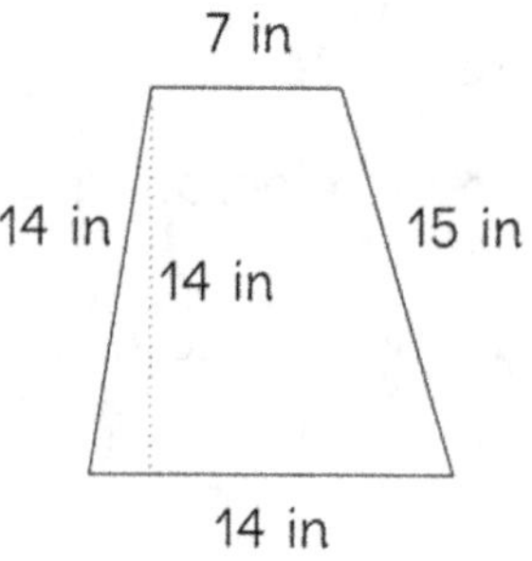

Let's denote:

- The lengths of the parallel sides of the trapezoid as $a = 7$ and $b = 14$.

- The lengths of the non-parallel sides as $c = 14$ and $d = 15$.

- The height of the trapezoid (the perpendicular distance between the parallel sides) as $h=14$.

Area of the Trapezoid:

The area of a trapezoid is given by the formula:

$$\text{Area} = \frac{1}{2} \times \text{Height} \times (\text{Sum of the lengths of the parallel sides})$$

$$\text{Area} = \frac{1}{2} \times h \times (a + b)$$

$$\text{Area} = \frac{1}{2} \times 14 \times (7 + 14)$$

$$\text{Area} = \frac{1}{2} \times 14 \times 21$$

$$\text{Area} = 147 \text{ in}^2$$

Perimeter of the Trapezoid:

$$\text{Perimeter} = 7 + 14 + 14 + 15$$

$$= 50 \text{ in}^2$$

<u>Pythagorean Theorem</u>

The Pythagorean Theorem is a fundamental principle in geometry that relates the lengths of the sides of a right triangle. It states that in any right triangle, the square of the length of the hypotenuse (the side opposite the right angle) is equal to the sum of the squares of the lengths of the other two sides.

$$a2 + b2 = c2$$

Let's use the Pythagorean Theorem to find the length of the hypotenuse (c) when $a=44$ and $b=78$.

$$c^2 = 44^2 + 78^2$$
$$c^2 = 1936 + 6084$$
$$c^2 = 8020$$
$$c = \sqrt{8020}$$
$$c \approx 89.554$$

<u>Volume and surface Area</u>

Volume refers to the amount of space occupied by a three-dimensional object. For shapes like cubes or rectangular prisms, we calculate volume by multiplying their length, width, and height.

To find the volume V of a rectangular prism, we use the formula:

$$Volume = length \; x \; width \; x \; height$$

Surface Area represents the total area covering all the faces of a three-dimensional object. For shapes like cubes or rectangular prisms, we find the surface area by summing the areas of all its faces.

The formula for surface area SA of a cube or rectangular prism is:

$$Surface\ Area\ =\ 2lw\ +\ 2lh\ +\ 2wh$$

Where: l is the length, w is the width, and h is the height of the object.

For example: Let's find the Volume and Surface Area of following rectangular prisms:

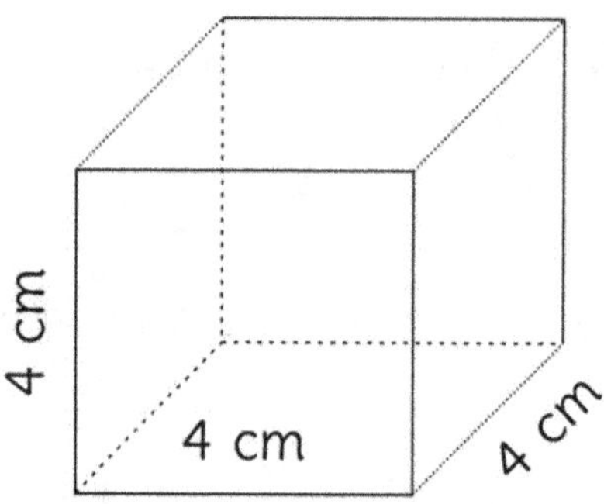

$$Volume\ =\ length\ \times\ width\ \times\ height$$

$$= 4 \times 4 \times 4$$

$$= 64\ cm^2$$

$$Surface\ Area\ =\ 2lw\ +\ 2lh\ +\ 2wh$$

$$= 2(4 \times 4) + 2(4 \times 4) + 2(4 \times 4)$$

$$= 32 + 32 + 32$$

$$= 96\ cm2$$

Different 3D objects have unique formulas for finding their volume and surface area. Here are some common ones:

1. Cube:

    - Volume: $V = s^3$ (where s is the length of one side of the cube)

    - Surface area: $SA = 6s^2$

2. Sphere:

- Volume: $V = \left(\frac{4}{3}\right)\pi r^3$ (where r is the radius of the sphere)

- Surface area: $SA = 4\pi r^2$

3. Cone:

- Volume: $V = \left(\frac{1}{3}\right)\pi r^2 h$ (where r is the radius of the base and h is the height of the cone)

- Surface area: $SA = \pi r^2 + \pi r\sqrt{(r^2 + h^2)}$

4. Cylinder:

- Volume: $V = \pi r^2 h$ (where r is the radius of the base and h is the height of the cylinder)

- Surface area: $SA = 2\pi r^2 + 2\pi rh$

5. Pyramid:

- Volume: $V = \left(\frac{1}{3}\right)Bh$ (where B is the area of the base and h is the height of the pyramid)

- Surface area: $SA = B + \frac{1}{2}Pl$ (where P is the perimeter of the base and l is the slant height of the pyramid)

Area and Perimeter

1.
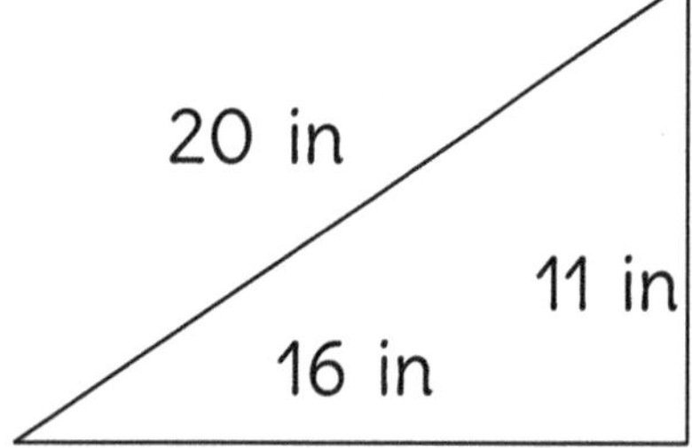

2.
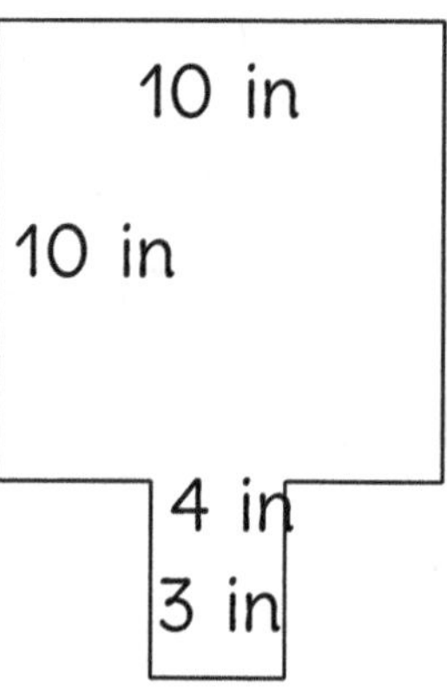

3.
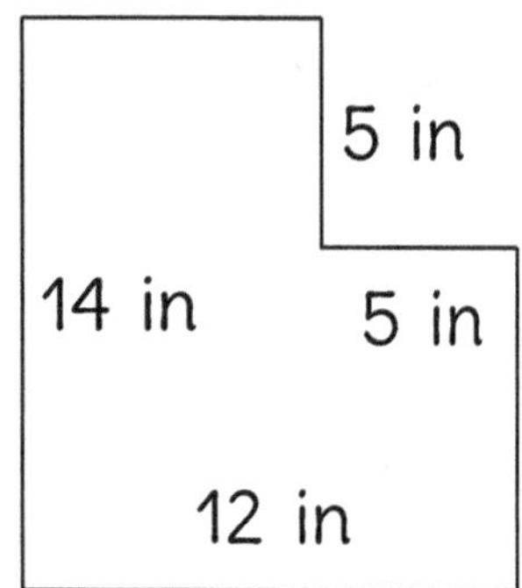

4.
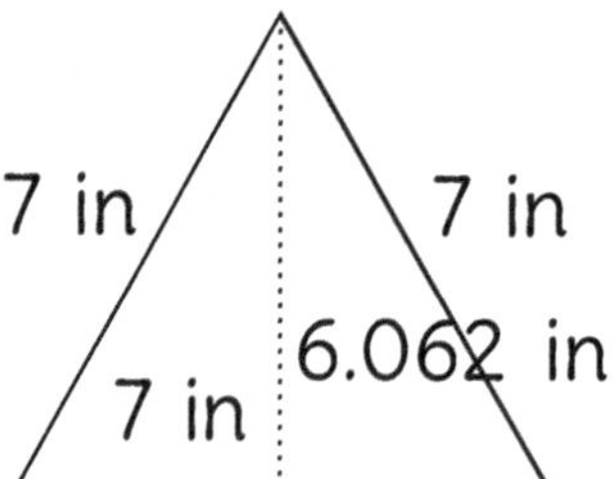

5. 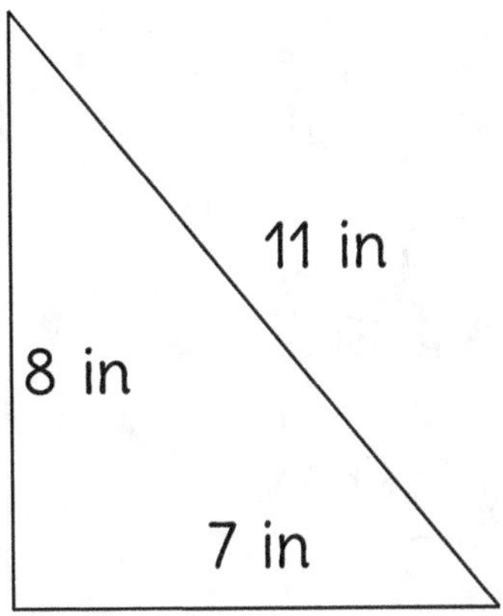

6. 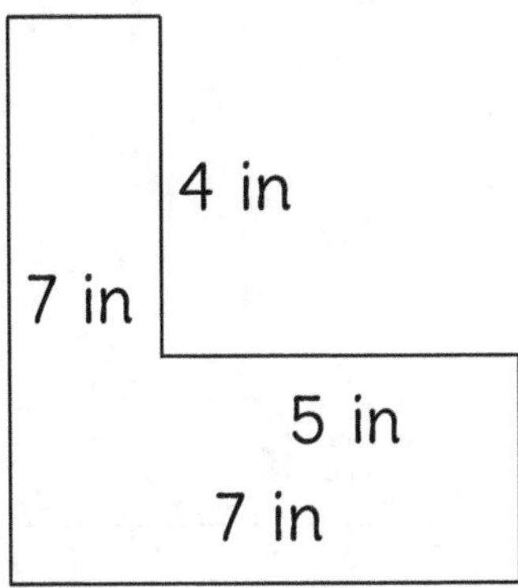

7. 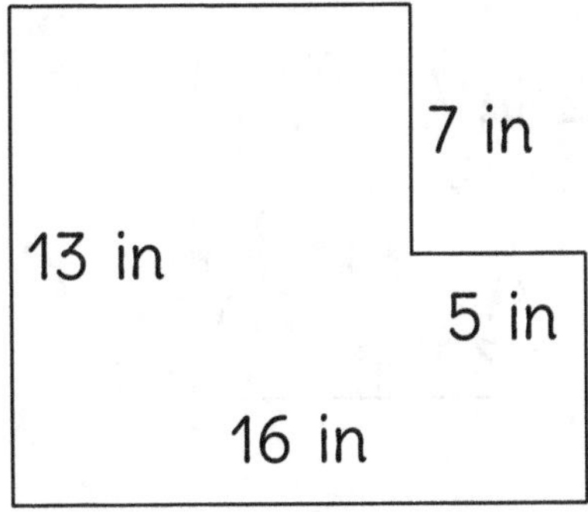

8. 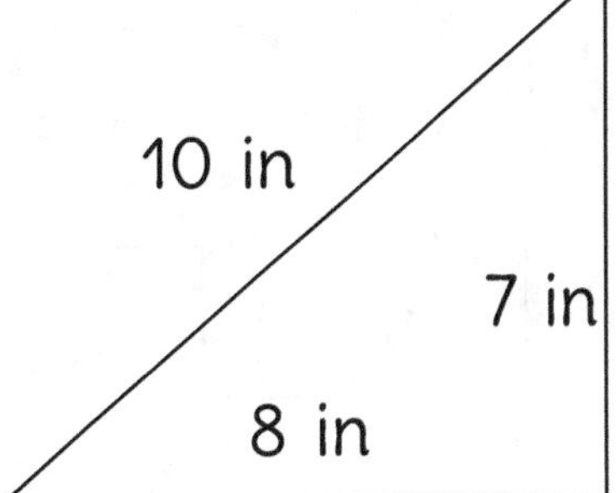

MATH
FLARE
Name:_______________
Date: ____________

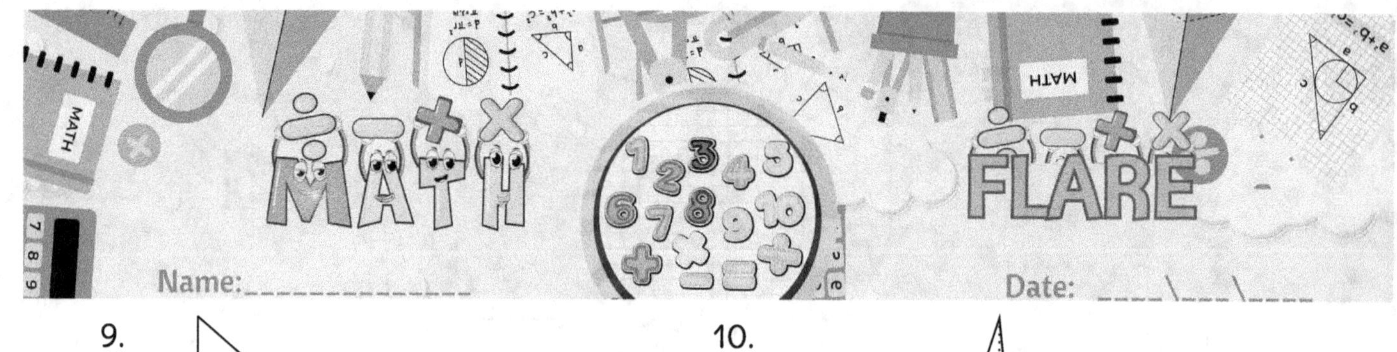

9.

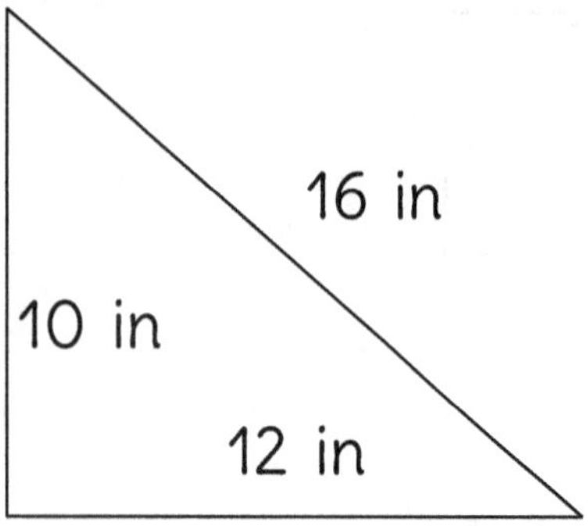

16 in
10 in
12 in

10.

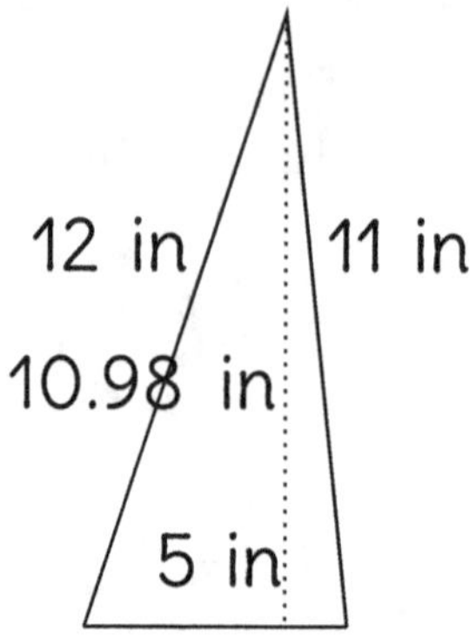

12 in
11 in
10.98 in
5 in

11.

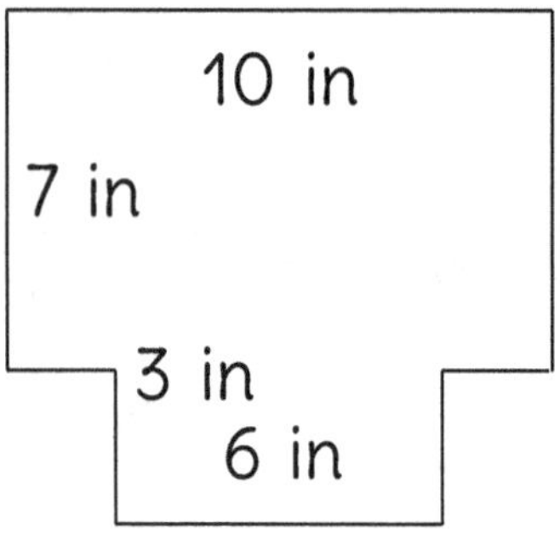

10 in
7 in
3 in
6 in

12.

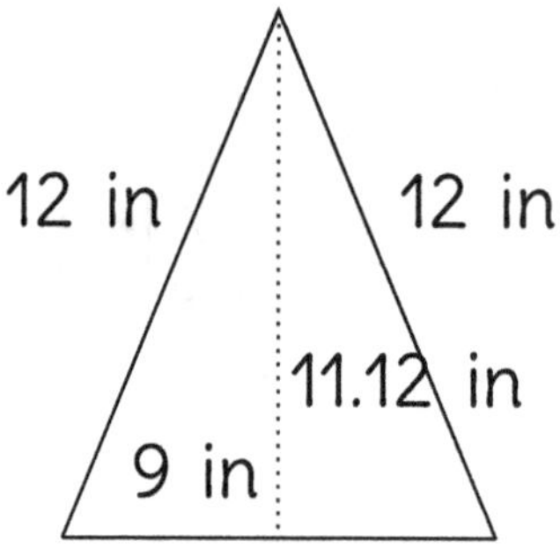

12 in
12 in
11.12 in
9 in

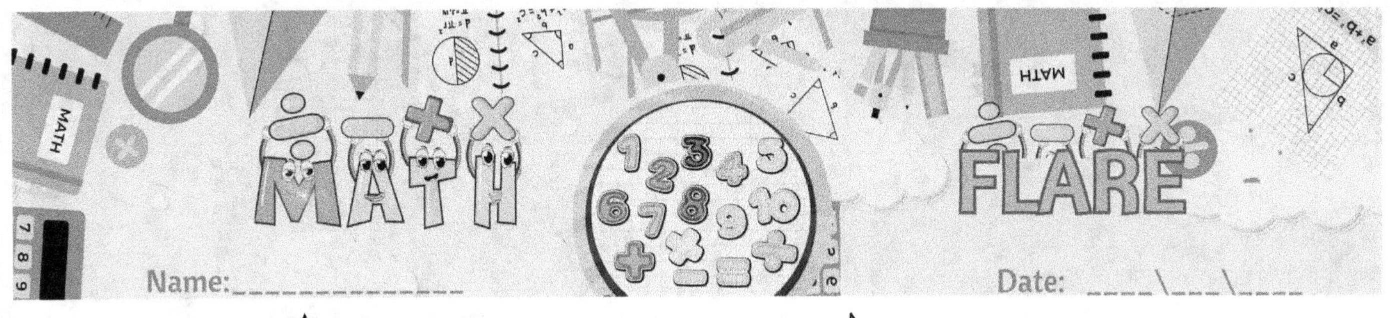

13.

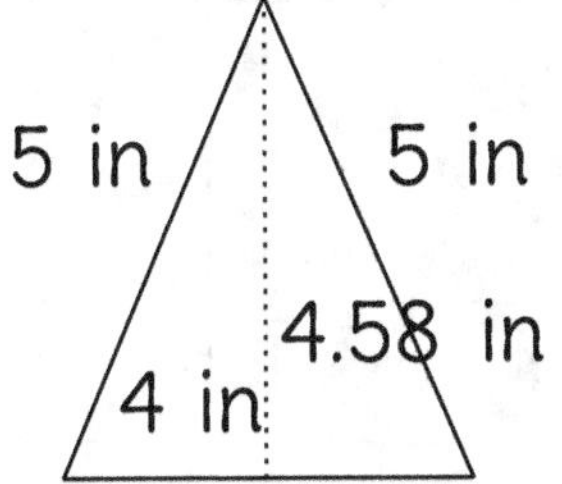

5 in   5 in

4.58 in

4 in

14.

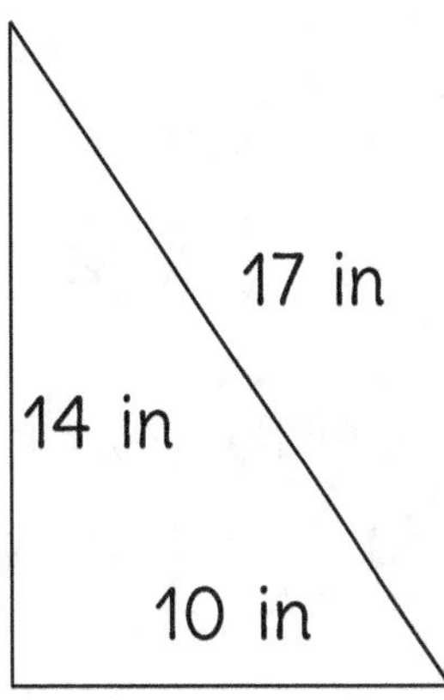

17 in

14 in

10 in

15.

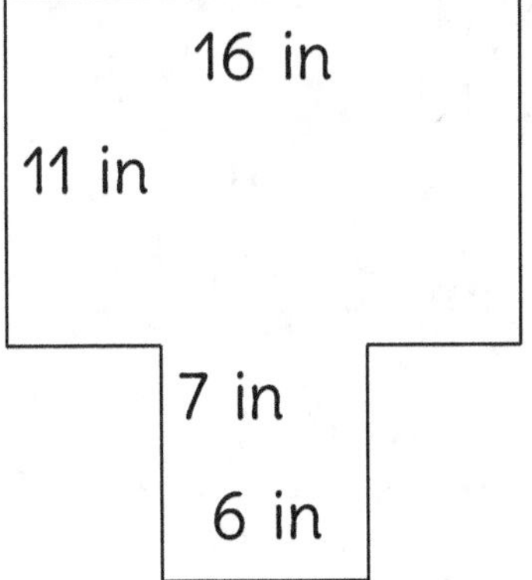

16 in

11 in

7 in

6 in

16.

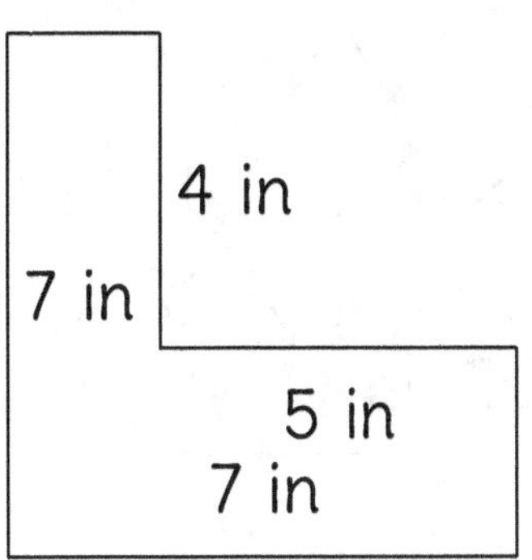

4 in

7 in

5 in

7 in

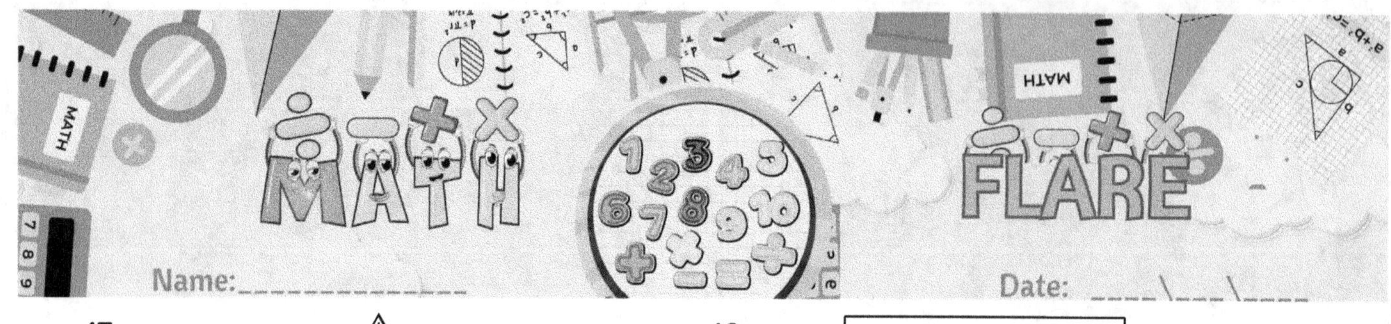

17.

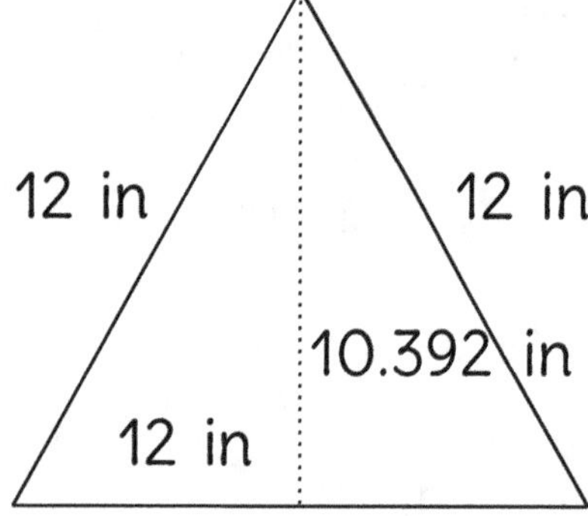

18.

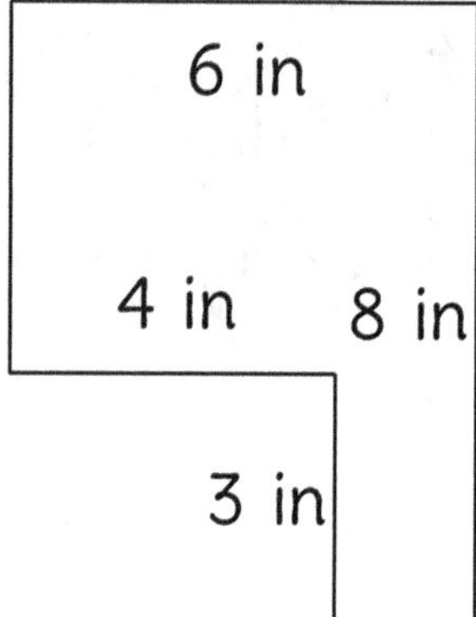

19.

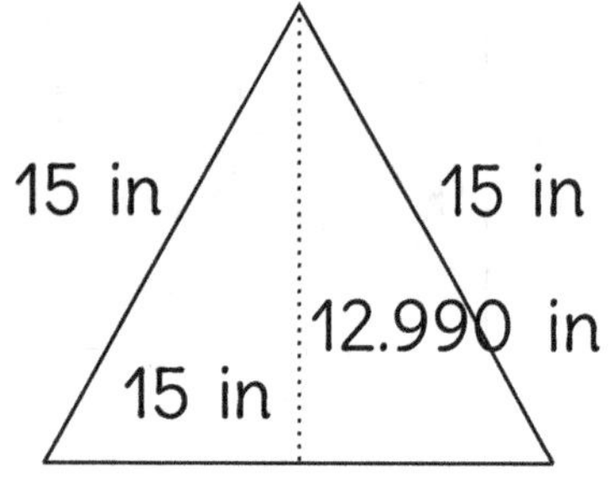

20.

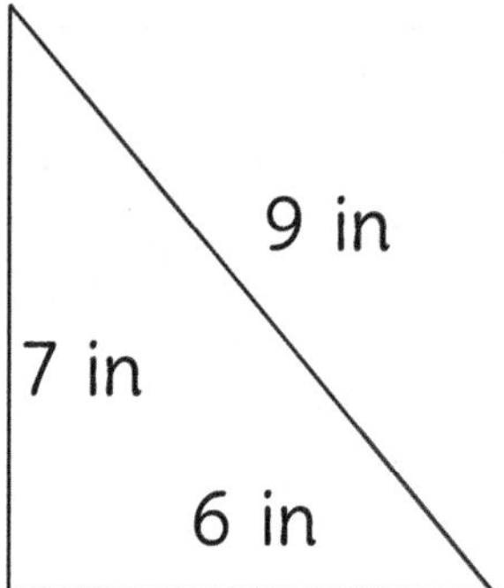

MATH
FLARE
Name:
Date:

21.

4 in
14 in
14 in
12 in
16 in

22.

11 in
8 in
10 in
6 in

23.

7 in
7 in
7.00 in
3 in

24.

8 in
13 in 5 in
11 in

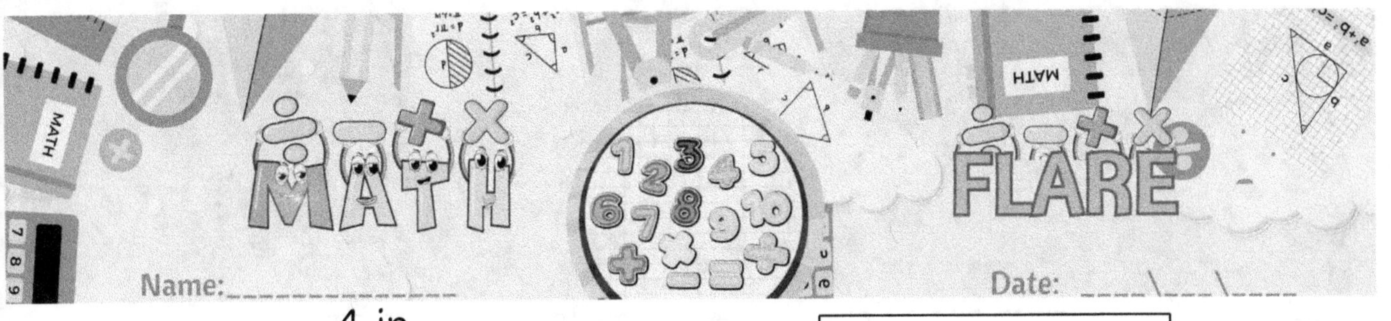

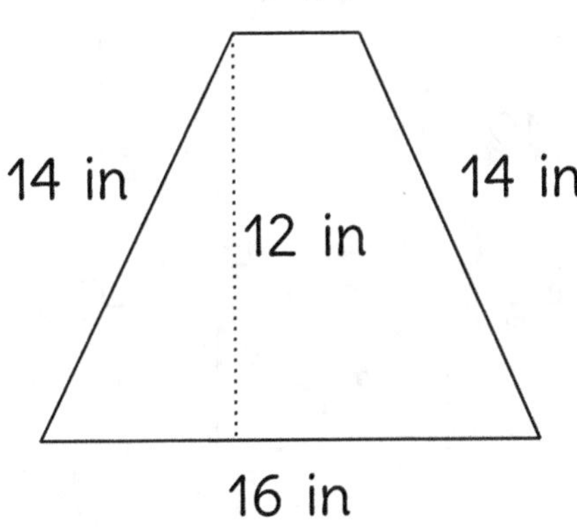

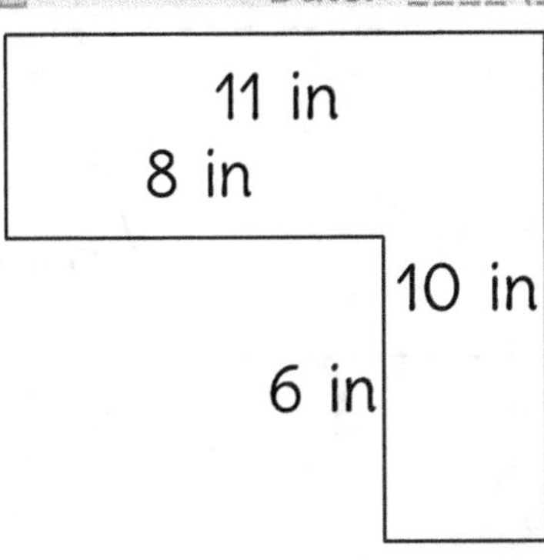

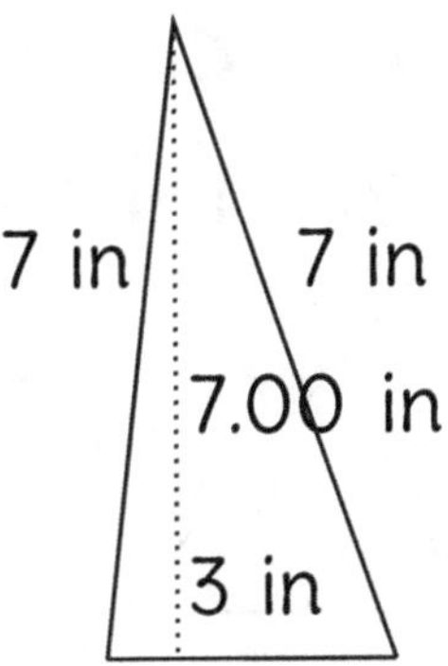

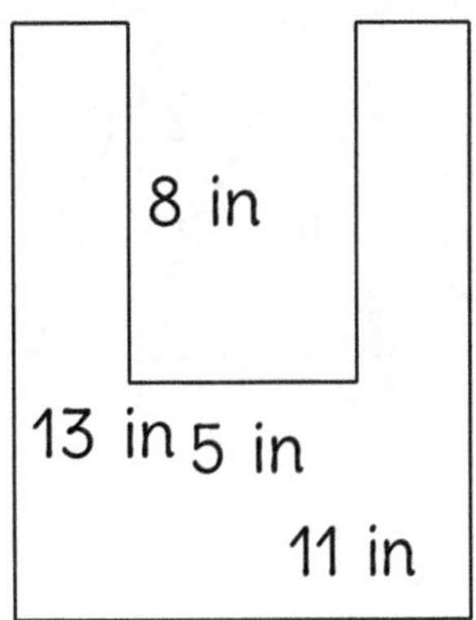

Name:
Date:

25.

4 in
5 in
6 in

26.

14 in
10 in
4 in
7 in

27.

12 in
12 in
12 in
10.392 in

28.

20 in
15 in
13 in

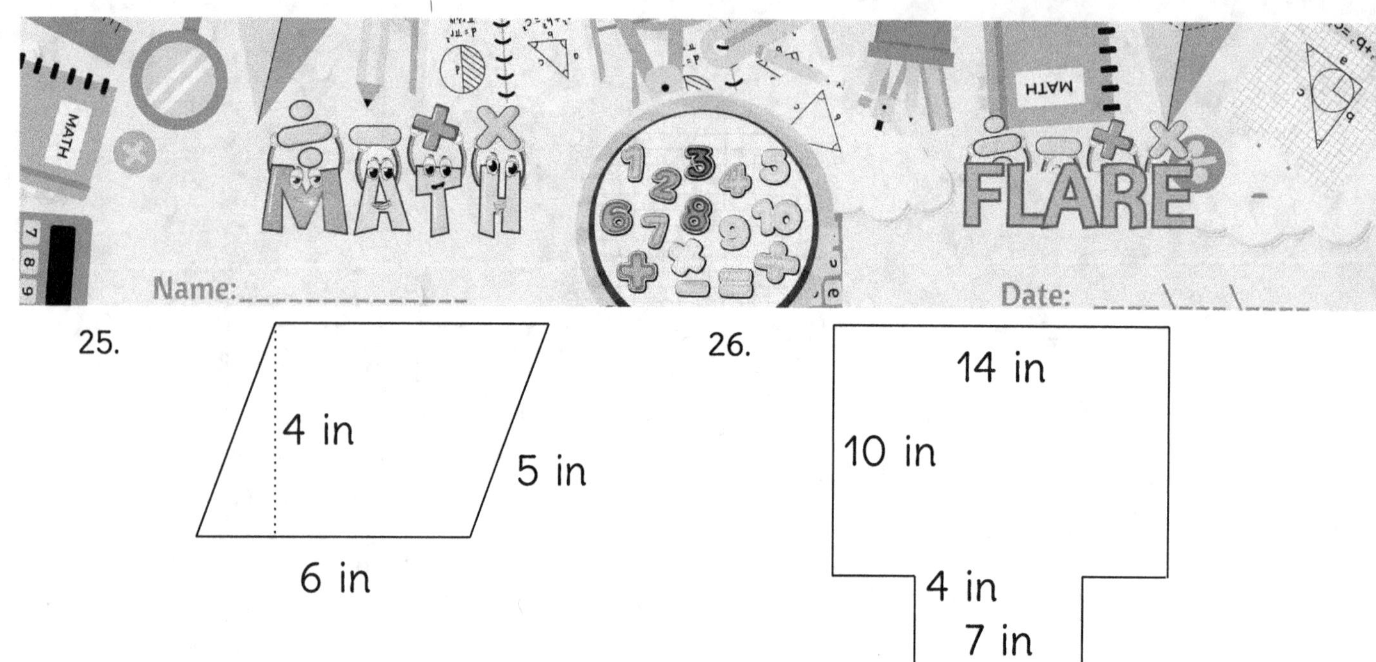

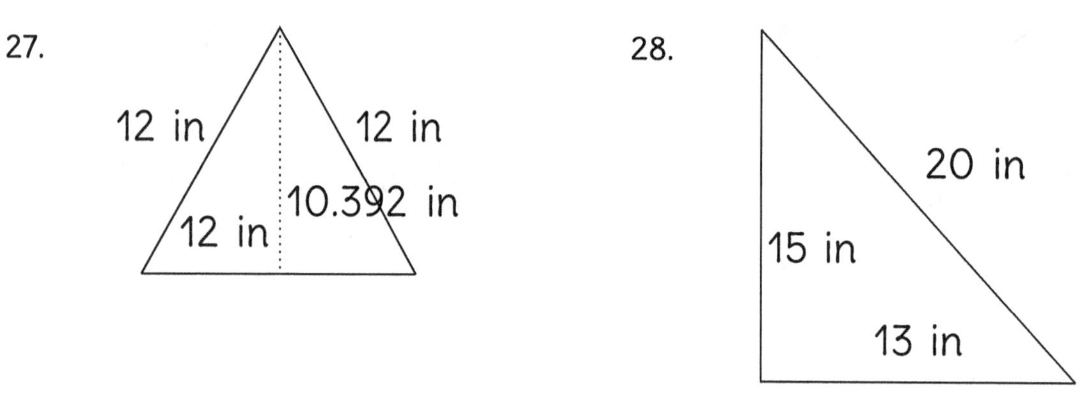

29.

11 in
11 in
10.50 in
5 in

30.

8 in
9 in
6 in

31.

5 in
14 in
15 in
14 in
16 in

32.

8 in
8 in
6.928 in
8 in

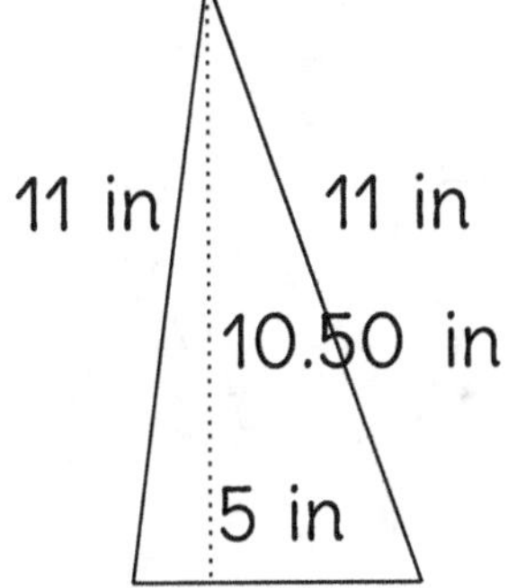

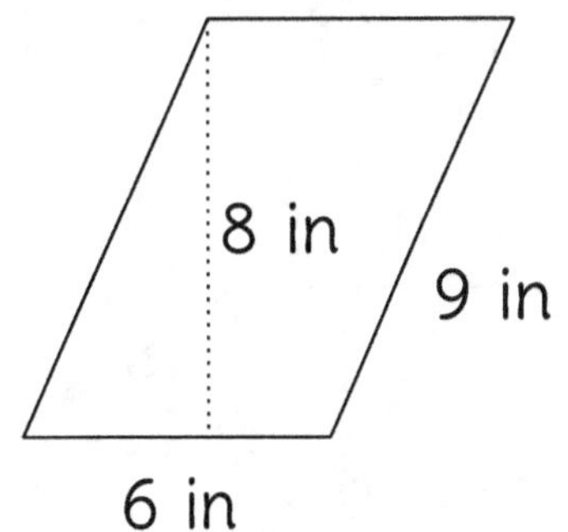

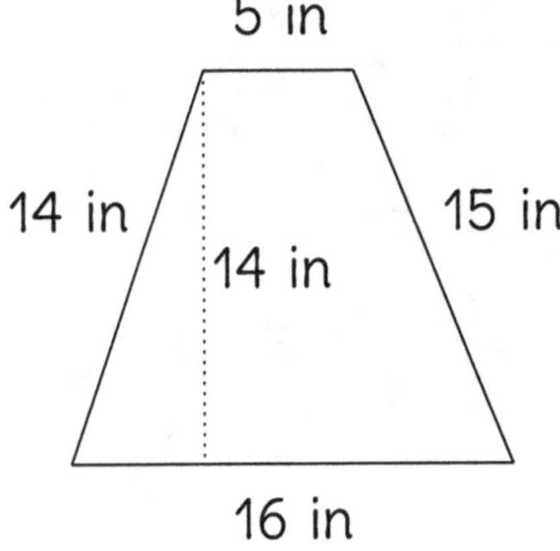

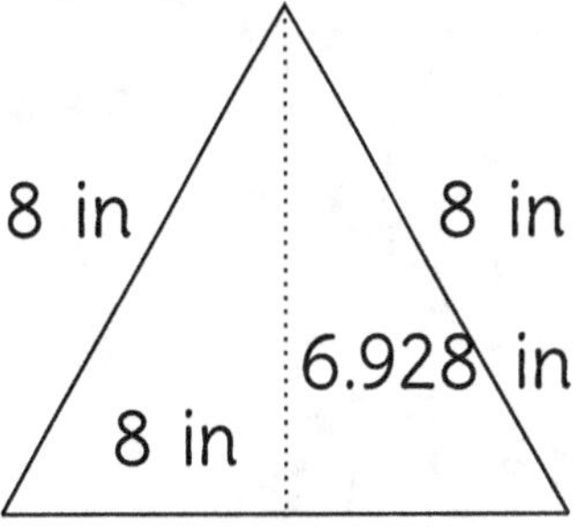

Name:
MATH
FLARE
MATH
Date:

33.

8 in
5 in
8 in
5 in

34.

2 in
4 in
4 in
3 in
7 in

35.

10 in
10 in
9.54 in
4 in

36.

8 in
8 in
8 in
6.928 in

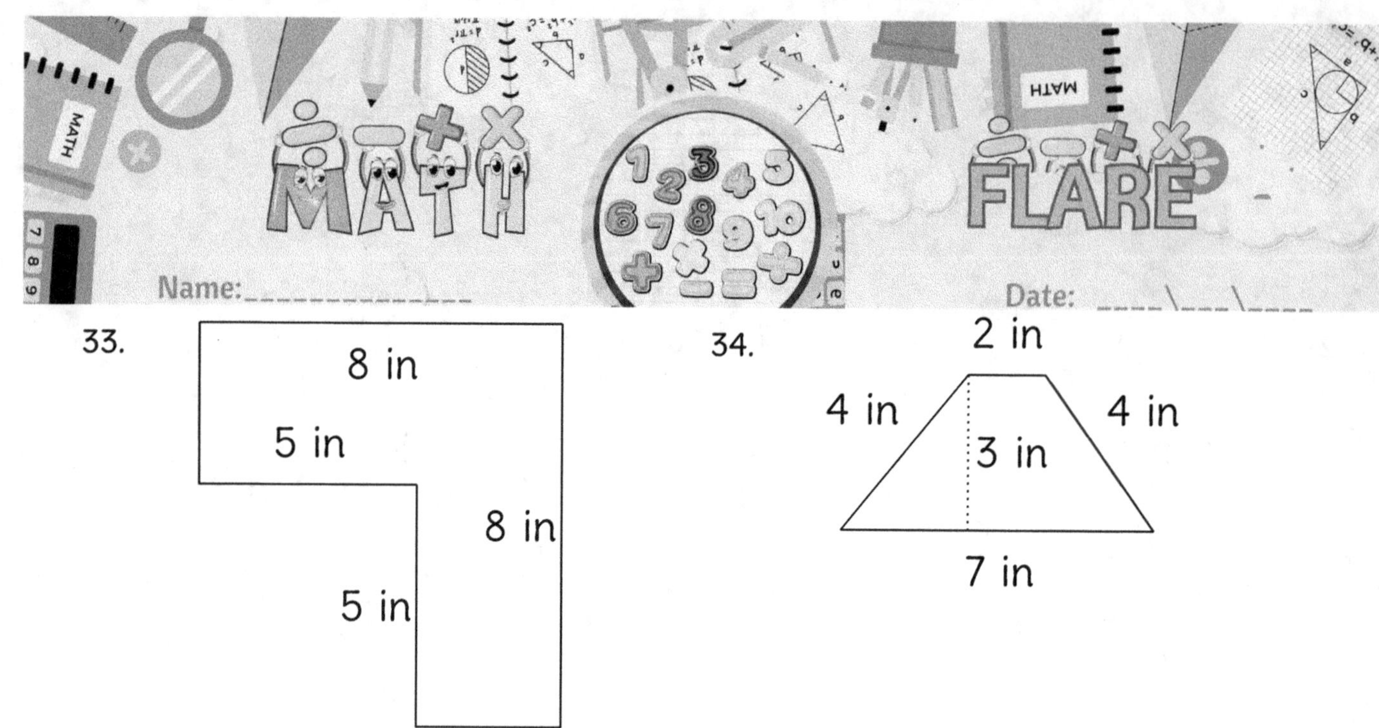

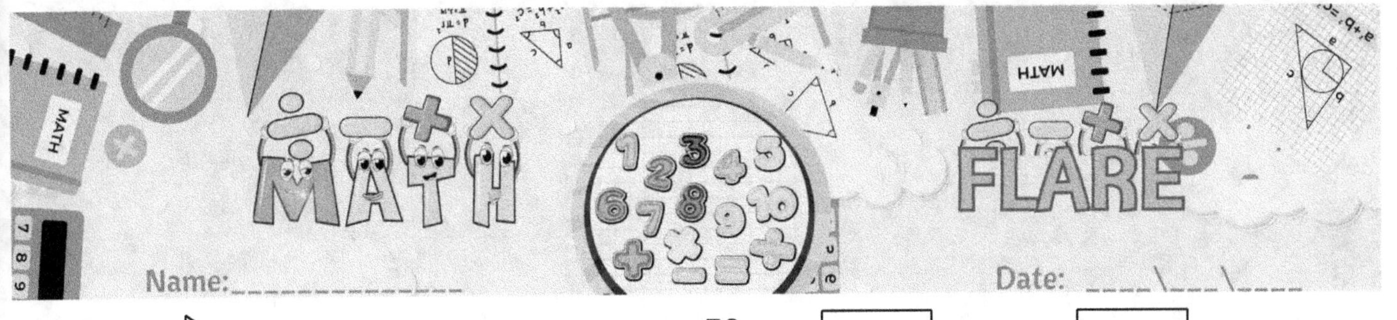

37.

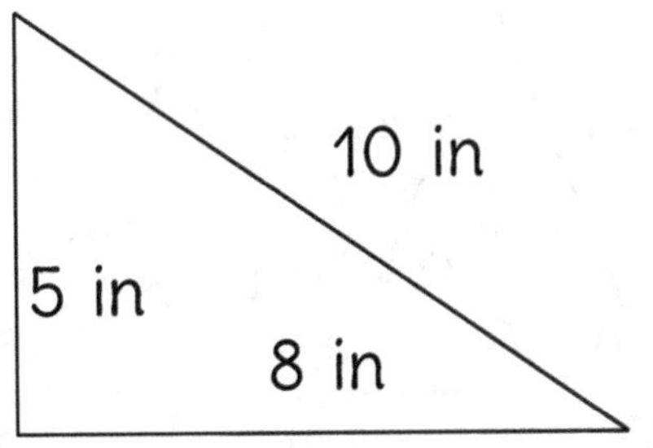

38.

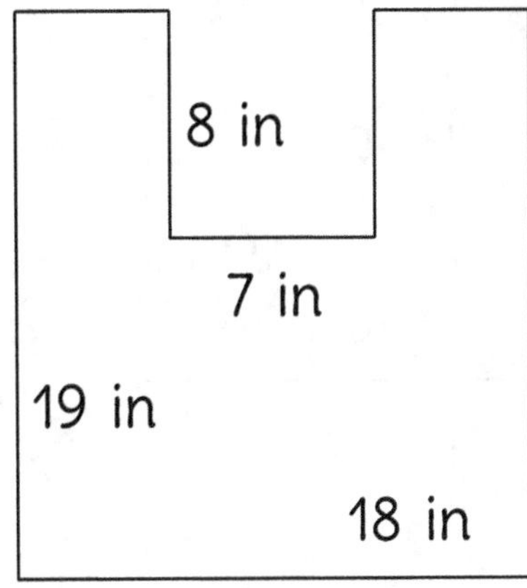

39.

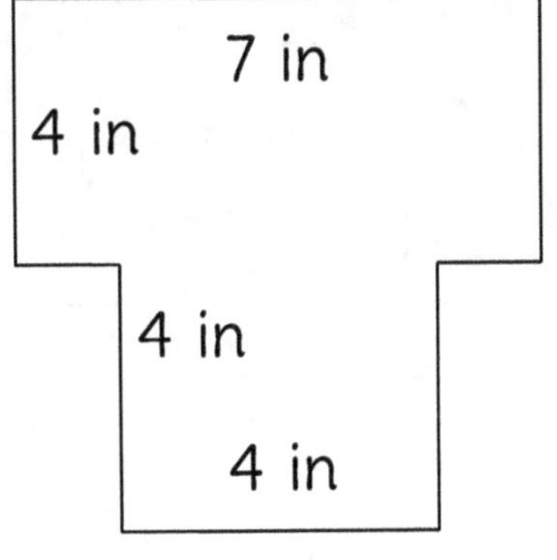

40.

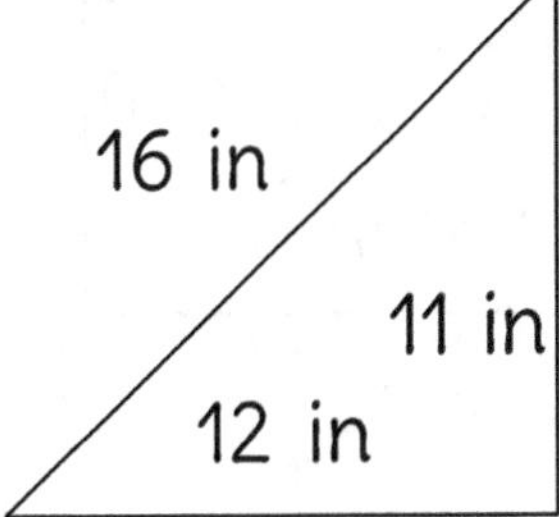

41.

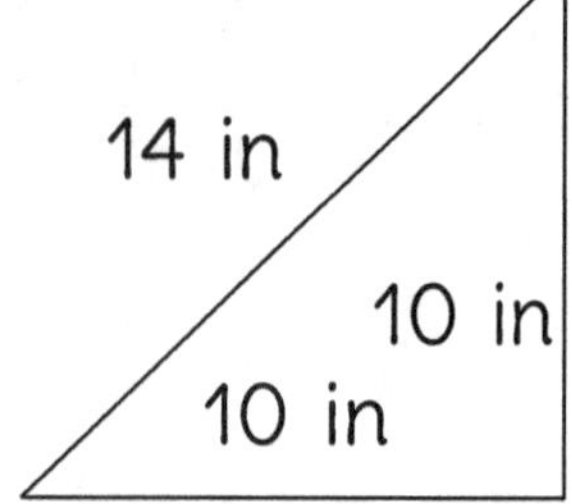

42.

43.

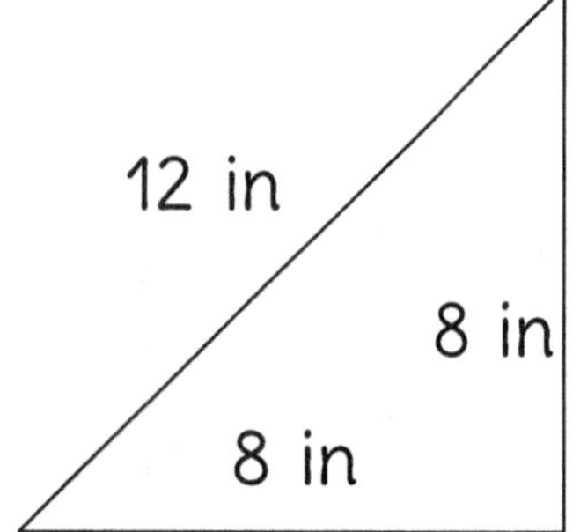

44.

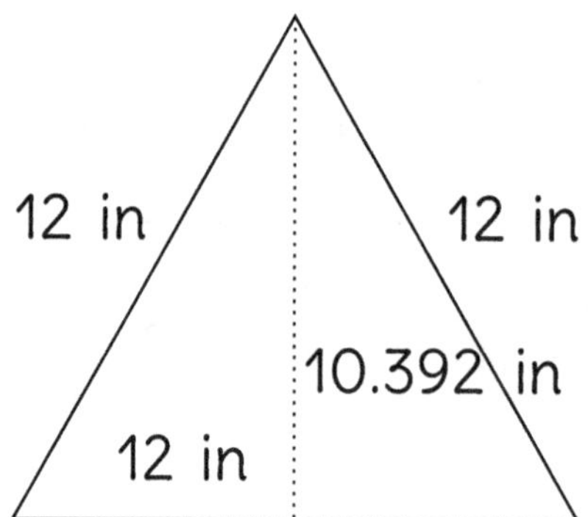

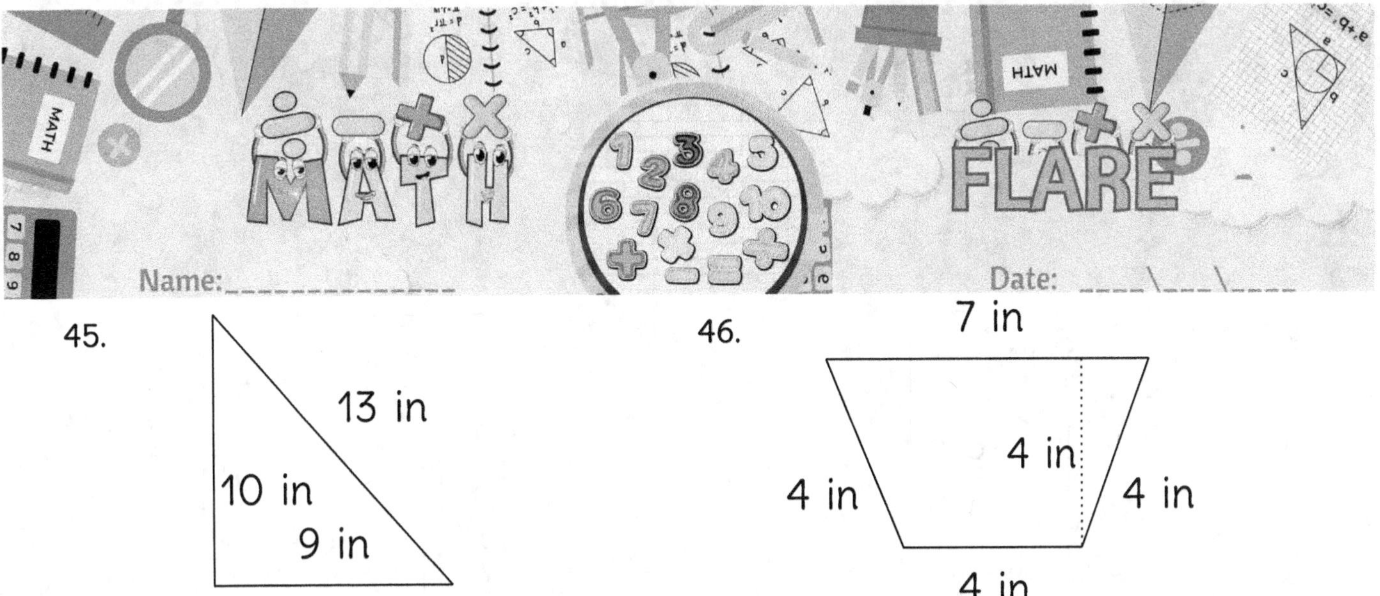

45.

46.

47.

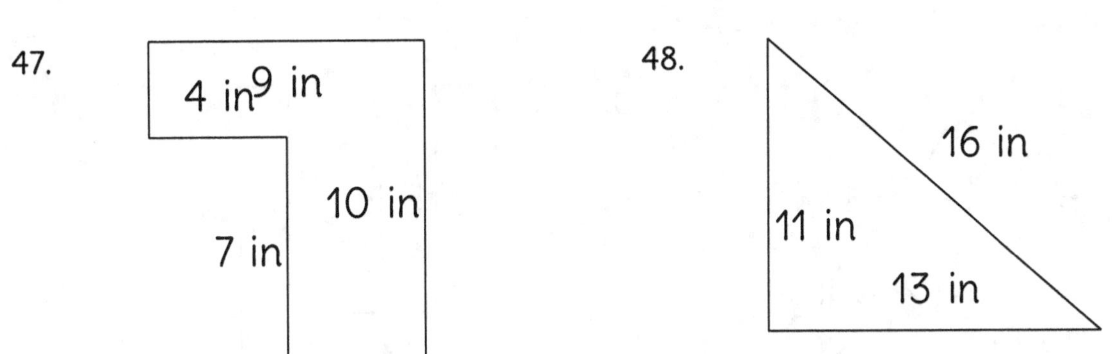

48.

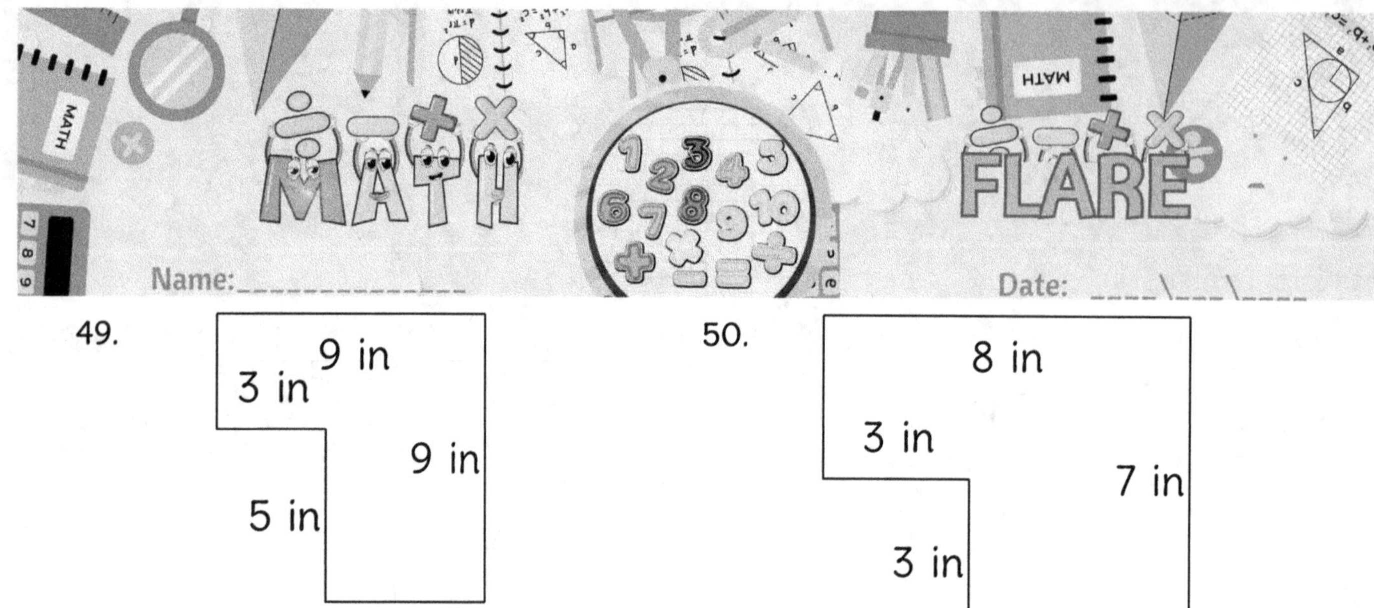

49.

50.

51.

52.

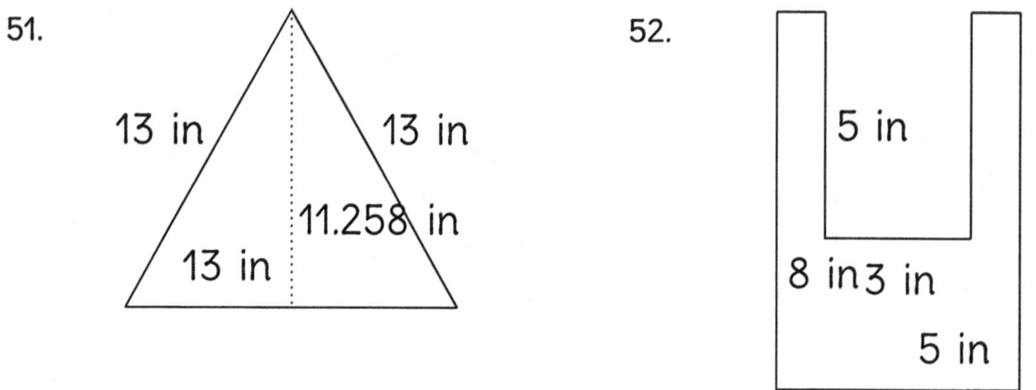

140

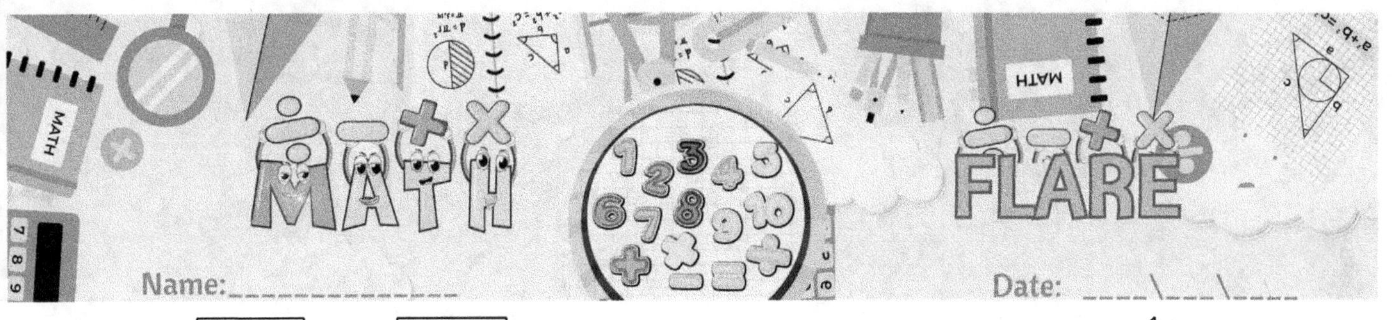

53.

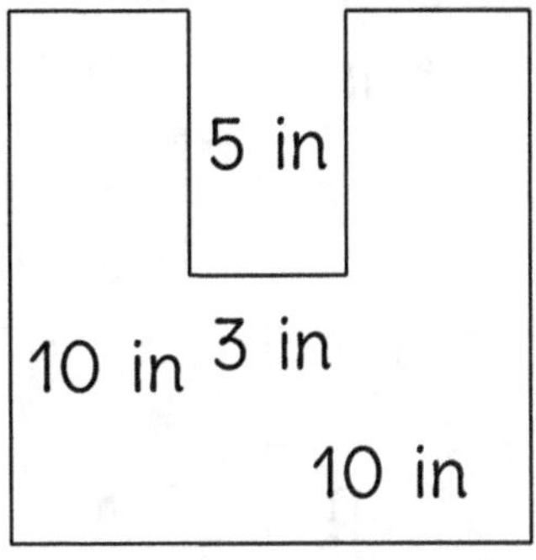

54.

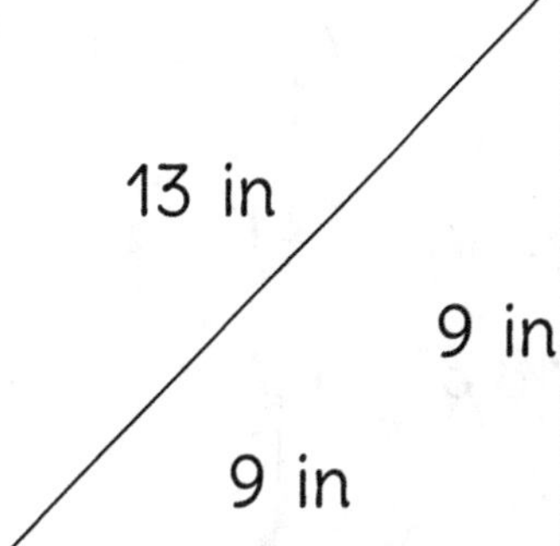

55.

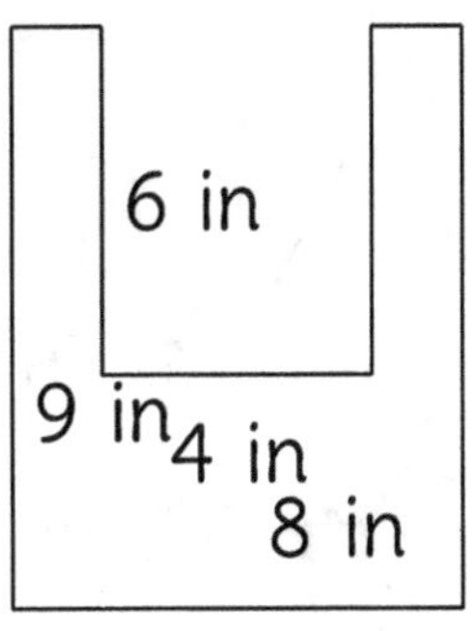

56.

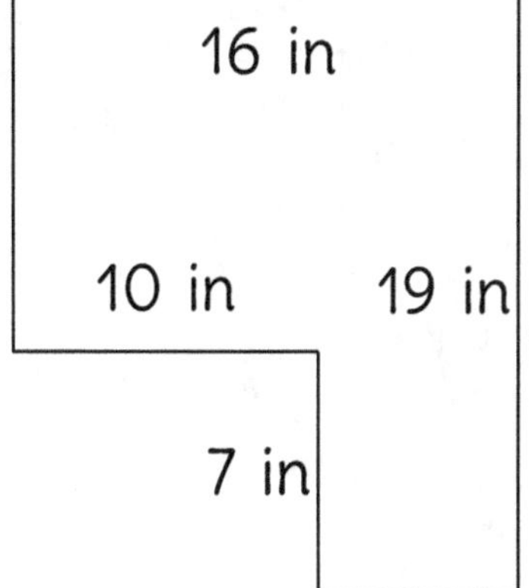

MATH
FLARE
Name:
Date:

57.

20 in
19 in
18.63 in
9 in
6 in
4 in
4 in
4 in

58.

59.

13 in
12 in
12.40 in
5 in
12 in
12 in
10.392 in
12 in

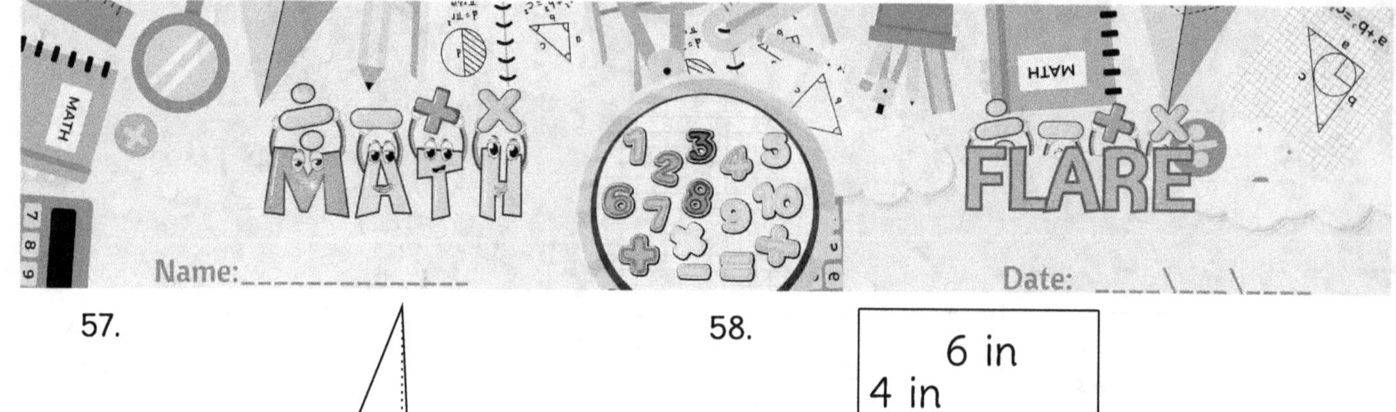

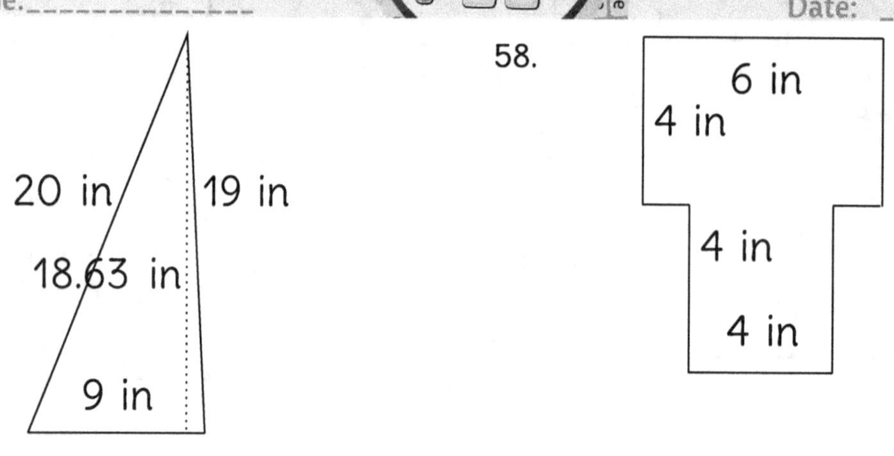

60.

Volume and Surface Area

61.

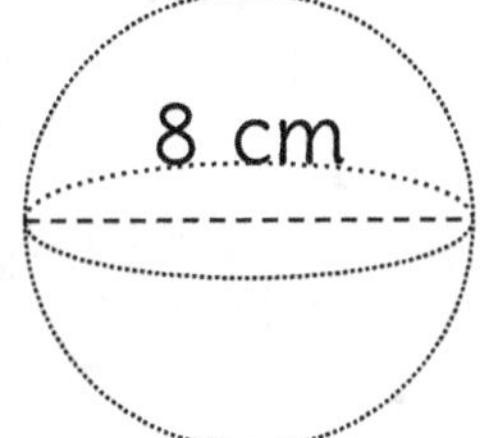

62.

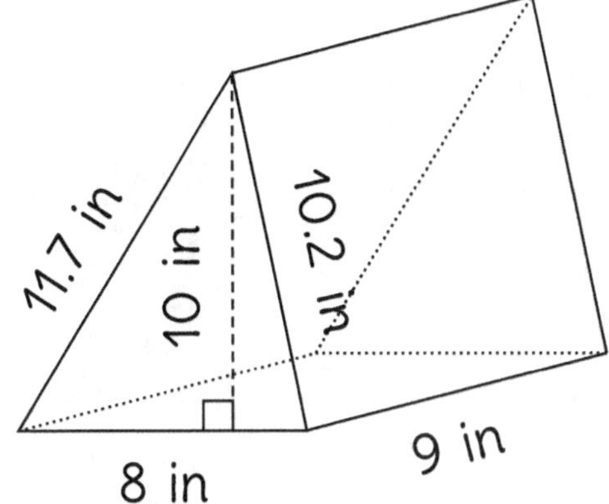

63.

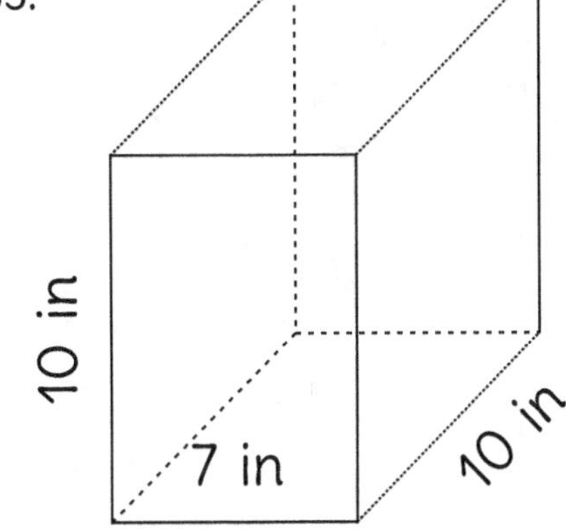

64.

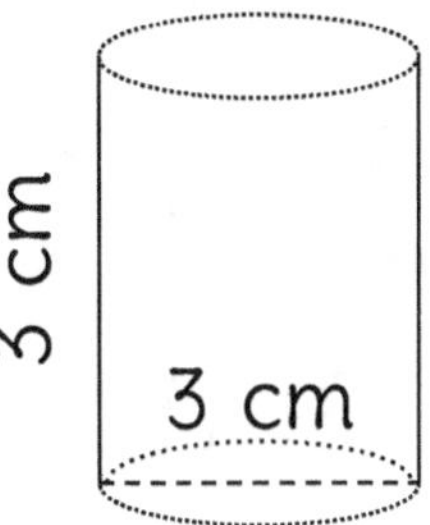

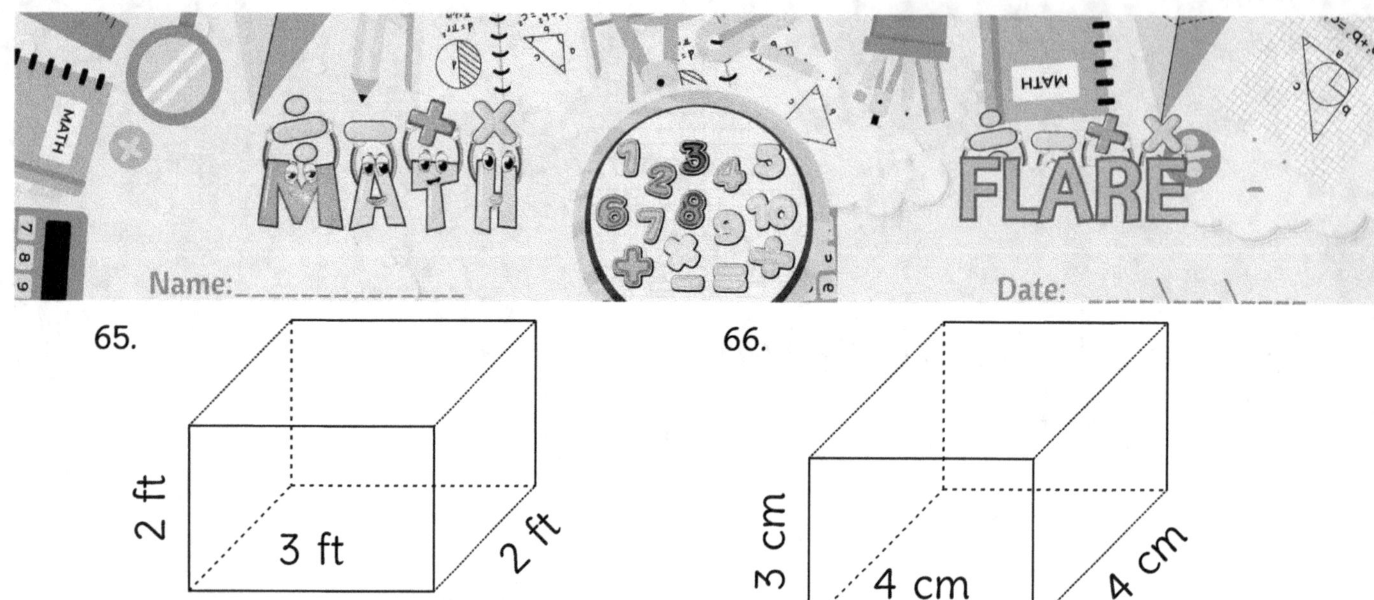

65.

2 ft
3 ft
2 ft

66.

3 cm
4 cm
4 cm

67.

6 in

68.

2 ft

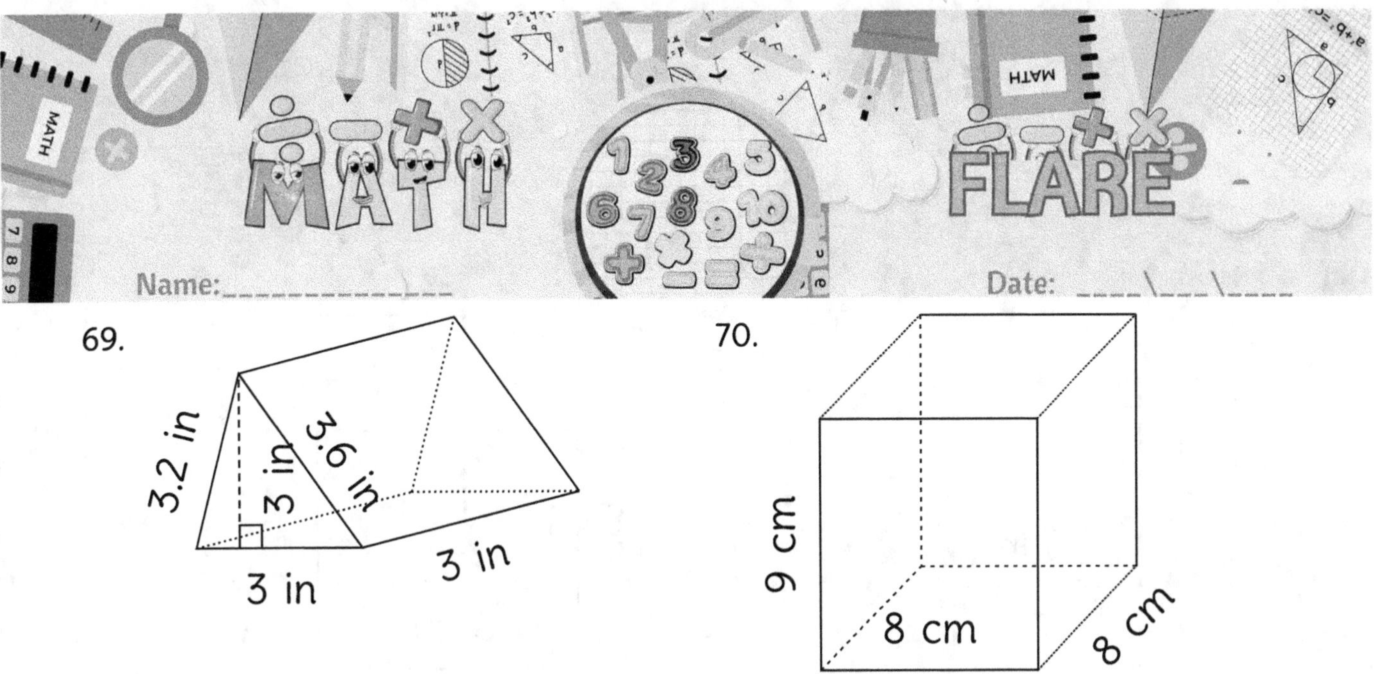
Name:
Date:
MATH
FLARE
69.
3.2 in
3 in
3.6 in
3 in
3 in
70.
9 cm
8 cm
8 cm

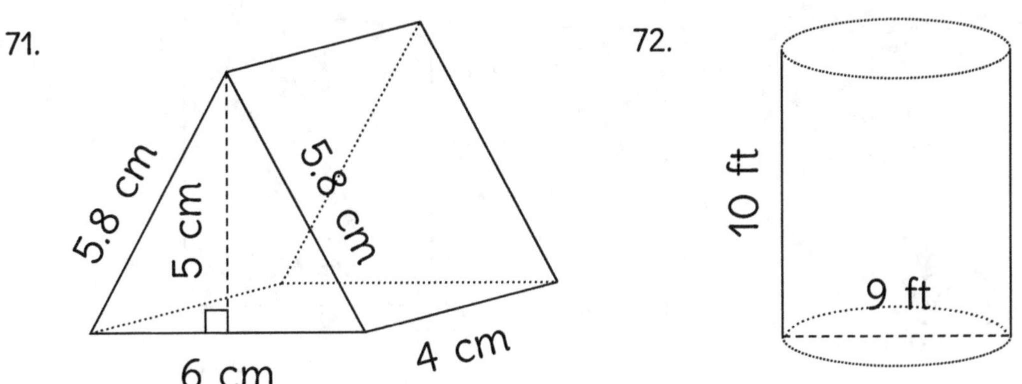
71.
5.8 cm
5 cm
5.8 cm
6 cm
4 cm
72.
10 ft
9 ft

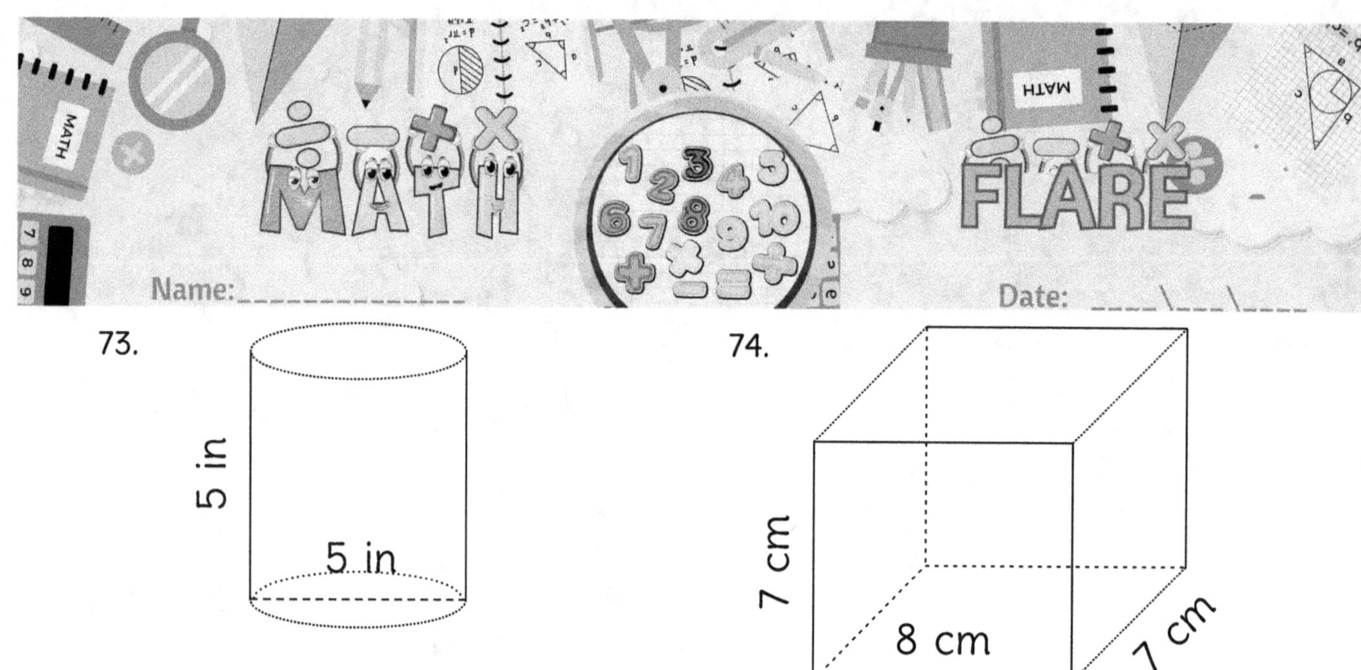

73.

74.

75.

76.

MATH
FLARE
Name:
Date:

77.

5 cm
6 cm
6 cm

78.

10.2 in
10 in
11.2 in
7 in
8 in

79.

6.3 ft
6.3 ft
6 ft
4 ft
5 ft

80.

5 ft
5 ft
4 ft

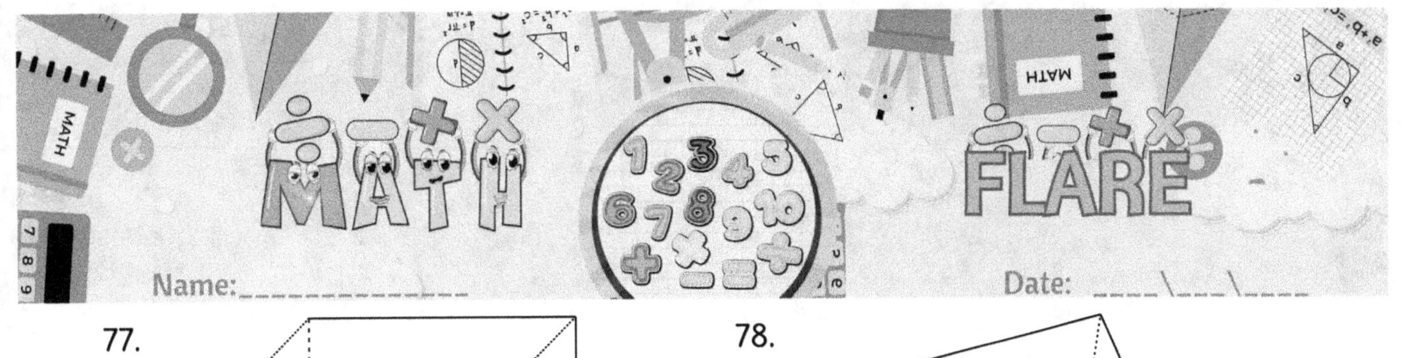

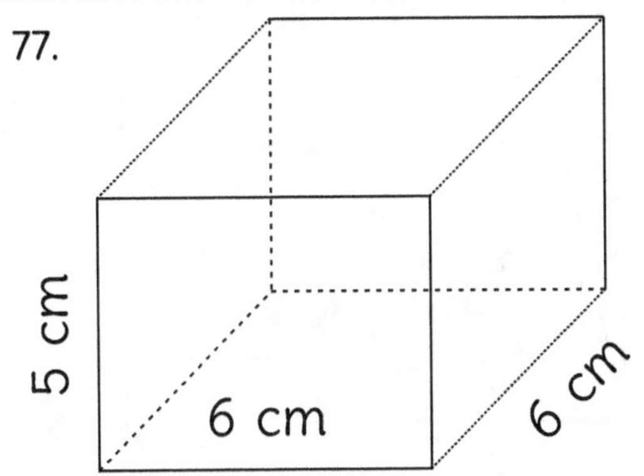

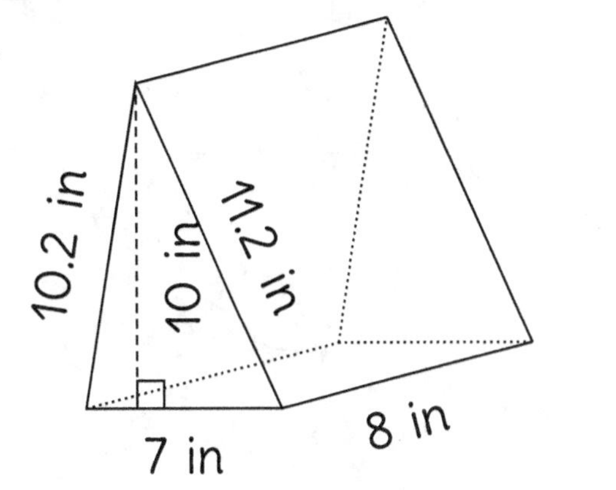

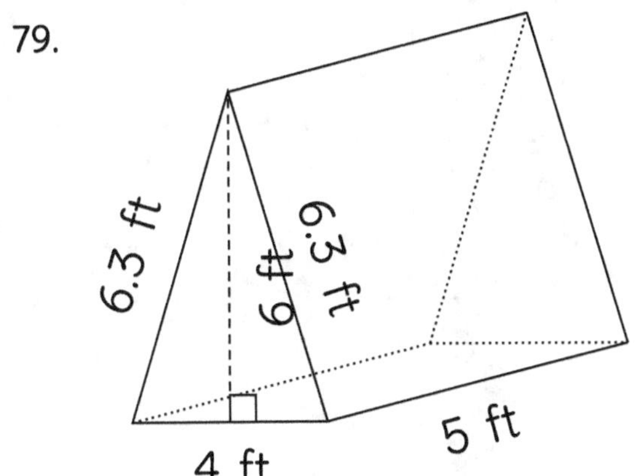

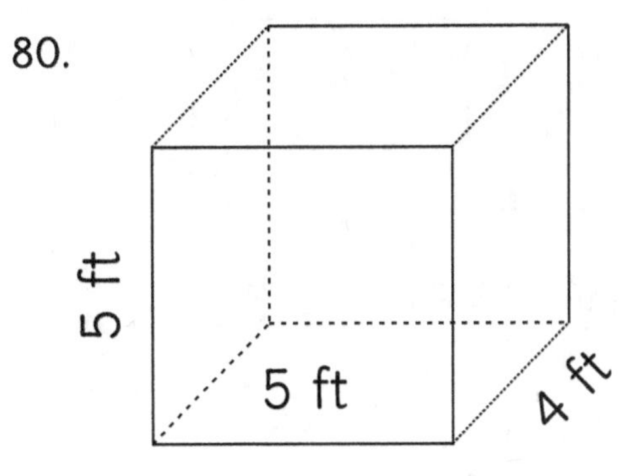

MATH
FLARE
Name:
Date:

81.

10 in

82.

3.2 ft
3 ft
3.6 ft
3 ft
2 ft

83.

5 in
5 in
8 in

84.

5.8 in
5 in
5.8 in
6 in
5 in

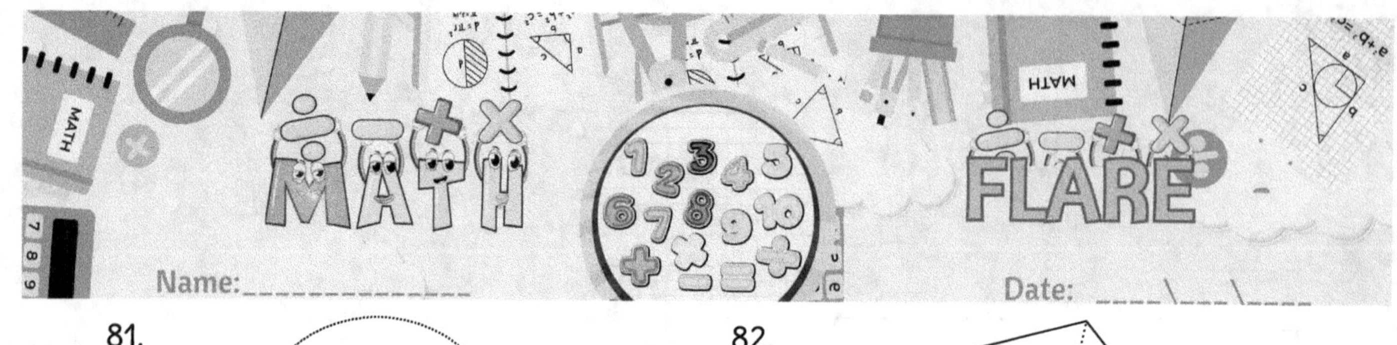

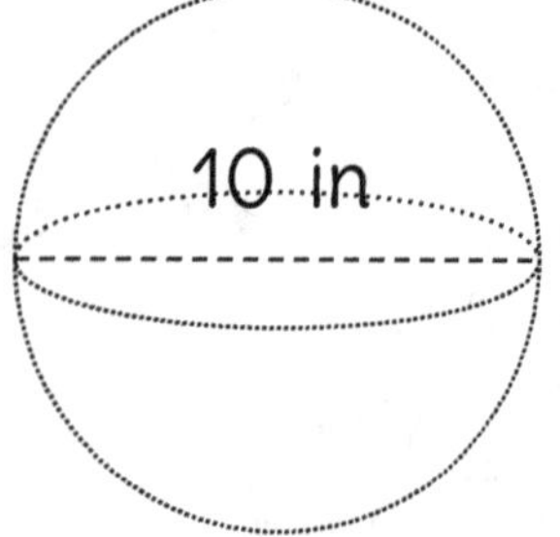

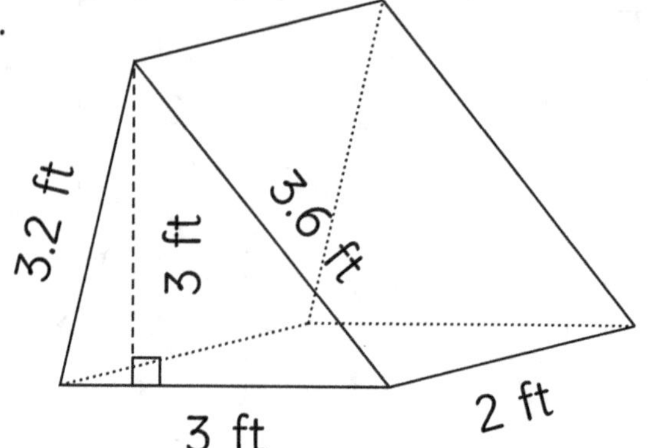

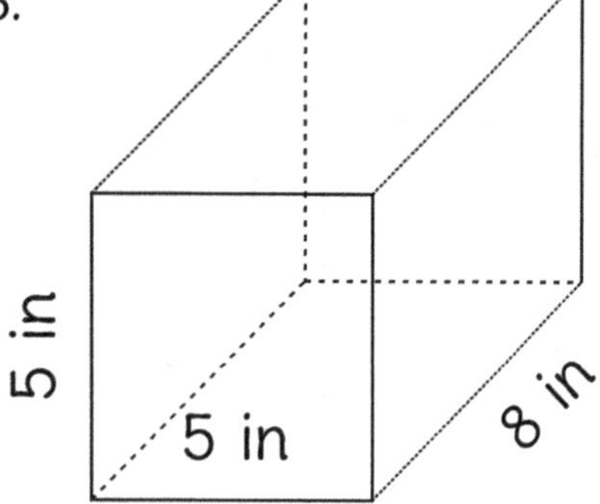

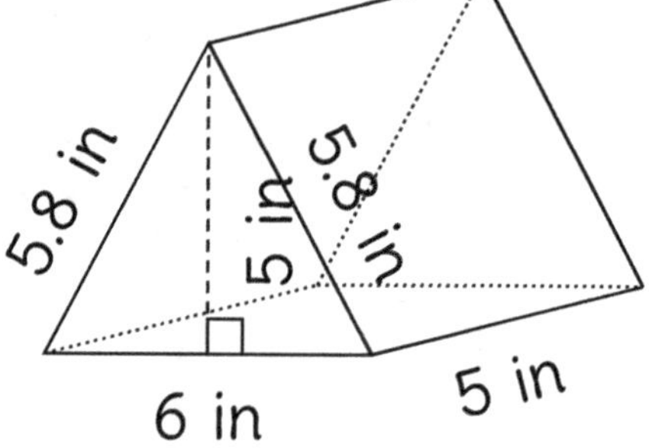

MATH
FLARE
Name:
Date:

85.

2.2 ft
2 ft
2.8 ft
3 ft
3 ft

86.

4 cm
3 cm

87.

7 ft
6 ft

88.

6 ft
7 ft
8 ft

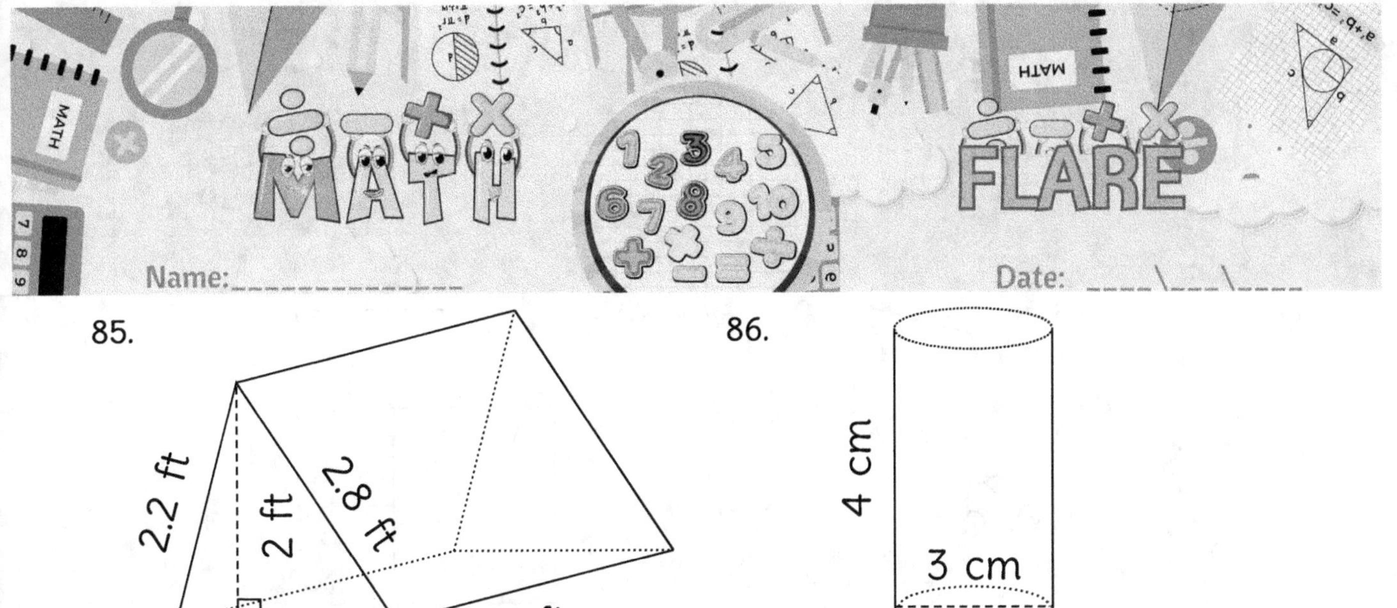

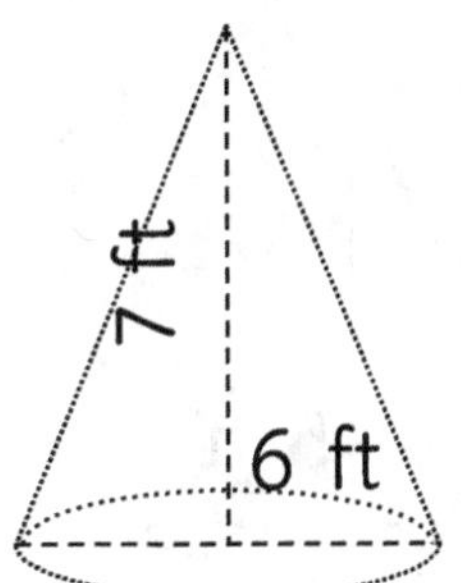

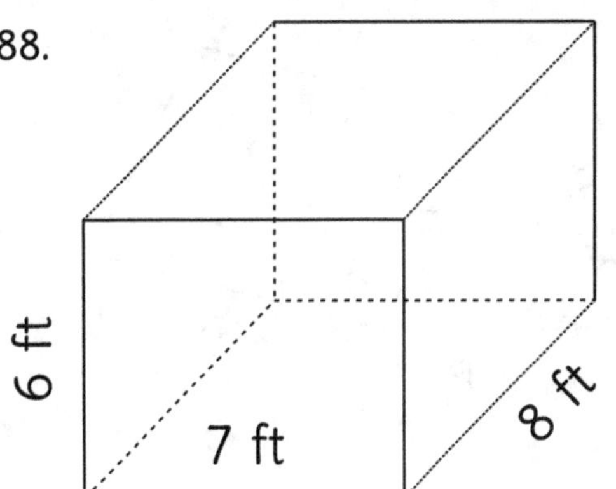

MATH
FLARE
Name:
Date:

89.

9.8 cm
9.8 cm
6 cm
9.8 cm
8 cm
7 cm

90.

4 cm
3 cm
4 cm

91.

3.2 ft
3.2 ft
3 ft
2 ft
4 ft

92.

6 ft
5 ft

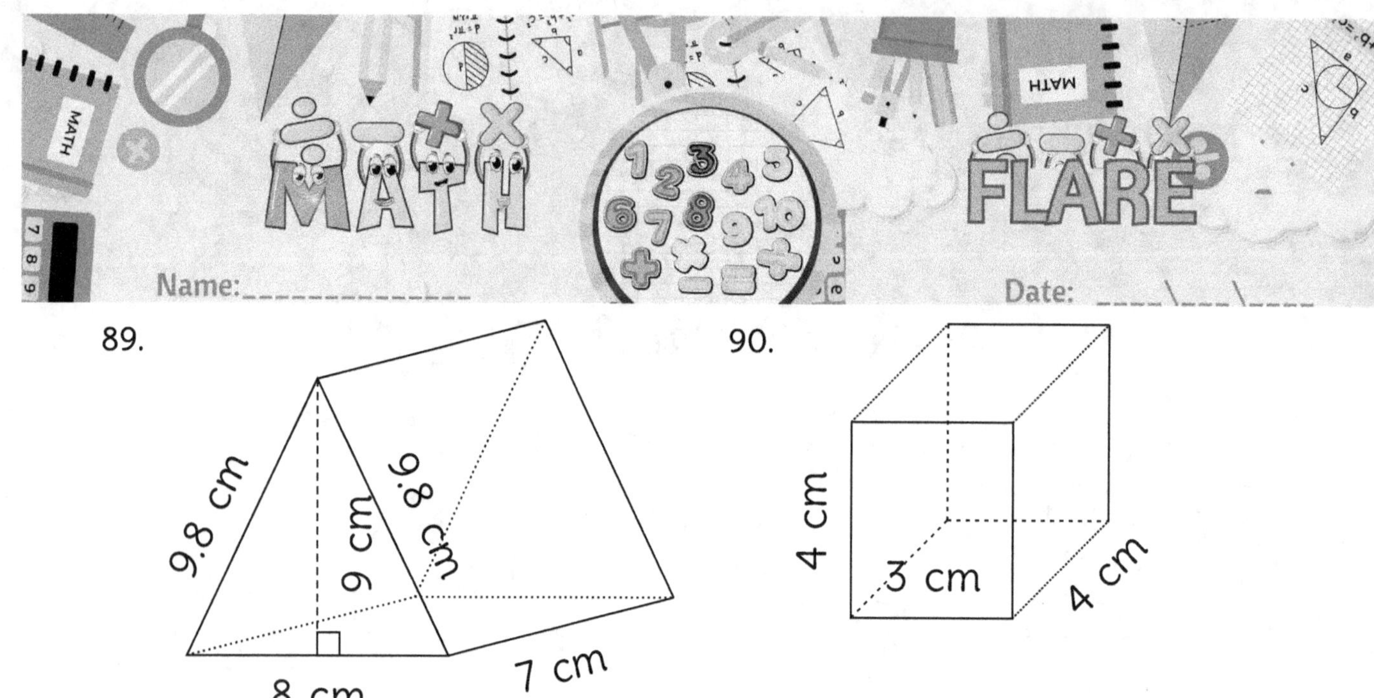

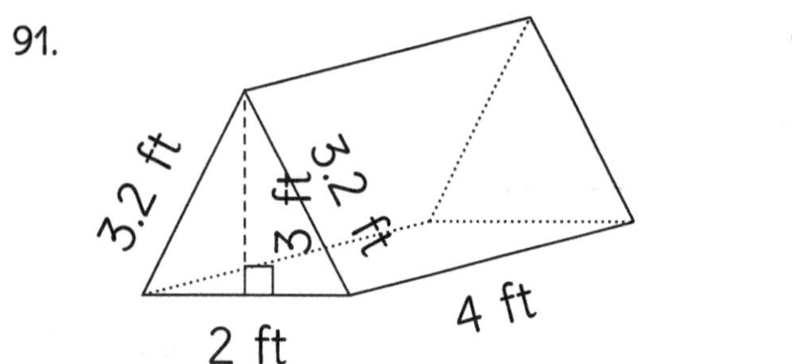

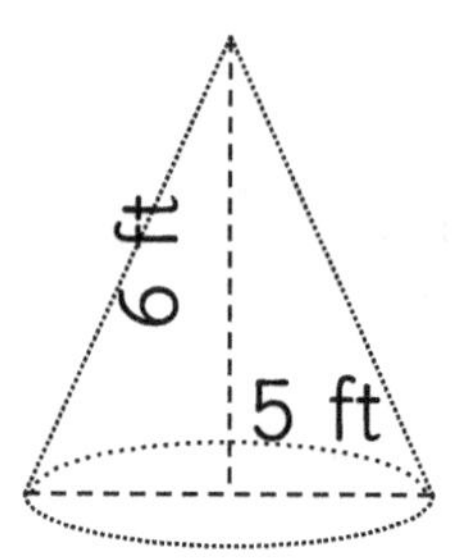

MATH
FLARE
Name:
Date:

93.

8 cm
10 cm

94.

3 in
3 in
2 in

95.

9 cm
9 cm

96.

4 in
5 in
3 in
5 in

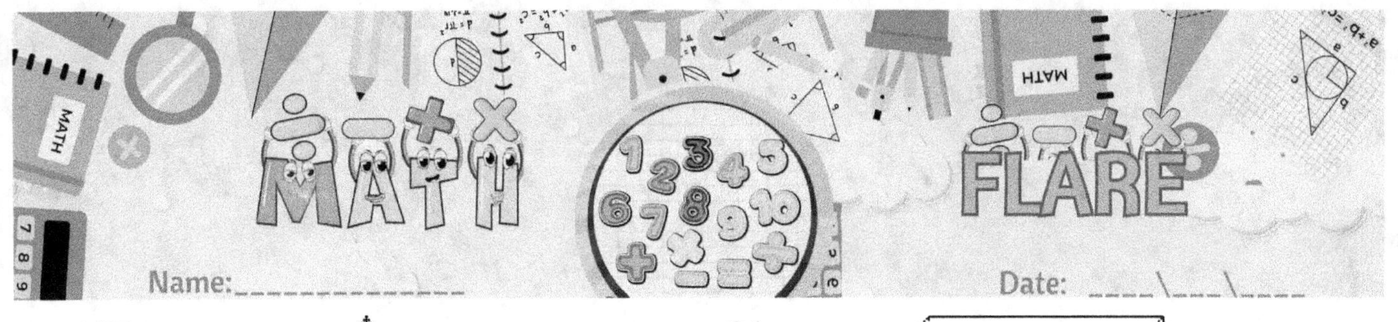

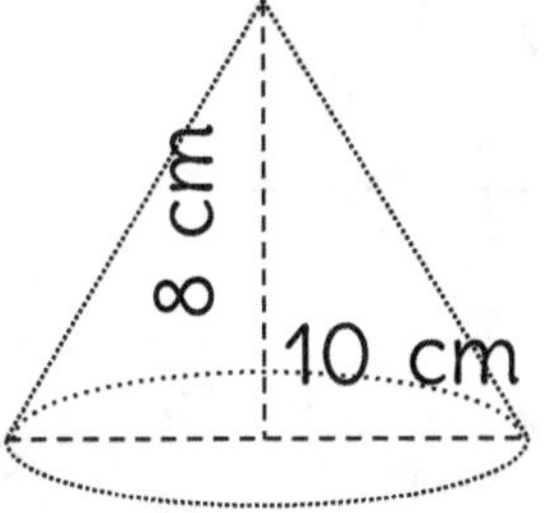

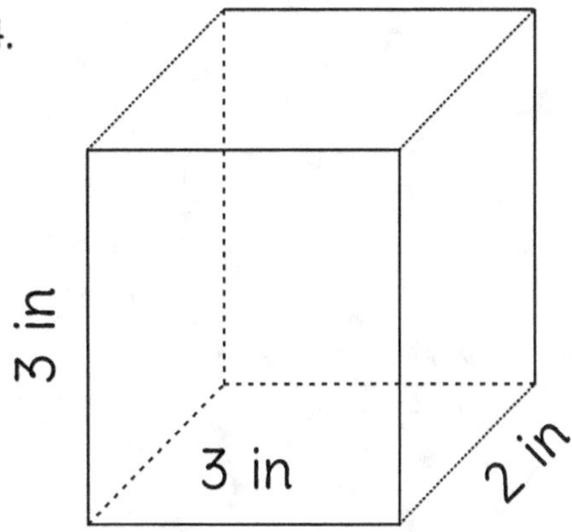

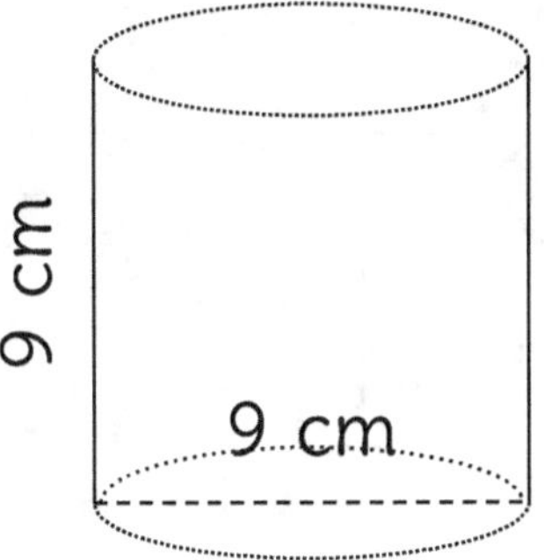

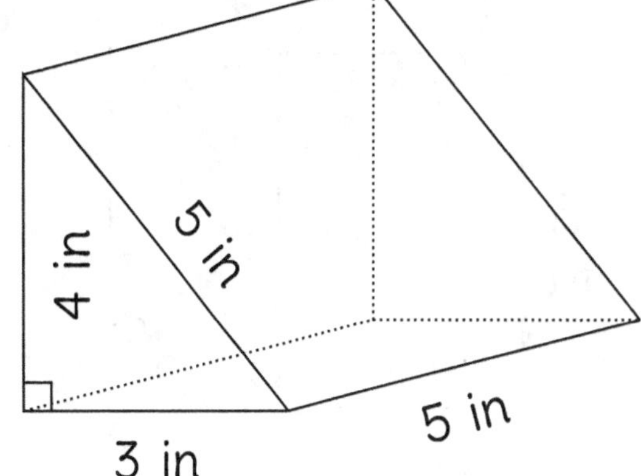

MATH
FLARE
Name:
Date:

97.

4 ft
4 ft
4 ft

98.

4 ft
5 ft
4 ft

99.

3 cm
2 cm
3 cm

100.

4 in
5 in
8 in

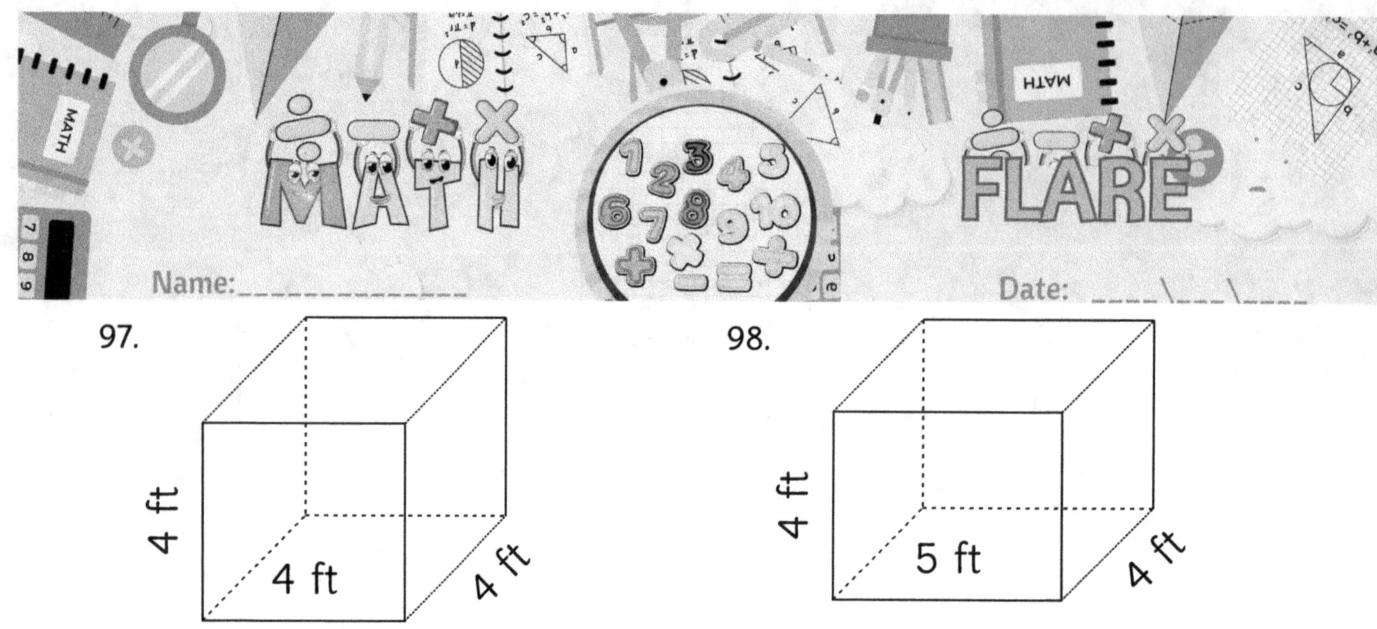

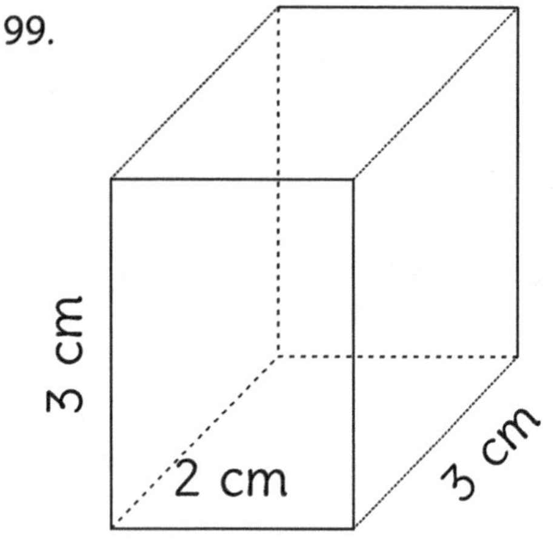

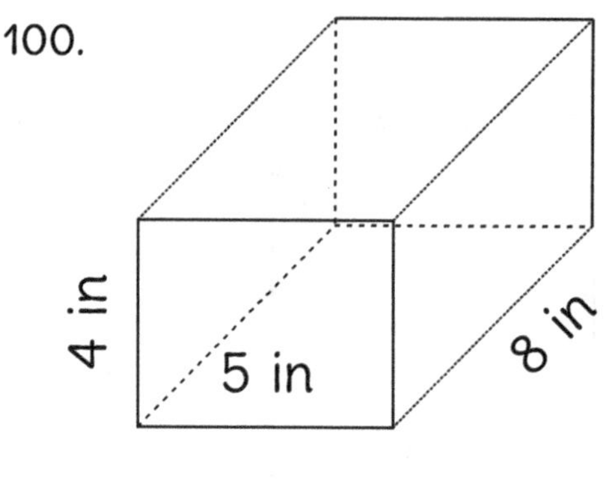

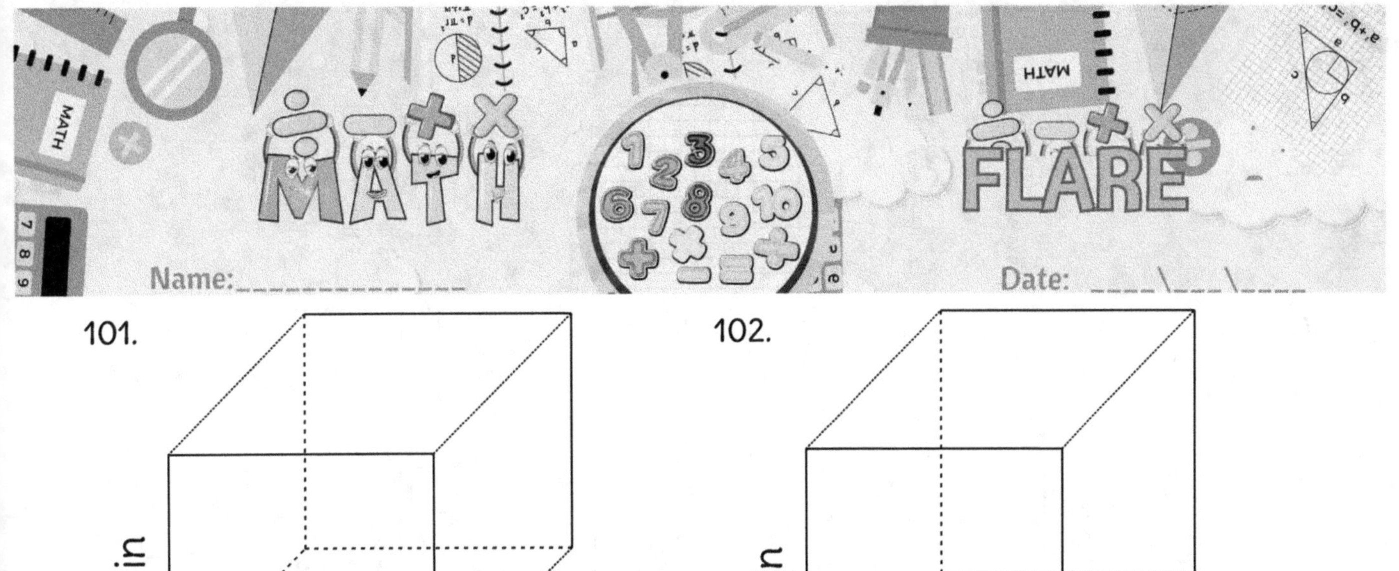

101.
4 in
4 in
4 in
102.
7 in
7 in
7 in

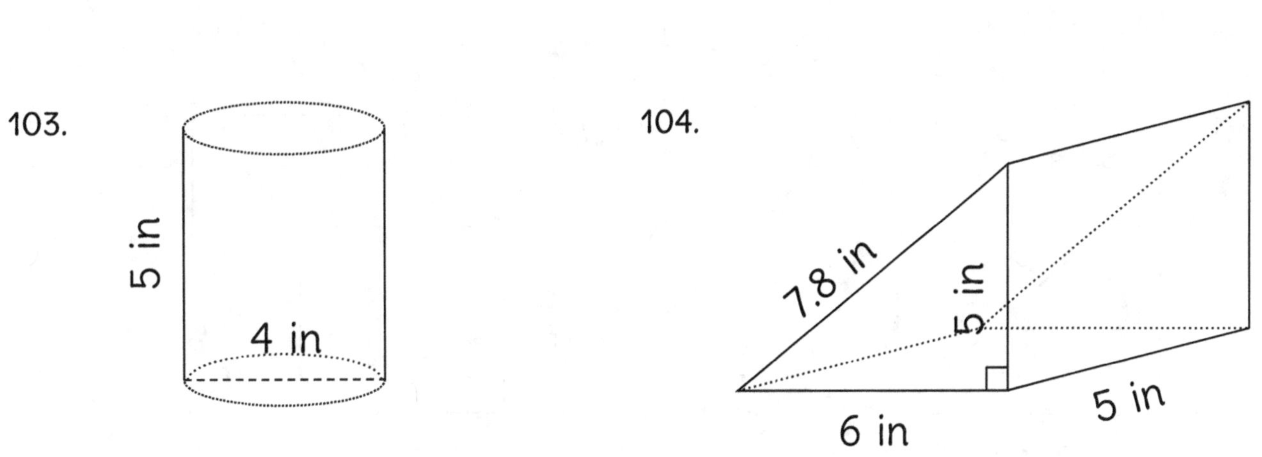

103.
5 in
4 in
104.
7.8 in
5 in
6 in
5 in

105.

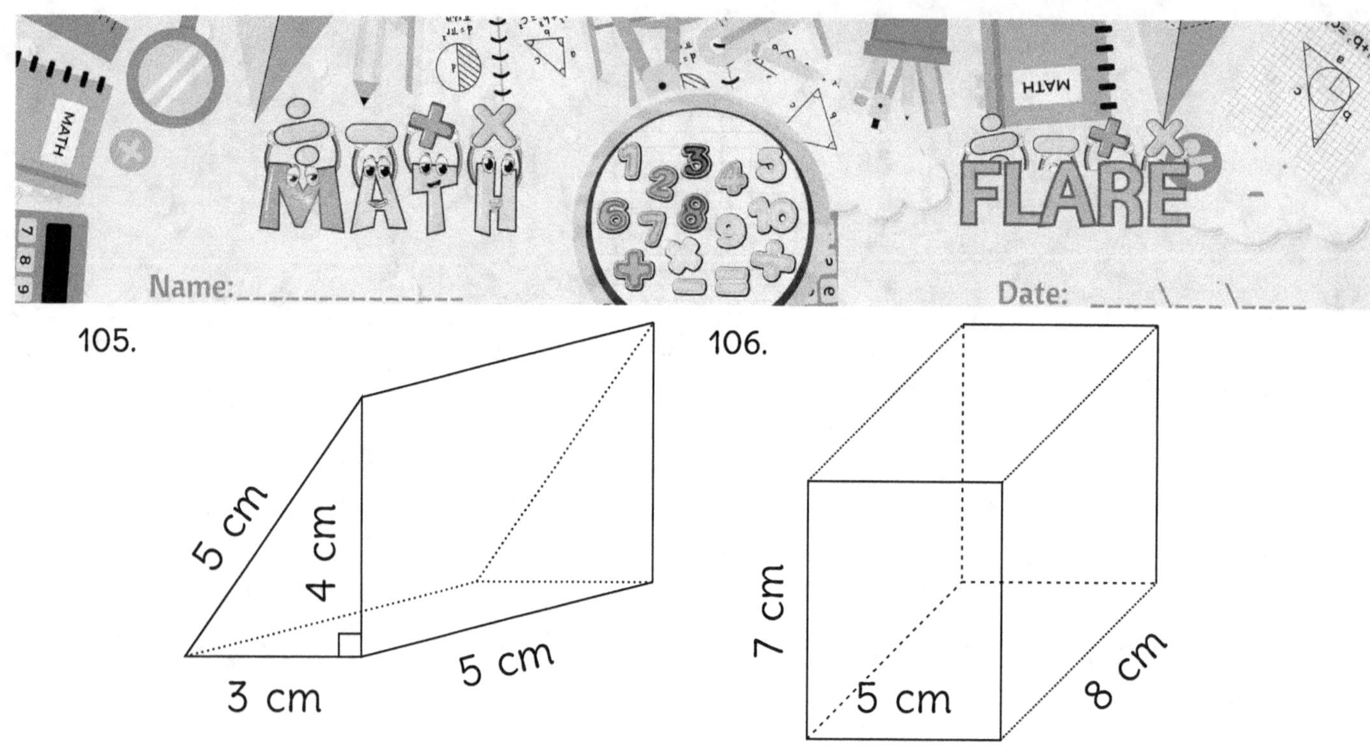

107.

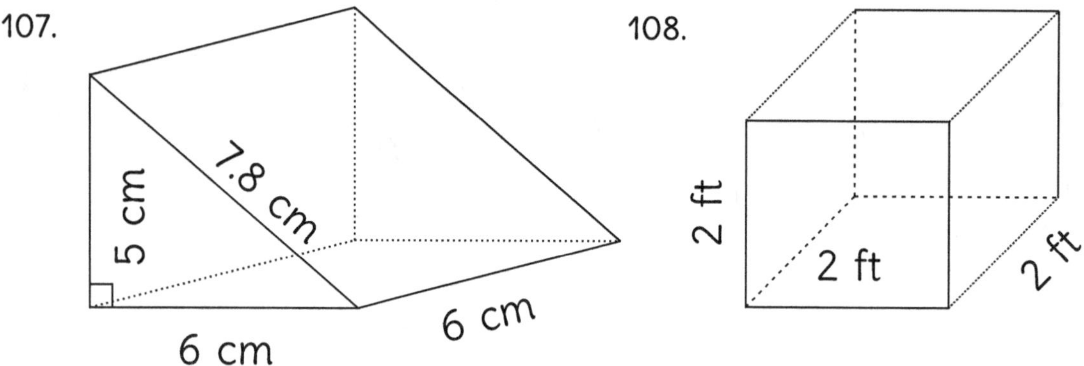

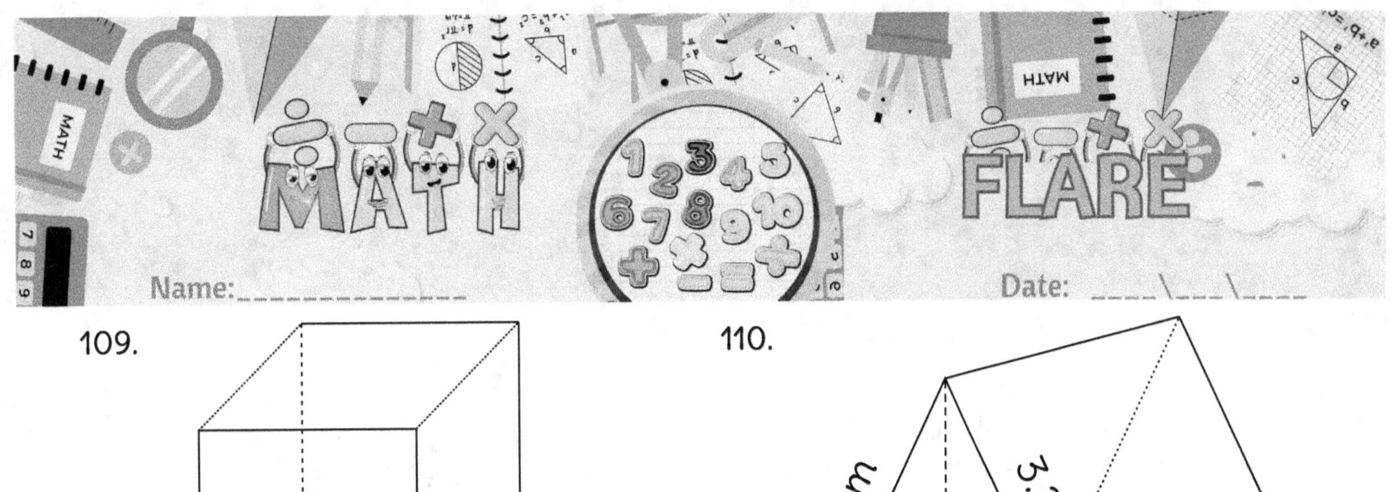

109.

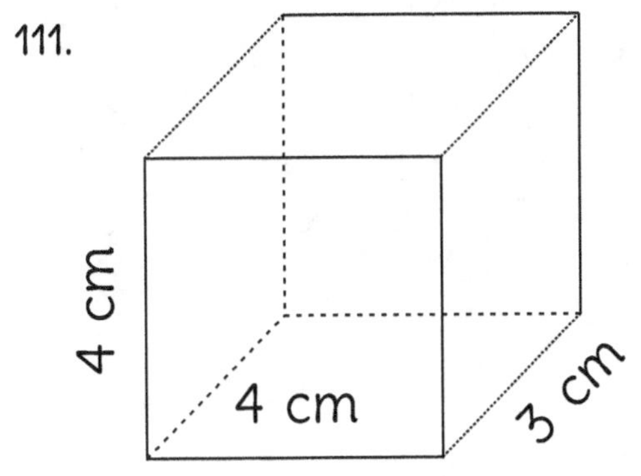

110.

111.

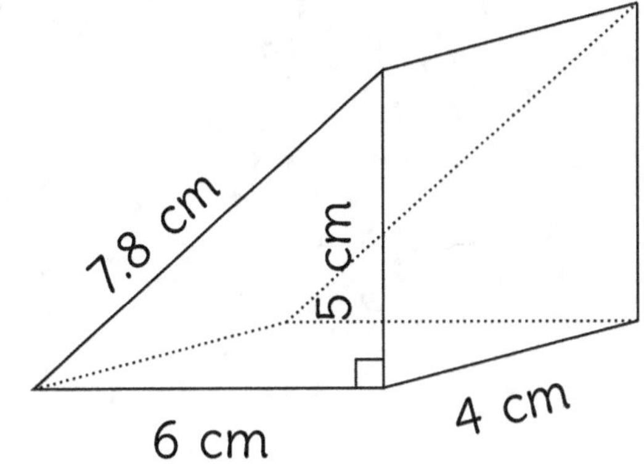

112.

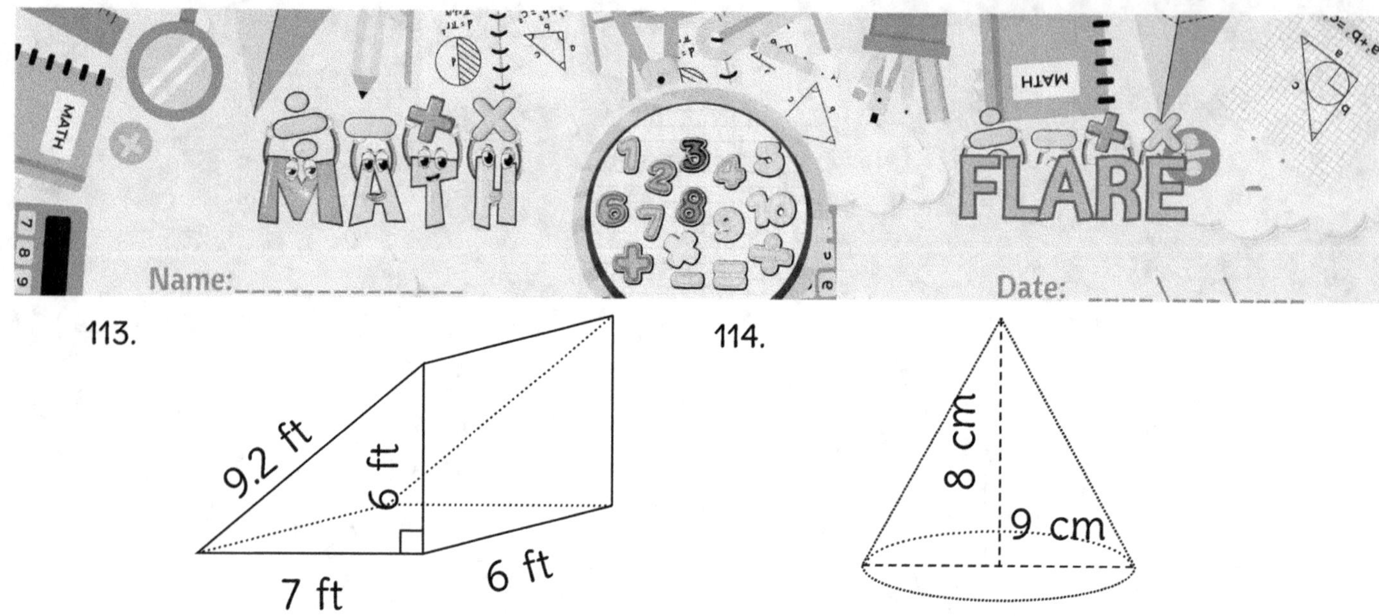

113.

114.

115.

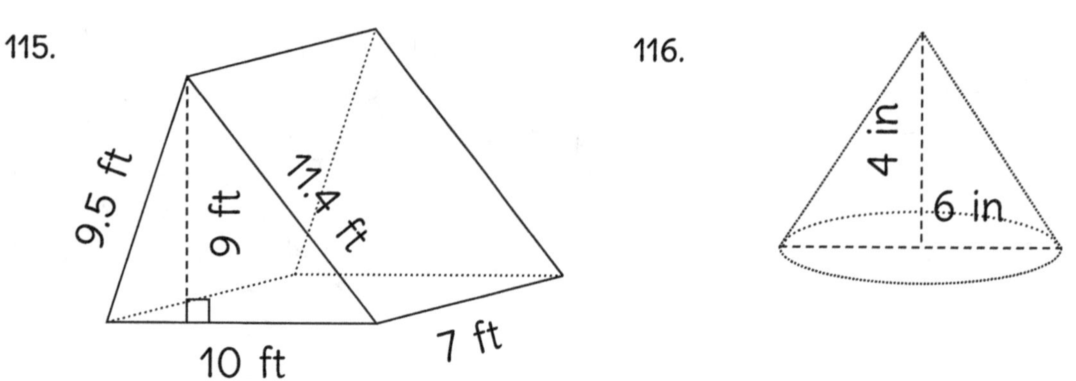

116.

117.

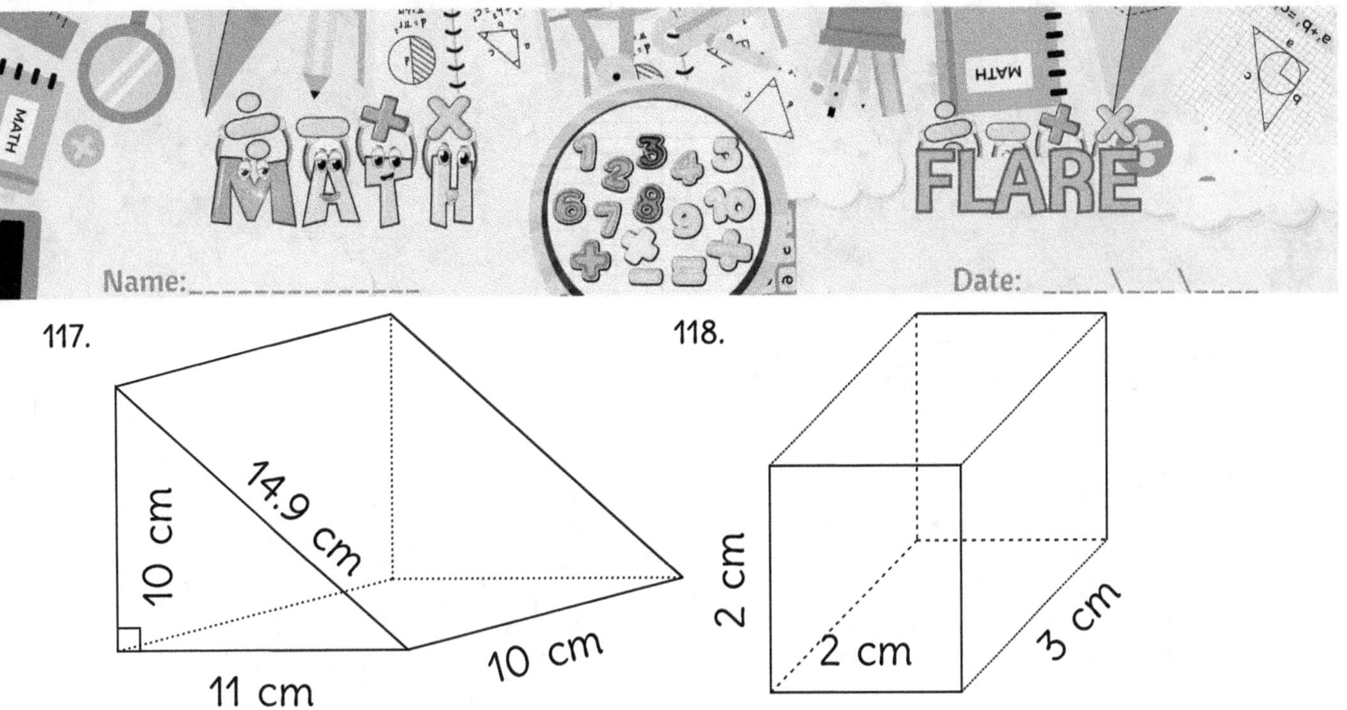

118.

119.

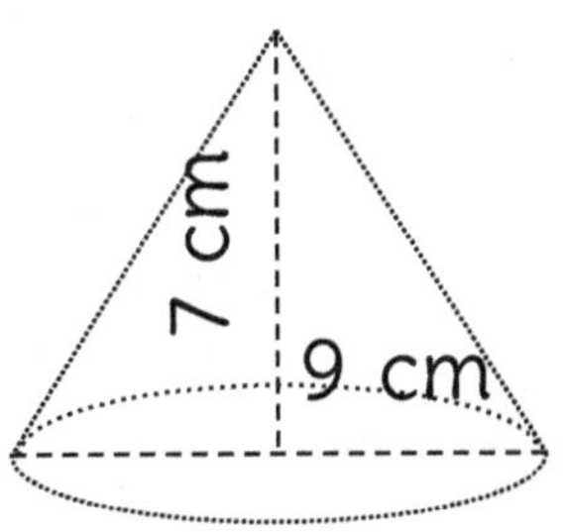

120.

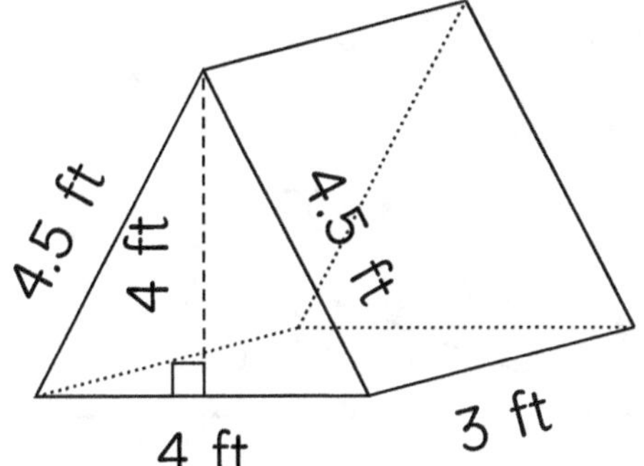

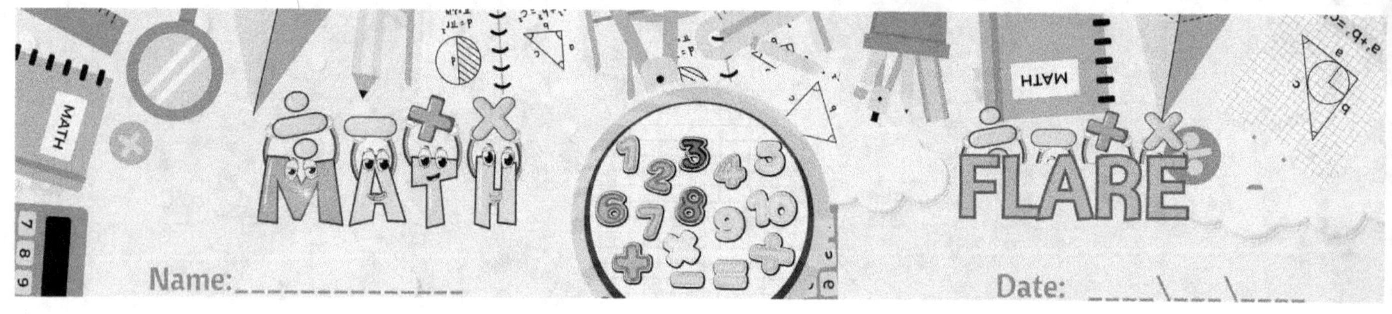

Pythagorean Theorem

121. 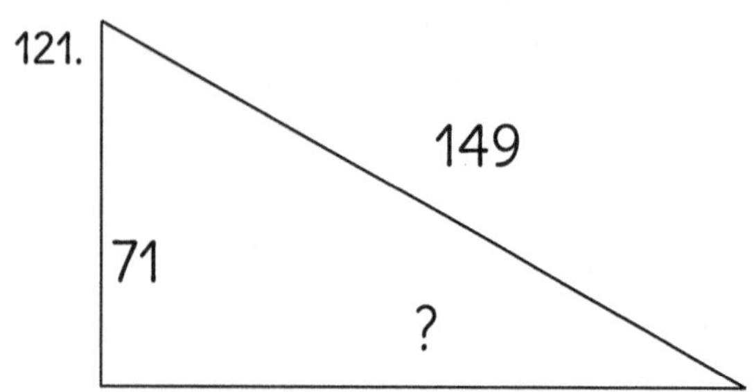

122. 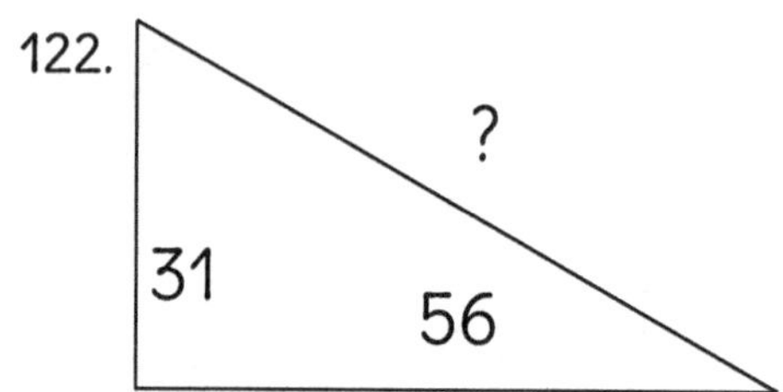

123. 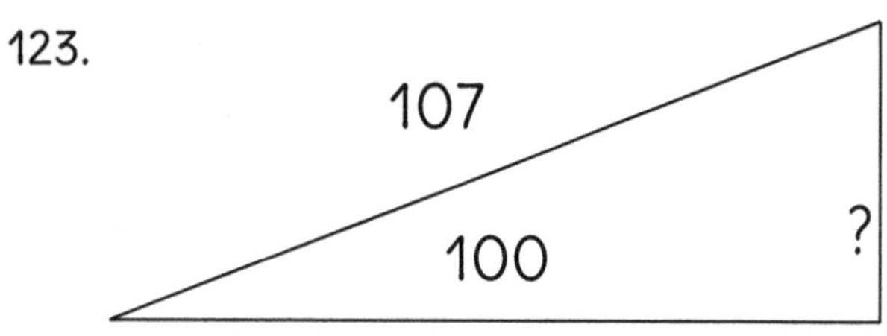

124. 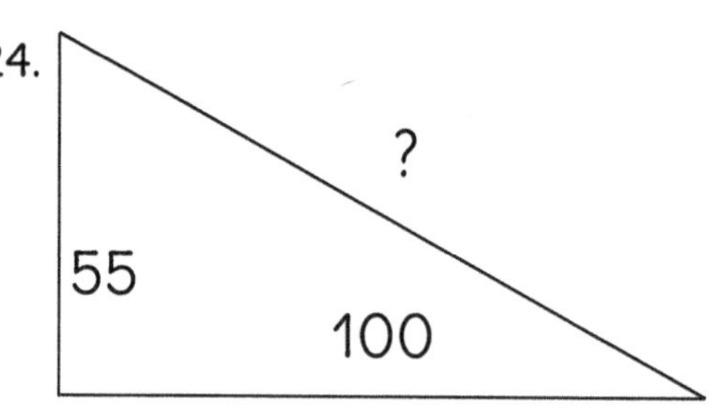

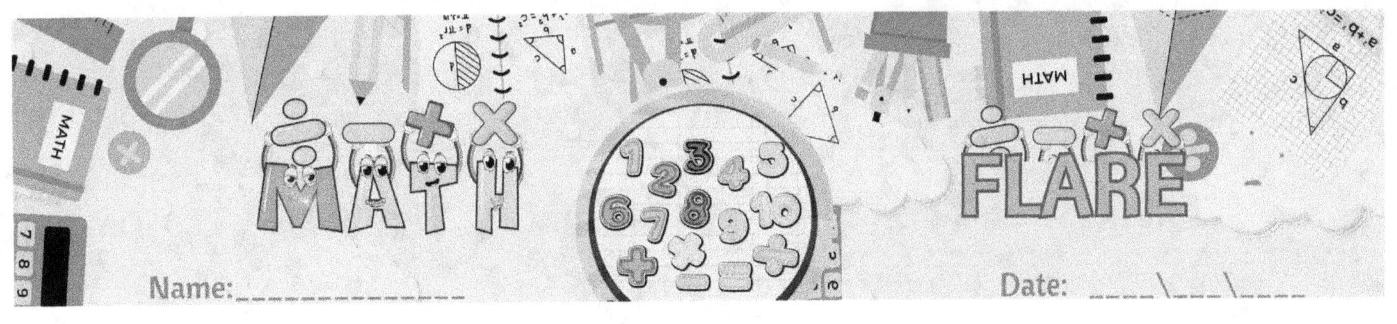

125.

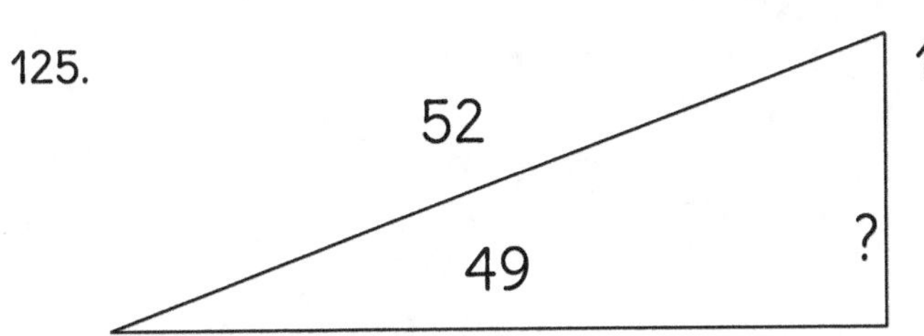

126.

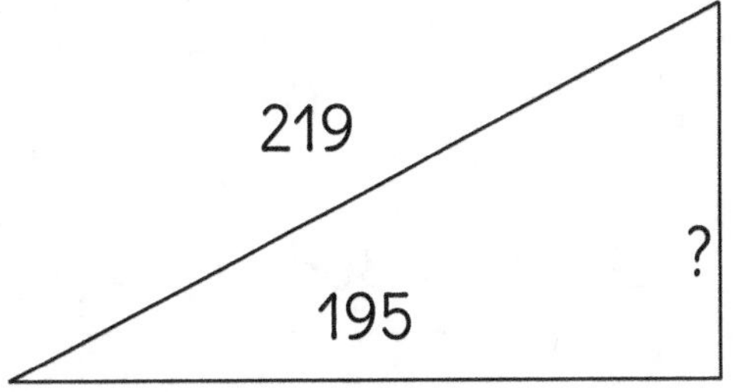

127.

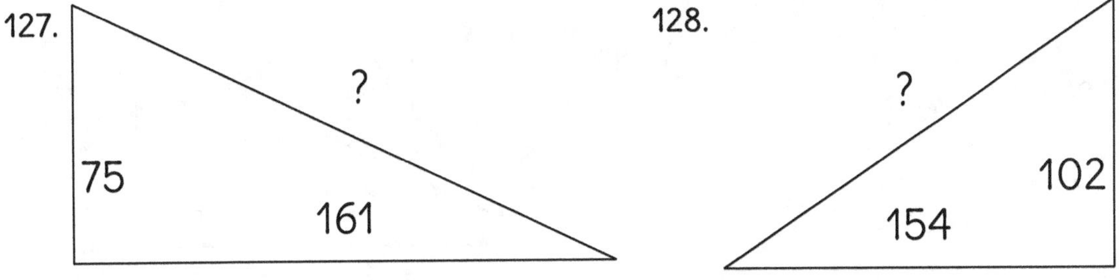

128.

129.

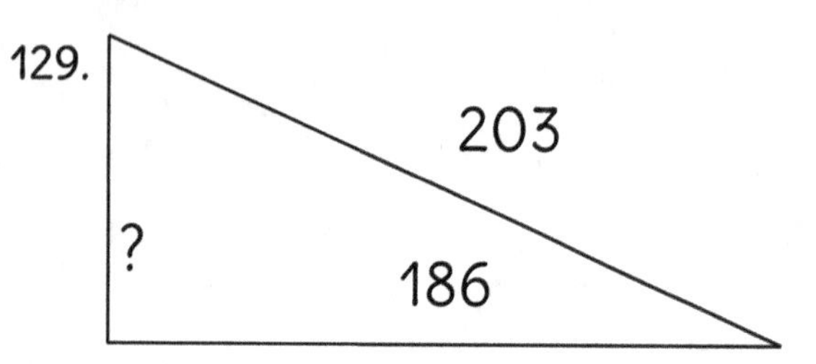

130.

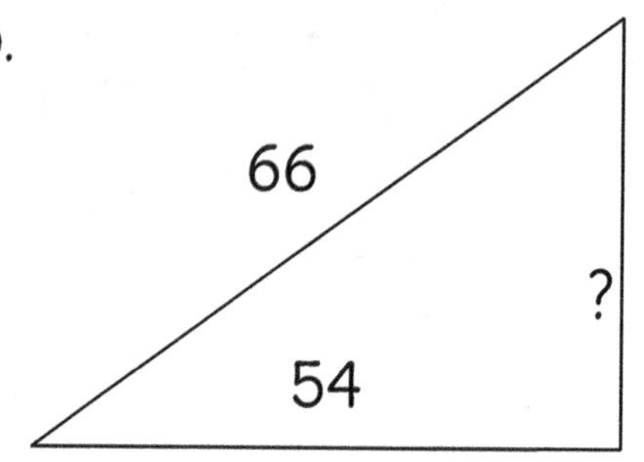

131.

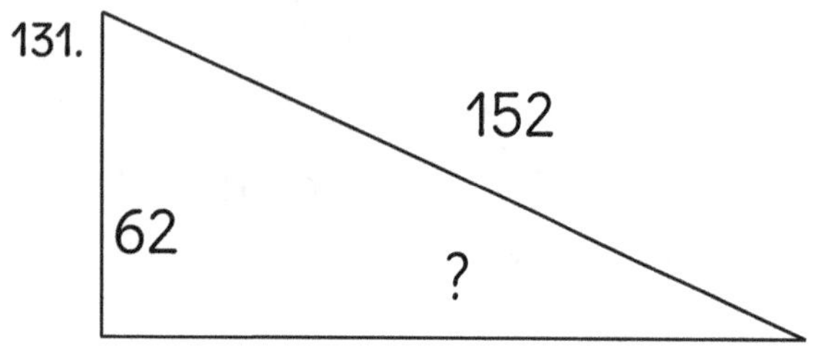

132.

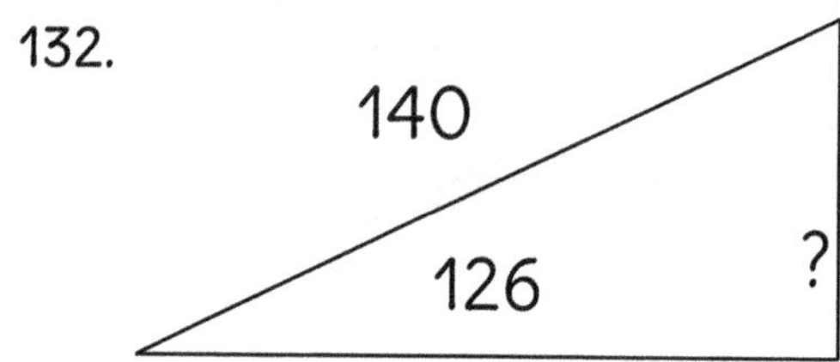

133.

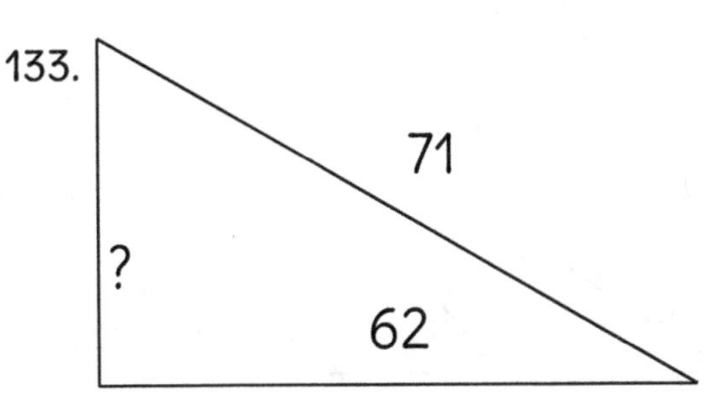

134.

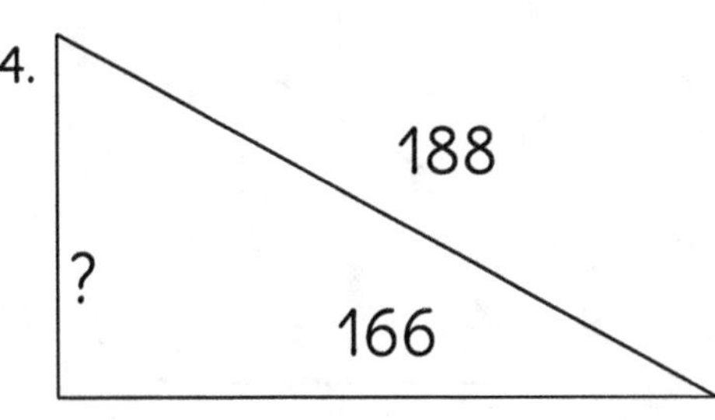

135.

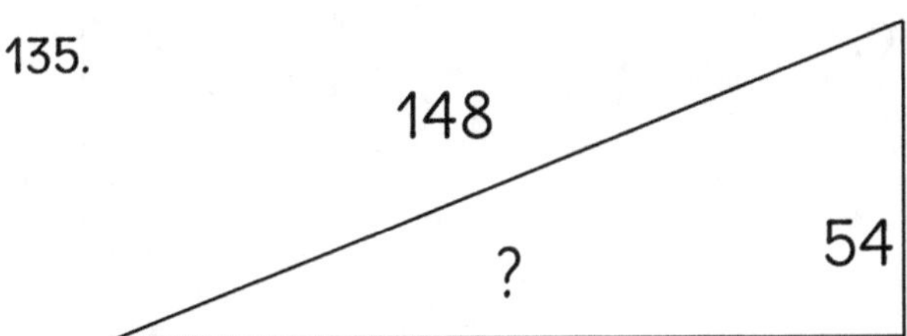

136.

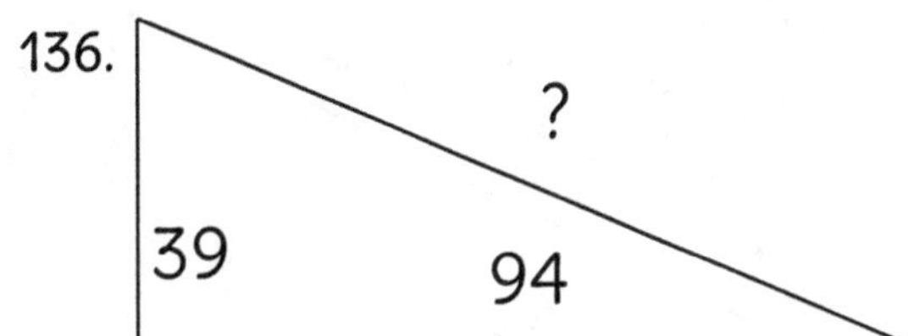

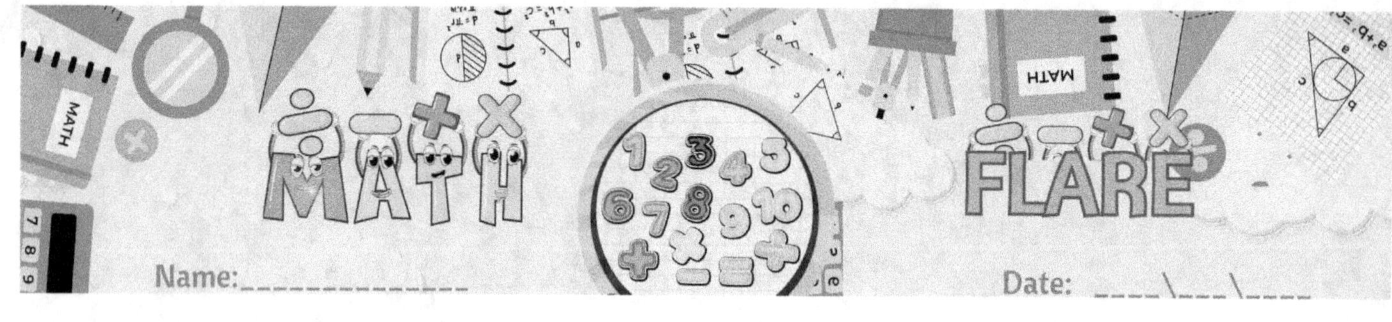

137.

138.

139.

140.

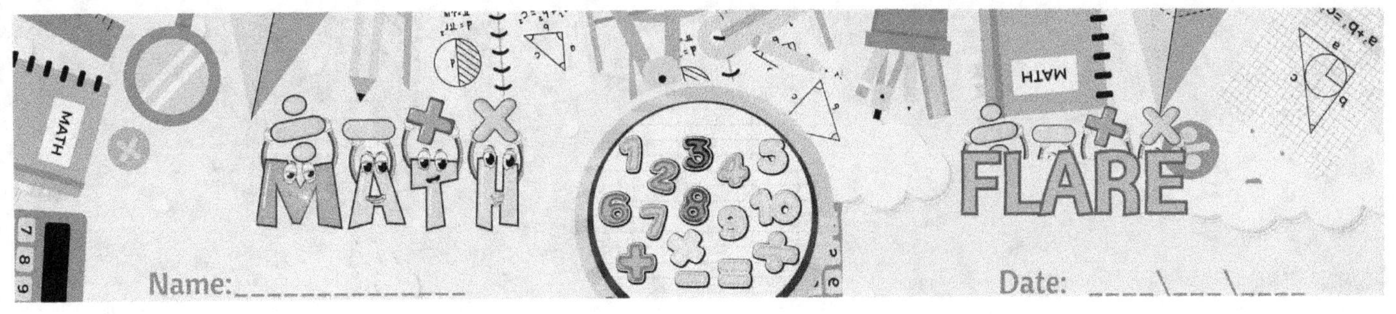

141.

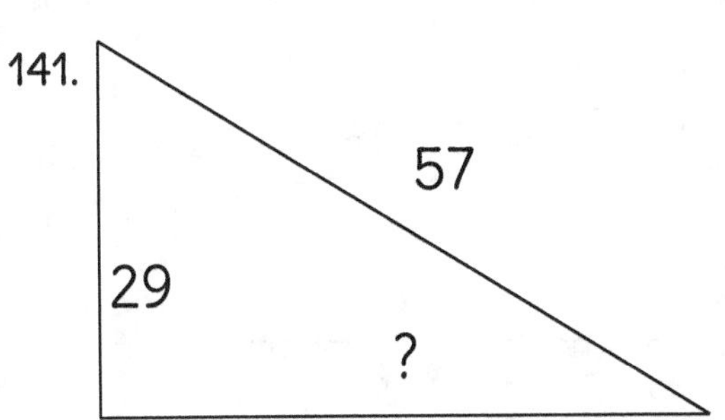

142.

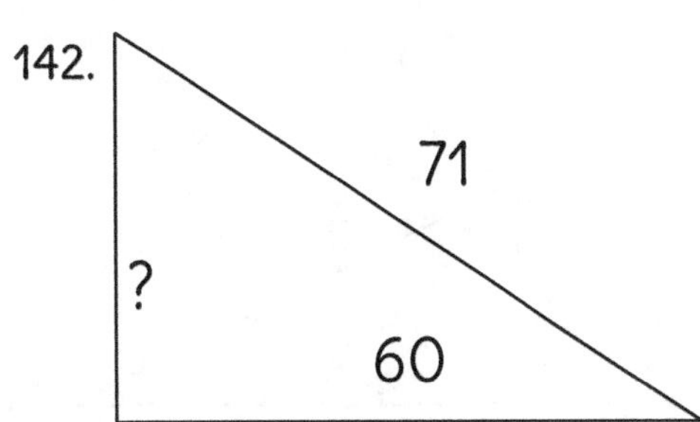

143.

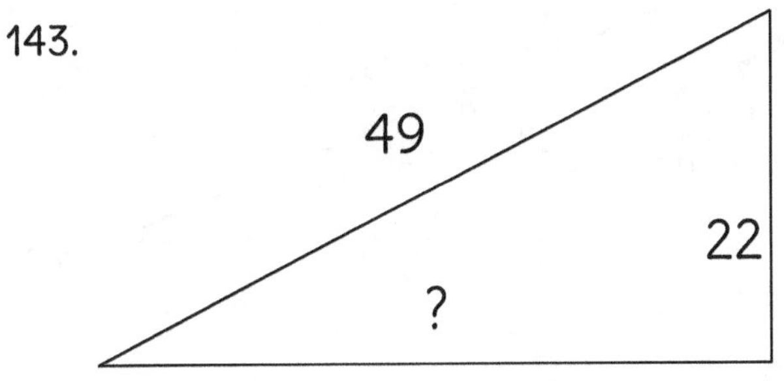

144.

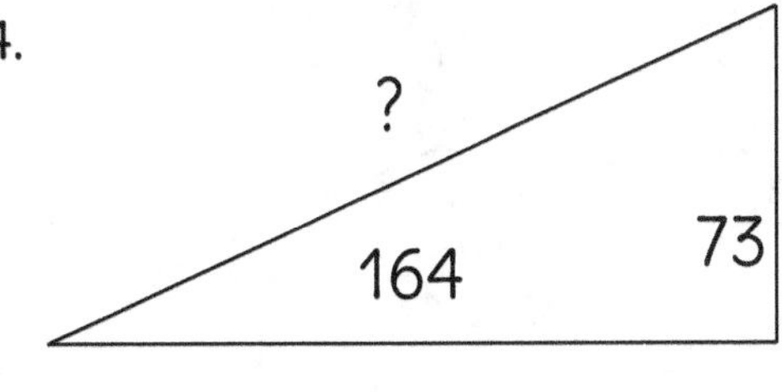

145. 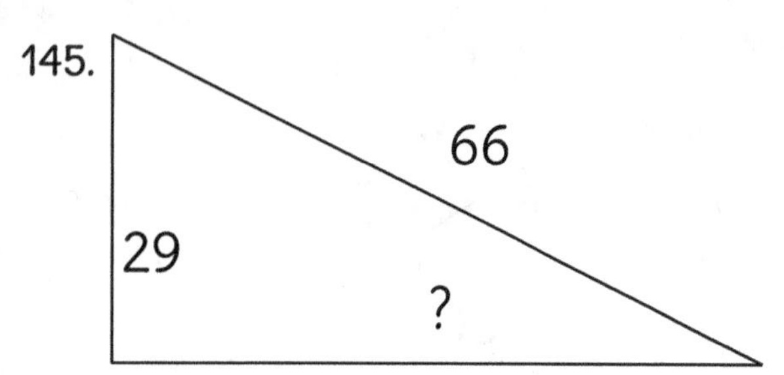

146. 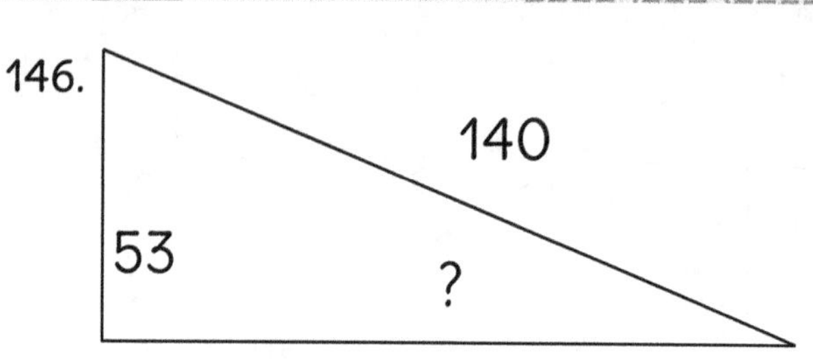

147. 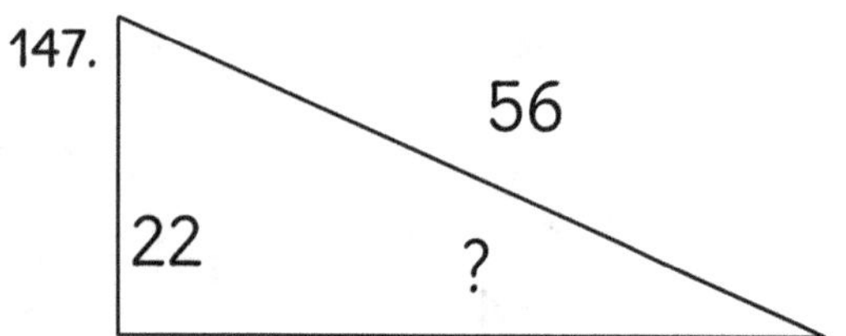

148. 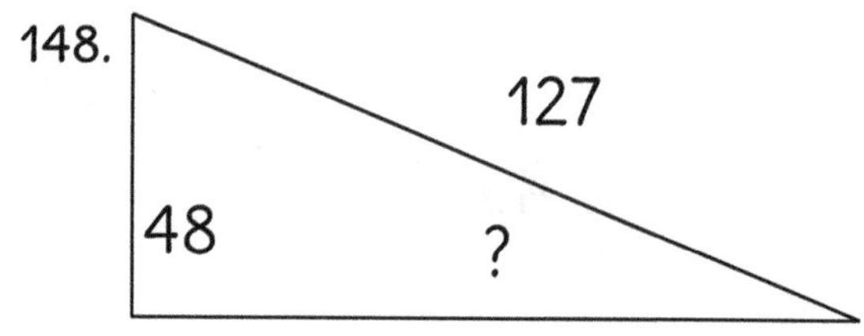

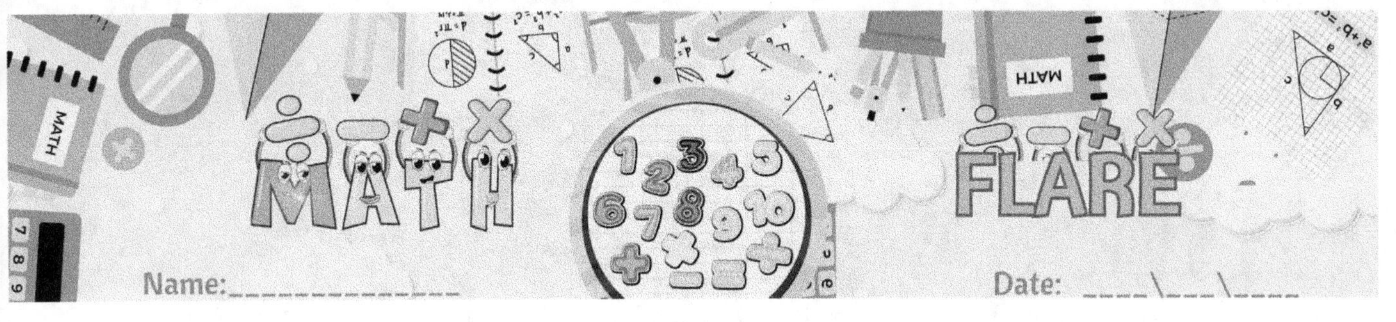

149. 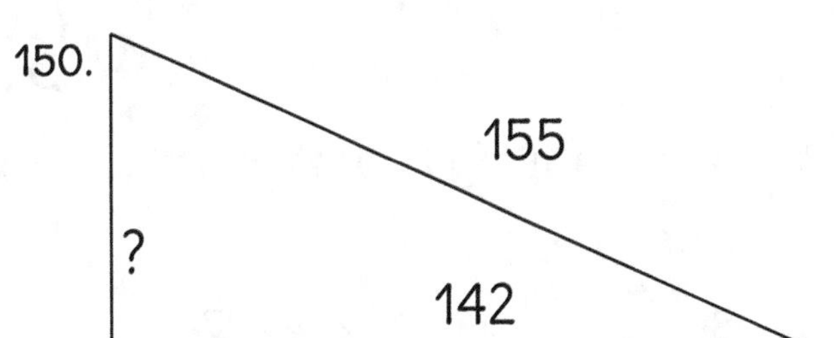

150.

151. 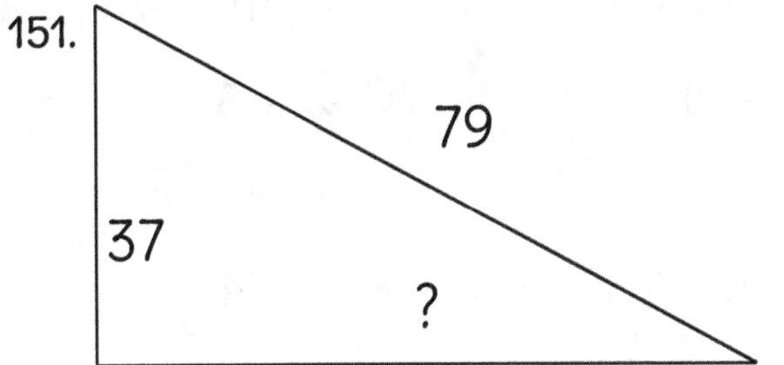

152. 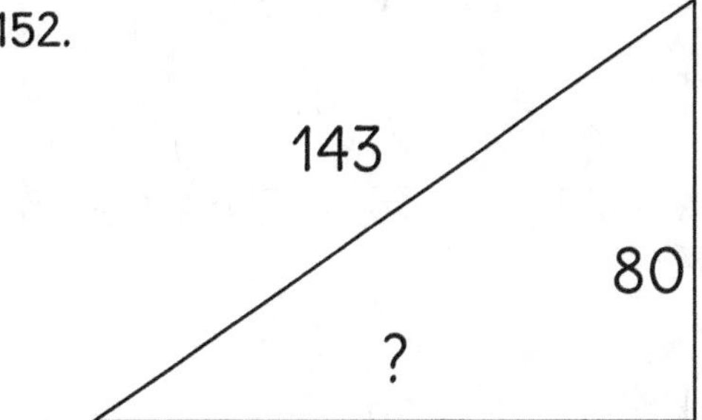

ANSWERS

Page 1:   Simplify Expressions

1. -28m + 6

2. -21x + 20

3. -5y

4. 10k + 9

5. -8y

6. 21z + 17

7. -20k

8. -21m + 71

9. -9z

10. -18k + 26

11. 9m - 8

12. 32k - 31

13. 3k - 1

14. -12x

15. -9m + 12

16. -84z + 97

17. -24k + 12

18. 11k + 25

19. -29z

20. 3k - 4

21. -17x

22. 9x + 9

23. 8y - 13

24. 8k

25. 16z - 8

26. -26y + 38

27. 6m + 1

28. -255x + 257

29. 10k

30. -17x

31. -8z - 20

32. -28y + 19

33. 16x

34. 4x

35. -11k

36. 9x + 3

37. -10x - 24

38. -12m + 55

39. -6

40. -17m + 8

41. 14z

42. 8z

43. 42k + 39

44. x + 24

45. -34k + 34

46. -7

47. 37m + 25

48. -16m + 4

49. m - 3

50. -18y

51. -y - 1

52. 34

53. 6m - 16

54. 7y + 1

55. 2m - 15

56. 26z - 10

57. 13z - 25

58. 75y - 81

59. -15k - 13

60. 5k + 17

61. -11y + 20

62. -9x

63. -15k + 52

64. 19x + 10

65. -9k

66. -5x - 1

67. 8x - 23

68. -30x + 24

69. -17m - 5

70. 16y + 34

71. -27x - 11

72. -30z + 5

73. 13x + 15

74. -7x + 19

75. -21k - 5

76. -5x

77. 39m - 54   78. -4k   79. 19z + 11   80. -13x + 17

81. x   82. 4z   83. -15m - 7   84. -140m + 34

85. 7y + 14   86. 50z - 19   87. 9x   88. 2z + 22

89. 16k   90. 12m + 5   91. 7y + 1   92. 6y + 28

93. 7m - 3   94. -15x   95. y + 7   96. 3x + 17

97. -5z   98. -14y + 2   99. 36m + 21   100. 20x - 12

Page 21: Solving Equations

1. 12   2. 40   3. -2   4. 5   5. 76   6. 2   7. 62   8. 32   9. 74

10. 10

Page 22: Solving Equations

1. 2   2. 18   3. 6   4. 19   5. 3   6. 22   7. 22   8. 2   9. 24

10. 45

Page 23: Solving Equations

1. 13   2. 12   3. 43   4. 12   5. 15   6. 28   7. 9   8. 49   9. 40   10. 11

Page 24: Solving Equations

1. 5   2. 10   3. 6   4. -76   5. 5   6. 29   7. 29   8. 11   9. 40

10. 64

Page 25: Solving Equations

1. 70   2. 27   3. 12   4. 8   5. 7   6. 54   7. 250   8. 5

9. 56   10. -19

Page 26: Solving Equations

1. 33   2. 3   3. 25   4. 9   5. -28   6. 30   7. 192   8. 13   9. -1

10. 22

Page 27:   Solving Equations
1. 60   2. 1   3. 1   4. 4   5. 2   6. 16   7. 7   8. 72

9. 29   10. 30

Page 28:   Solving Equations
1. 1   2. 24   3. 3   4. 19   5. 32   6. 18   7. 22   8. 22   9. 2   10. 0

Page 29:   Solving Equations
1. 7   2. 74   3. 7   4. 98   5. 61   6. 44   7. 7   8. 44   9. 42

10. 15

Page 30:   Solving Equations
1. 7   2. 42   3. 21   4. 28   5. 44   6. -5   7. 1   8. 36   9. 136

10. 8

Page 31:   Solving Equations
1. 12   2. 5   3. 56   4. 1   5. 40   6. 42   7. 27   8. 12   9. 75   10. 6

Page 32:   Solving Equations
1. 1   2. -6   3. 7   4. -5.5   5. 11   6. -43   7. 6   8. 13

9. 3   10. 4

Page 33:   Solving Equations
1. 10   2. 24   3. 41   4. 42   5. 59   6. 38   7. 200

8. 35   9. 15   10. -5.6

Page 34:   Equations (One Side)
1. 13   2. 4

3. 18

5. 18

7. 9

9. 15

11. 4

13. 4

15. 1

17. 14

19. 9

21. 4

23. 19

25. 14

27. 7

29. 16

31. 18

33. 14

35. 2

37. 10

39. 1

41. 7

43. 12

4. 6

6. 8 or -8

8. 13

10. 9

12. 16 or -16

14. 9

16. 4

18. 14

20. 17

22. 11

24. 10

26. 2

28. 14

30. 12

32. 2

34. 16

36. 9 or -20

38. 1

40. 2

42. 14

44. 1

45. 16

46. 3

47. 18

48. 2

49. 10

50. 16

51. 2

52. 5

53. 16

54. 14

55. 6

56. 8

57. 3 or -3

58. 4

59. 12

60. 4

61. 2 or -2

62. 16

63. 14

64. 14

65. 8

66. 1

67. 18

68. 4 or -199 or -198 or -197 or...

69. 10

70. 8

71. 5

72. 11 or -11

73. 13

74. 15

75. 20

76. 5

77. 6

78. 18

79. 2

80. 1

81. 20

82. 10

83. 20

84. 14

85. 2

86. 9

87. 15

88. 16

89. 10 or -10

90. 1

91. 16

92. 12 or -12

93. 13

94. 2 or -2

95. 1

96. 4 or -4

97. 10

98. 2

99. 13

100. 2

Page 59: Equations (Two Sides)

1. $x = 1$	2. $x = 4$	3. $z = 1$	4. $k = 4$	5. $y = 2$	6. $k = 8$
7. $k = 4$	8. $x = 3$	9. $m = 9$	10. $x = 1$	11. $z = 6$	12. $x = 3$
13. $k = 1$	14. $x = 5$	15. $k = 7$	16. $x = 1$	17. $k = 5$	18. $m = 2$
19. $y = 2$	20. $k = 2$	21. $k = 8$	22. $x = 3$	23. $m = 7$	24. $m = 3$
25. $x = 6$	26. $y = 8$	27. $z = 3$	28. $z = 2$	29. $m = 9$	30. $m = 3$
31. $y = 7$	32. $k = 5$	33. $m = 4$	34. $m = 6$	35. $m = 3$	36. $k = 7$
37. $y = 8$	38. $k = 1$	39. $y = 6$	40. $m = 6$	41. $m = 8$	42. $x = 9$
43. $x = 5$	44. $m = 1$	45. $z = 4$	46. $m = 7$	47. $k = 5$	48. $y = 7$
49. $m = 2$	50. $k = 5$	51. $m = 4$	52. $k = 9$	53. $m = 9$	54. $k = 8$
55. $x = 4$	56. $k = 2$	57. $m = 6$	58. $x = 5$	59. $x = 4$	60. $z = 3$
61. $k = 7$	62. $m = 1$	63. $k = 6$	64. $z = 7$	65. $y = 1$	66. $z = 3$
67. $m = 8$	68. $z = 6$	69. $k = 9$	70. $z = 9$	71. $z = 2$	72. $z = 5$
73. $y = 9$	74. $x = 9$	75. $y = 5$	76. $y = 8$	77. $z = 2$	78. $k = 7$

79. x = 4   80. k = 8   81. x = 6   82. m = 9   83. x = 5   84. m = 6

85. k = 5   86. x = 4   87. z = 8   88. m = 4   89. z = 8   90. k = 9

91. z = 6   92. m = 1   93. x = 2   94. y = 1   95. k = 5   96. k = 1

Page 69: Verbal Algebra Expressions

1. 64

2. 7, 8

3. 10

4. 2

5. 36

6. 7, 9

7. 39, 6

8. 1, 5

9. 1, 2

10. 4, 2

11. 11

12. 80

13. 9, 17

14. 5, 6

15. 9

16. 2

17. 5, 50

18. 24

19. 2

20. 4

21. 2

22. 4

23. 6

24. 7

25. 15, 9

26. 5

27. 3, 5

28. 12, 9

29. 8

30. 4, 6, 8, 10

31. 7, 45

32. 27

33. 16

34. 12, 3

35. 3, 12

36. 0

37. 3

38. 6

39. 12

40. 6

41. 10

42. 7, 35

43. 11, 7

44. 0

45. 5

46. 38, 5

47. 8

48. 15

49. 14

50. 4

51. 1, 8

52. 21

53. 4

54. 4, 36

55. 19, 9

56. 12

57. 20

58. 9

59. 2

60. 6

61. 1, 3

Page 83: Standard Linear Equations

1. -8	11. 5	21. 5	31. 5	41. -10
2. -2	12. 7	22. 0	32. 8	42. 6
3. 6	13. 1	23. 7	33. 8	43. -4
4. 1	14. 3	24. 1	34. -6	44. -2
5. 7	15. 2	25. -10	35. 7	45. -10
6. 4	16. 5	26. 1	36. 1	46. -3
7. -4	17. -8	27. 10	37. -4	47. 7
8. 2	18. 8	28. -10	38. 1	48. 9
9. -2	19. -4	29. 1	39. 1	
10. 1	20. -5	30. -3	40. 10	

Page 87: Find Slope from Two Points

1. -5	11. 4	21. -10	31. 7	41. -7
2. 6	12. 2	22. 3	32. -9	42. 9
3. -5	13. -3	23. 0	33. -8	43. 6
4. -3	14. -10	24. 7	34. 3	44. -8
5. -1	15. 10	25. -3	35. -10	45. 5
6. 6	16. -5	26. 2	36. -3	46. -2
7. 6	17. 9	27. -7	37. 7	47. -1
8. 9	18. -1	28. 7	38. 5	48. -5
9. -4	19. -3	29. 7	39. 2	49. 1
10. 9	20. -2	30. 3	40. 9	50. 7

Page 91: System of Equations

1. x = 4.6, y = -4.2

2. x = 0.72, y = -0.62

3. x = 1.06, y = -0.37

4. x = 1.6, y = -0.6

5. x = 3.38, y = -0.04

6. x = 0.97, y = 0.19

7. x = 0.18, y = 0.24

8. x = -0.4, y = 2.0

9. x = -1.0, y = 0.89

10. x = 1.33, y = -0.58

11. x = 5.75, y = -2.75

12. x = 1.68, y = 0.59

13. x = 0.82, y = 0.27

14. x = 2.67, y = -3.67

15. x = 4.33, y = -2.5

16. x = 4.12, y = -2.38

17. x = 1.0, y = -0.0

18. x = 1.42, y = -0.69

19. x = -0.12, y = 1.16

20. x = 0.97, y = 0.19

21. x = -0.06, y = 0.71

22. x = -1.8, y = 1.6

23. x = -0.25, y = 0.88

24. x = 11.0, y = -8.0

25. x = 2.0, y = -2.0

26. x = 0.93, y = -0.5

27. x = 0.88, y = 0.44

28. x = 2.5, y = -4.0

29. x = 1.19, y = -0.32

30. x = -1.35, y = 1.58

Page 101: Quadratic Equations

1. (0.899, -0.809)
2. (1.667, -2)
3. (1.726, -3.476)
4. (5, -3.2)
5. (0.825, -0.269)
6. (0.89, -0.14)
7. (2.57, -1.07)
8. (5.5, -6.5)
9. (1, -4)
10. (1.237, -1.537)
11. (0.935, -0.713)
12. (-2, -8)
13. (1.5, -0.667)
14. (1, 0.667)
15. (1.333, -3)
16. (-2, -2.5)
17. (0.811, -2.311)
18. (1.851, -1.351)
19. (1.318, -1.518)
20. (1, -2.8)
21. (1.808, -1.475)
22. (1.759, -1.634)
23. (1, -2)
24. (1.5, -3)
25. (-1, -2)
26. (3, 1)
27. (3.852, -0.519)
28. (1.8, -4)
29. (1.621, -2.621)
30. (0.591, -2.257)
31. (16, -6)
32. (2.4, -4)
33. (5, 3)
34. (1, -10)
35. (2.299, -0.87)
36. No real solution.
37. No real solution.
38. (7.5, -2)
39. (0.703, -2.37)
40. (2.25, -3)
41. (9, -3)
42. (1.6, -1)
43. No real solution.
44. (2.735, -1.535)
45. (1.667, -2)
46. (0.557, -12.557)
47. (4, -7.667)
48. No real solution.
49. No real solution.
50. (1, -1.833)
51. (1.119, -1.519)
52. No real solution.
53. (2, 0.2)
54. (2.5, -4)
55. (13, -9)
56. (1.674, -0.299)
57. No real solution.
58. (8, -5)
59. (1.58, -0.723)
60. (3, -1.6)

Page 107: Polynomials: Addition and Subtraction

1. $9x^2 - 8x$
2. $4x^3 + 7x^2$
3. $10n^4 - 8$
4. $4n^2 - 3$
5. $6v^4 + 15v^2$
6. $-2n^3 + 7n^2 - 4n$
7. $2r^4 + 3$
8. $12n^4 + 14$
9. $4v$
10. $10m^2 + 3m$
11. $7m^3$
12. $-9n^2 + 10$
13. $7v^4 + 3v^3$
14. $2n^2 + 5n$
15. $2n^4 + 12n^2$
16. 0
17. $15x^2 + 8x$
18. $v^3 + 3$
19. $5n^4 - 3$
20. $4p^4 + p^3$
21. $-7n - 3$
22. 2
23. $10n^3 + 6n$
24. $-n^2 - n$
25. $-r^3 - r$
26. $-3x^2 + 8$
27. $2p^3 - 3p$
28. $-9n + 8$
29. $-3x^2$
30. $5x^4$
31. $6b^3 + 4b^2 + 12$
32. $4b^4 + 10b + 4$
33. $2x^4 + 3x^3 - 6x^2$
34. $-4n^4 - 9n$
35. $-8a^3 + 7a$
36. $-2x^3 - 15x^2 - 6$
37. $14r^4 - 15r^3 - 4r^2$
38. $-14x^4 + 2x + 5$
39. $2n^3 + 4n$
40. $-2n^4 - 6n^3 + 11$
41. $4r^2$
42. $-2n^3 - 9n^2 + 4$
43. $4x^4 + 13x + 12$
44. $9p^4 - 6p^3 - 1$
45. $-10x^2 - 7x$
46. $-4k^3 + 3k^2 + 9k$
47. $-x^4 + 7x^3 + 1$
48. $6n^4 + 9n - 5$
49. $7v^3 - 8v$
50. $3x - 8$
51. $2n - 5$
52. $8x^4 - 6x^3 - 6x$
53. $-3v^2 + 8v + 14$
54. $7a^3 - 2a^2 - 6$
55. $5x^4 + 3x + 1$
56. $2k^3 + 7k^2 - 3$
57. $6m^3 + 6m^2 - 13m$
58. $p^4 + 8p^2 - 15$
59. $-2x^3 - 6x^2 + 5$
60. $-4v^4 + 7v^3 - 3v$
61. $4v^4 + 10v^2 - 3v + 2$
62. $-x^4 - 2x^2 + 6x$
63. $3n^3 + 13n^2 - 7n + 6$
64. $2n^4 - 4n^2 + 12n$
65. $3n^4 + 8n^3 - 6n + 4$
66. $8x^4 - 7x^3 - x^2 + 11x$
67. $-9p^4 + 2p^3 + 5p - 6$
68. $-5x^4 + 6x^3 - 3$
69. $-12n^3 + 11$
70. $3n^4 - 2n + 1$
71. $-m^4 + 3m^3 + m^2 + 3m$
72. $-2m^4 + 12m^3 + 11m^2 + 3$
73. $-x^4 + 10x^2 + 10x$
74. $-4k^3 - 4k^2 + 9$
75. $r^4 + 6r^3 - 5r^2 + 11r$
76. $v^4 + v^3 - 7v + 7$
77. $3p^3 + 12p$
78. $-3r^2 + 4r$
79. $-7b^4 - 4b^3 + b^2 - 4$
80. $-m^4 + 8m^2 + 5m + 1$
81. $-3a^2 + 3a + 1$
82. $13x^4 - 9x^3 - 6x^2$
83. $-4v^4 + 14v^2 + 3v + 7$
84. $-5m^4 - m^3 + 15m$
85. $8n^4 - 2n^3 - n^2 + 3$
86. $-2n^4 + 2n$
87. $3p^4 - 2p^3$
88. $-3x^4 + x^3 - 7x^2 - 2$

Page 116: Polynomials: Multiplication

1. $14x^2 - 52xy + 30\,y^2$
2. $18x^2 - 45xy + 28\,y^2$
3. $21x^2 - 38xy + 16\,y^2$
4. $12m^2 + 50mn + 42n^2$
5. $6x^2 + 10xy - 4\,y^2$
6. $40a^2 - 64ab + 24b^2$
7. $56x^2 + 3xy - 9\,y^2$
8. $18x^2 + 12xy - 16\,y^2$
9. $42m^2 - 40mn + 8n^2$
10. $15x^2 - 16xy - 7\,y^2$
11. $12x^2 + 8xy - 15\,y^2$
12. $8x^2 + 20xy - 28\,y^2$
13. $40x^2 - 54xy - 16\,y^2$
14. $3a^2 + 32ab + 64b^2$
15. $16m^2 - 60mn + 36n^2$
16. $8u^2 - 2uv - v^2$
17. $56m^2 + 77mn + 21n^2$
18. $32u^2 - 52uv + 20v^2$
19. $24x^2 - 19xy - 35\,y^2$
20. $10x^2 + 14xy - 48\,y^2$
21. $10m^2 + 14mn - 12n^2$
22. $6a^2 + 41ab - 7b^2$
23. $12u^2 + 2uv - 24v^2$
24. $7x^2 + 9xy + 2\,y^2$
25. $48x^2 - 46xy + 10\,y^2$
26. $12m^2 + 38mn - 40n^2$
27. $8x^2 - 8xy + 2\,y^2$
28. $32x^2 - 20xy - 3\,y^2$
29. $24x^2 - 23xy - 12\,y^2$
30. $10u^2 + 26uv + 16v^2$
31. $6x^3 - 7x^2y - 16xy^2 - 5\,y^3$
32. $40u^3 + 11u^2v - 17uv^2 - 6v^3$
33. $20x^3 - 40x^2y + 30xy^2 - 10\,y^3$
34. $24m^3 - 2m^2n - 50mn^2 - 12n^3$
35. $4x^3 + 18x^2y + 23xy^2 + 15\,y^3$
36. $16x^3 + 10x^2y + 17xy^2 + 2\,y^3$
37. $30m^3 - 63m^2n - 11mn^2 + 56n^3$
38. $48x^3 + 16x^2y - 38xy^2 + 4\,y^3$
39. $4m^3 + 8m^2n - 22mn^2 - 20n^3$
40. $8a^3 - 24a^2b - 56ab^2 - 24b^3$
41. $15x^3 - 7x^2y - 48xy^2 + 30\,y^3$
42. $56x^3 + 78x^2y - 24xy^2 - 10\,y^3$
43. $21m^3 - 13m^2n + 16mn^2 - 4n^3$
44. $8x^3 - 40x^2y - 32xy^2 + 64\,y^3$
45. $9x^3 + 36x^2y + 14xy^2 - 24\,y^3$
46. $24x^3 - 61x^2y + 40xy^2 + 6\,y^3$
47. $48x^3 - 66x^2y - 30xy^2 + 48\,y^3$
48. $9u^3 + 15u^2v + 28uv^2 + 32v^3$
49. $7x^3 + 57x^2y + 15xy^2 + 56\,y^3$
50. $14u^3 - 50u^2v - 59uv^2 - 15v^3$
51. $6x^3 - 10x^2y - xy^2 + y^3$
52. $35m^3 - 16m^2n - 52mn^2 - 16n^3$
53. $8u^3 - 26u^2v + 3uv^2 + 9v^3$
54. $6x^3 - 39x^2y + 22xy^2 - 24\,y^3$
55. $12u^3 - 8u^2v - 27uv^2 + 18v^3$
56. $35x^3 - 51x^2y - 50xy^2 - 6\,y^3$
57. $18x^3 + 15x^2y - 49xy^2 - 49\,y^3$
58. $2x^3 + 6xy^2 - 8\,y^3$
59. $m^3 - 8m^2n + 5mn^2 + 42n^3$
60. $8x^3 + 53x^2y - 15xy^2 + 42\,y^3$
61. $48x^4 + 50x^3y + 78x^2y^2 + 30xy^3 + 18\,y^4$
62. $6x^4 - 40x^3y - 36x^2y^2 - 22xy^3 - 8\,y^4$
63. $14x^4 - 36x^3y - 27x^2y^2 + 51xy^3 - 8\,y^4$
64. $48x^4 + 4x^3y + 22x^2y^2 + 18xy^3 + 12\,y^4$
65. $6a^4 - 19a^3b + 57a^2b^2 - 46ab^3 - 40b^4$
66. $3u^4 - 4u^3v - 18u^2v^2 + 84uv^3 - 49v^4$
67. $35x^4 + 82x^3y - 29x^2y^2 - 90xy^3 + 42\,y^4$
68. $20x^4 - 11x^3y - 33x^2y^2 - 60xy^3 - 18\,y^4$

69. $40u^4 + 60u^3v + 44u^2v^2 - 8uv^3 - 64v^4$

70. $8a^4 + 14a^3b + 50a^2b^2 + 34ab^3 + 20b^4$

71. $40x^4 + 21x^3y - 23x^2y^2 + 4y^4$

72. $14x^4 + 22x^3y - 12x^2y^2 - 14xy^3 + 6y^4$

73. $12x^4 + 34x^3y - 102x^2y^2 + 64xy^3 - 8y^4$

74. $14x^4 + 41x^3y - 10x^2y^2 + 6xy^3 + 4y^4$

75. $4a^4 + 9a^3b - 38a^2b^2 + 29ab^3 - 6b^4$

76. $14x^4 - 54x^3y + 81x^2y^2 - 60xy^3 + 25y^4$

77. $42x^4 + 104x^3y + 72x^2y^2 + 8xy^3 - 2y^4$

78. $6x^4 - 45x^3y + 26x^2y^2 + 4xy^3 - y^4$

79. $16x^4 - 52x^3y - 24x^2y^2 + 23xy^3 - 40y^4$

80. $48u^4 + 34u^3v - 6u^2v^2 - 80uv^3 - 40v^4$

81. $2x^4 - 11x^3y - 44x^2y^2 - 31xy^3 - 6y^4$

82. $24x^4 + 26x^3y - 84x^2y^2 + 32y^4$

83. $24a^4 - 27a^3b - 10a^2b^2 - ab^3 - 2b^4$

84. $5a^4 + 37a^3b - 46a^2b^2 + 82ab^3 - 48b^4$

85. $14x^4 + 36x^3y - 16xy^3 + 28y^2x^2 - 32y^4$

86. $48a^4 - 4a^3b - 4a^2b^2 - 28ab^3 - 48b^4$

87. $3x^4 - 16x^3y + 40x^2y^2 - 41xy^3 - 40y^4$

88. $40a^4 - 66a^3b + 26a^2b^2 - 26ab^3 - 4b^4$

89. $16a^4 - 56a^3b - 52a^2b^2 + 68ab^3 + 48b^4$

Page 128: Area and Perimeter

1. P=47 A=88
2. P=48 A=112
3. P=52 A=143
4. P=21 A=21.22
5. P=26 A=28
6. P=28 A=29
7. P=58 A=173
8. P=25 A=28
9. P=38 A=60
10. P=28 A=27.45
11. P=40 A=88
12. P=33 A=50.04
13. P=14 A=9.16
14. P=41 A=70
15. P=68 A=218
16. P=28 A=29
17. P=36 A=62.35
18. P=28 A=36
19. P=45 A=97.42
20. P=22 A=21
21. P=48 A=120
22. P=42 A=62
23. P=17 A=10.5
24. P=64 A=103
25. P=22 A=24
26. P=56 A=168
27. P=36 A=62.35
28. P=48 A=97.5
29. P=27 A=26.25
30. P=30 A=48
31. P=50 A=147
32. P=24 A=27.71
33. P=32 A=39
34. P=17 A=14
35. P=24 A=19.08
36. P=24 A=27.71
37. P=23 A=20
38. P=90 A=286
39. P=30 A=44
40. P=39 A=66
41. P=34 A=50
42. P=34 A=54.55
43. P=28 A=32
44. P=36 A=62.35
45. P=32 A=45
46. P=19 A=22
47. P=38 A=62
48. P=40 A=71.5
49. P=36 A=66
50. P=30 A=47
51. P=39 A=73.18
52. P=36 A=25
53. P=50 A=85
54. P=31 A=40.5

55. P=46 A=48
56. P=70 A=234
57. P=48 A=83.84

58. P=28 A=40
59. P=30 A=31
60. P=36 A=62.35

Page 143: Volume and Surface Area

61. V=268 cm³ cm³ SA=201 cm² cm²

62. V=360 in³ in³ SA=349.1 in² in²

63. V=700 in³ in³ SA=480 in² in²

64. V=21.21 cm³ cm³ SA=42 cm² cm²

65. V=12 ft³ ft³ SA=32 ft² ft²

66. V=48 cm³ cm³ SA=80 cm² cm²

67. V=113 in³ in³ SA=113 in² in²

68. V=4 ft³ ft³ SA=13 ft² ft²

69. V=14 in³ in³ SA=38.4 in² in²

70. V=576 cm³ cm³ SA=416 cm² cm²

71. V=60 cm³ cm³ SA=100.4 cm² cm²

72. V=636.17 ft³ ft³ SA=410 ft² ft²

73. V=98.17 in³ in³ SA=118 in² in²

74. V=392 cm³ cm³ SA=322 cm² cm²

75. V=75.40 in³ in³ SA=101 in² in²

76. V=50.27 in³ in³ SA=75 in² in²

77. V=180 cm³ cm³ SA=192 cm² cm²

78. V=280 in³ in³ SA=297.2 in² in²

79. V=60 ft³ ft³ SA=107.0 ft² ft²

80. V=100 ft³ ft³ SA=130 ft² ft²

81. V=524 in³ in³ SA=314 in² in²

82. V=9 ft³ ft³ SA=28.6 ft² ft²

83. V=200 in³ in³ SA=210 in² in²

84. V=75 in³ in³ SA=118.0 in² in²

85. V=9 ft³ ft³ SA=30.0 ft² ft²

86. V=28.27 cm³ cm³ SA=52 cm² cm²

87. V=66 ft³ ft³ SA=100 ft² ft²

88. V=336 ft³ ft³ SA=292 ft² ft²

89. V=252 cm³ cm³ SA=265.2 cm² cm²

90. V=48 cm³ cm³ SA=80 cm² cm²

91. V=12 ft³ ft³ SA=39.6 ft² ft²

92. V=39 ft³ ft³ SA=71 ft² ft²

93. V=209 cm³ cm³ SA=227 cm² cm²

94. V=18 in³ in³ SA=42 in² in²

95. V=572.56 cm³ cm³ SA=382 cm² cm²

96. V=30 in³ in³ SA=72 in² in²

97. V=64 ft³ ft³ SA=96 ft² ft²

98. V=80 ft³ ft³ SA=112 ft² ft²

99. V=18 cm³ cm³ SA=42 cm² cm²

100. V=160 in³ in³ SA=184 in² in²

101. V=64 in³ in³ SA=96 in² in²

102. V=343 in³ in³ SA=294 in² in²

103. V=62.83 in³ in³ SA=88 in² in²

104. V=75 in³ in³ SA=124.0 in² in²

105. V=30 cm³ cm³ SA=72 cm² cm²

106. V=280 cm³ cm³ SA=262 cm² cm²

107. V=90 cm³ cm³ SA=142.8 cm² cm²

108. V=8 ft³ ft³ SA=24 ft² ft²

109. V=120 cm³ cm³ SA=148 cm² cm²

110. V=9 cm³ cm³ SA=31.2 cm² cm²

111. V=48 cm³ cm³ SA=80 cm² cm²

112. V=60 cm³ cm³ SA=105.2 cm² cm²

113. V=126 ft³ ft³ SA=175.2 ft² ft²

114. V=170 cm³ cm³ SA=193 cm² cm²

115. V=315 ft³ ft³ SA=306.3 ft² ft²

116. V=38 in³ in³ SA=75 in² in²

117. V=550 cm³ cm³ SA=469.0 cm² cm²

118. V=12 cm³ cm³ SA=32 cm² cm²

119. V=148 cm³ cm³ SA=181 cm² cm²

120. V=24 ft³ ft³ SA=55.0 ft² ft²

Page 158: Pythagorean Theorem

121. S=130.996   122. S=64.008   123. S=38.066   124. S=114.127

125. S=17.407   126. S=99.679   127. S=177.612   128. S=184.716

129. S=81.320   130. S=37.947   131. S=138.780   132. S=61.025

133. S=34.598   134. S=88.250   135. S=137.797   136. S=101.769

137. S=64.086   138. S=134.302   139. S=13.964   140. S=31.780

141. S=49.071   142. S=37.961   143. S=43.784   144. S=179.513

145. S=59.287   146. S=129.580   147. S=51.498   148. S=117.580

149. S=164.730   150. S=62.137   151. S=69.800   152. S=118.528

www.ingramcontent.com/pod-product-compliance
Lightning Source LLC
Chambersburg PA
CBHW080936120726

48003CB00011B/3185